ZEMKE'S WOLFPACK

The 56th Fighter Group in World War II

William N. Hess

Motorbooks International
Publishers & Wholesalers

First published in 1992 by Motorbooks International Publishers & Wholesalers, PO Box 2, 729 Prospect Avenue, Osceola, WI 54020 USA

Library of Congress Cataloging-in-Publication Data
Hess, William N.
   Zemke's Wolfpack / William N. Hess.
      p.   cm.
   Includes index.
   ISBN 0-87938-622-3
   1. World War, 1939-1945—Aerial operations, American.   2. United States. Army Air Forces. Fighter Group, 56th—History.   3. Zemke, Hub, 1914-   .   4. World War, 1939-1945—Regimental histories—United States.   5. World War, 1939-1945— Campaigns—Western. I. Title.
   D790.H486   1992
   940.54′4973—dc20   92-20643

On the front cover: The painting *Little Chief's War Dance* by noted historical aviation artist Jerry Crandall authentically depicts the Thunderbolt flown by Lt. Frank Klibbe of the 56th Fighter Group. Prints of this painting are available through Eagle Editions Ltd., P.O. Box 1830, Sedona, AZ 86336, USA. Painting copyright Eagle Editions Ltd.

On the back cover: Top, Maj. Harold ("Bunny") Comstock in UN-V leads his 52nd Fighter Squadron over England. Center, Lt. Frank McCauley, a 5.5-victory ace in the cockpit of his P-47 *Rat Racer*. Bottom, Lt. Col. Dave Schilling taxis out for takeoff in his Thunderbolt *Hairless Joe*.

Printed and bound in the United States of America

Contents

Acknowledgments 4

Introduction 5

Chapter 1   Genesis and Training 7

Chapter 2   Becoming Operational 11

Chapter 3   Victory and Frustration 24

Chapter 4   Carrying the Fight to Germany 39

Chapter 5   Winter Doldrums and Big Week 56

Chapter 6   Momentous March 1944 75

Chapter 7   Sweeps and Fans 96

Chapter 8   D-day and Ground Support 113

Chapter 9   A Slower Pace 130

Chapter 10   Winter Actions 145

Chapter 11   Final Acts 157

Appendix 172

Index 191

Acknowledgments

Since this book has been years in the making, a number of people have been involved. I would like particularly to thank Col. Harold Comstock, Col. Paul Conger, Col. Francis Gabreski, Lt. Col. Steven Gerick, Lt. Gen. Gerald Johnson, and Col. Frank Klibbe—all U.S. Air Force, retired—for their most welcome assistance and for their friendship, which I have enjoyed during my many years of close relationship with the American Fighter Aces Association. I would also like to thank Col. Ralph Johnson, Mr. Randel Murphy, Jr., and Robert Gill for their contributions. Most of the photos were processed and printed by my old friend John Bardwell, and a number of the color photos are due to the kind assistance of my friend Sam Sox, Jr. To all, my profound gratitude.

Introduction

Over the years a lot of material has been published about the 56th Fighter Group, but most of it has tended to be centered around a few individuals or limited periods of time. My reason for doing this book is to attempt to give an overall narrative combat history of the 56th from its introduction to combat to the end of World War II in Europe.

The 56th Fighter Group did not meet with immediate success in the skies over Europe, nor did their fellow fighter pilots in the other U.S. Army Air Force groups or their counterparts in the Royal Air Force think that they would be successful in the massive Thunderbolt. Blessed with some outstanding leaders and well-trained, disciplined pilots, the 56th Group fought its way to the forefront and downed more Luftwaffe aircraft in the air than did any group in the 8th Air Force. Most of its victories were also accomplished early in the operations of the fighters of the 8th Air Force when the Luftwaffe pilots were combat veterans with a great deal of experience. The group proved that through teamwork it could defeat the Luftwaffe at its own game.

Some outstanding books have been written by and about some of the leading pilots of the 56th Fighter Group. I heartily recommend Col. Hubert ("Hub") Zemke's *Hub-Fighter Leader,* done with Roger Freeman; Col. Francis S. ("Gabby") Gabreski's story *Gabby,* done with Carl Molesworth; *Honest John,* by Col. Walker M. ("Bud") Mahurin; and *Thunderbolt,* by Lt. Col. Robert S. Johnson, done with Martin Caidin. Articles and such about 56th Fighter Group aces abound in back issues of various magazines.

Throughout its career the Thunderbolt was well known by its sobriquet Jug, given because of its appearance and certainly not short for *juggernaut.* I have not used it in this text purely to simplify identifying the aircraft by its designation, P-47, and its more universally known name, Thunderbolt.

I trust that the reader will gain an overall look at the 56th Group and its accomplishments in these pages and relish the photos that I have been able to gather over the years.

William N. Hess

Chapter 1

Genesis and Training

Late 1940 and early 1941 saw the United States frantically forming new units in the Army Air Corps as it sought to build up its drastically depleted defenses. The year 1940 saw the fall of France and the Battle of Britain. Relations between the United States and Japan were already becoming strained over economic sanctions, but it was the war in Europe that was keeping America's interest. President Franklin Roosevelt had made lend-lease agreements with Great Britain, and feelings ran high that sooner or later the United States would become involved in the conflict.

Among the new units formed in early 1941 was the 56th Fighter Group. Three officers and 150 enlisted men reported to Savannah Air Base, Savannah, Georgia, on January 14, 1941, to become the nucleus of the unit, which consisted of a group headquarters and three fighter squadrons—the 61st, 62nd, and 63rd. Only a handful of men and fewer aircraft were available for the unit. After a few months the group received its first permanent commanding officer in the person of Maj. David D. Graves. Shortly after his arrival, the 56th Fighter Group was moved to Charlotte Army Air Base in North Carolina.

During the early months of training, a trickle of personnel were gained, and by early summer the group possessed three P-39 Airacobras, five P-40 Warhawks and a few AT-6 Texans. By the time the historic Carolina maneuvers began, the group boasted an additional ten P-39s and it was able to scramble its interception force against the "enemy" bombers.

When Pearl Harbor was attacked on December 7, 1941, the men of the 56th were eager for action, and when they were alerted for movement it was

hoped that they would be departing for the Pacific, but such was not the case. Group headquarters and the 61st Squadron were moved to Charleston Municipal Airport, the 62nd went to Wilmington, and the 63rd went to Myrtle Beach, all in South Carolina. The group continued to receive more men and aircraft, primarily P-39s, and a real fighter unit began to take shape.

In January 1942 the 56th Group became a part of 1st Fighter Command, headquartered at Mitchel Field, Long Island, New York. Group headquarters went to Teaneck Armory in New Jersey, and the squadrons were assigned as follows: the 61st to Bridgeport Municipal Airport in Connecticut, the 62nd to Bendix Airfield in New Jersey, and the 63rd to Farmingdale, Long Island, New York, where Republic Aviation Corporation was located. The group was now charged with the air defense of New York City. It gained considerable takeoff and navigation experience while scrambling to intercept any unidentified aircraft entering the air defense zone.

In March the group was joined by Capt. Hubert ("Hub") Zemke, who had just returned from Great Britain, where he had been a combat observer, and from Russia, where he had instructed Russian pilots in the operation of Curtiss P-40s. Zemke visited all three squadrons of the 56th and reported back to Graves, who informed him that he was to become group operations officer.

At this time the group was informed that it was to be equipped with the Republic P-47 Thunderbolt, which was just coming off the production line at Farmingdale. Just as the aircraft began to arrive, the headquarters squadron was disbanded and Graves was replaced by Col. John C. Crosswaithe. The 56th was on the move once more, with the 63rd

Capt. Hubert Zemke returned from England and Russia to find a new command in the 56th Fighter Group. USAAF

Capt. David Schilling was commanding officer of the 62nd Fighter Squadron when he flew the first mission on April 13, 1943. USAAF

Squadron going to Bridgeport and the 61st and the 62nd going to Bradley Field at Windsor Lock, Connecticut.

On September 16, Major Zemke replaced Colonel Crosswaithe as commander of the 56th Fighter

---

First Impressions

The overall appearance of the Republic P-47 Thunderbolt elicited various first impressions from the pilots who were to take it to combat. Most were awed at its size and could not believe that it was to become a first-line fighter. After the first flight, however, most were impressed with its power and particularly its performance at high altitude.

Lt. Gen. Jerry Johnson stated: I still remember so well my first impressions of the airplane. It was huge, and with an R-2800 radial engine it appeared the Republic engineers had completely overlooked any streamlining effort. There were steps built into the side of the fuselage so one could climb up to the cockpit. But there were eight .50-caliber machine guns, and they were arranged in such a way that jamming seemed unlikely. I must have spent at least 3 hours examining and studying the airplane the first day it arrived. I finally concluded that maybe it didn't really matter how big it was if it had enough power to handle the weight.

Col. Francis ("Gabby") Gabreski said: Seeing the P-47 for the first time after flying the Spitfire IX, I was horrified with the tremendous size of the aircraft. The cockpit of the Thunderbolt could accommodate a large pilot with room to spare, while an average person fit the Spitfire like a tight tailored glove. On the other hand I didn't permit the size to destroy my enthusiasm over flying a new aircraft that we would use to perform our mission. . . . Scared, NO—but very apprehensive. I could hardly wait to take my first flight and learn the performance of the P-47.

Col. Paul Conger was appalled. He was just out of flight training when he was sent to Bridgeport, Connecticut, to join the 56th Group. He caught a taxi from the hotel downtown and had it take him out to the base. Up to this point he had no idea what type of aircraft he would be flying. Upon arrival at the base he had the cab take him down by the flight line and was floored when he saw the massive Thunderbolts. There's no way I can survive flying that thing in combat, he thought. Such was his frustration that instead of getting out he had the taxi driver take him back to Bridgeport, where he proceeded to drown his troubles.

Col. Harold Comstock was a pilot with over 400 hours in the air before he went to flight training. By the time he reported to the 56th Group he had over 600 hours in his logbooks. For one who was used to putting along in low-horsepower aircraft, the Thunderbolt was most impressive. He remembered: It was a real powerhouse. I was never afraid of it. It handled very well in the air, and the performance at high altitude was most impressive. I was just happy to know that I would be going to combat in the P-47.

Group. The group was receiving its Thunderbolts regularly by this time, and Zemke did his utmost to get his pilots ready for combat. A new fighter such as the massive P-47 gives problems enough without pressing them into service with young second lieutenants just out of flying school. Zemke had been provided with three veteran squadron commanders who proved to be invaluable in molding these green units into combat capacity. They were Capts. Loren G. McCollom heading the 61st Squadron, David C. Schilling heading the 62nd, and Philip E. Tukey, Jr., heading the 63rd. Many modifications had yet to be inaugurated on the Thunderbolts, and these shortcomings combined with the exuberance

of the young pilots proved to be costly; eighteen pilots were lost in accidents before the group was committed to combat.

The group was alerted for overseas shipment on Thanksgiving Day, but it had to undergo a month of absolute boredom before it was shipped down to Camp Kilmer, New Jersey, which served as the port of embarkation. On January 3, 1943, the men of the 56th boarded the former British luxury liner *Queen Elizabeth* bound for the British Isles.

The trip overseas was made unescorted in five days, and the ship docked at Gourock, Scotland. The following day the men were unloaded and put on trains for King's Cliffe, which was in the East

This P-47C is virtually the same aircraft as the B-model. It was increased 8 inches in length. Its 400mph speed at *altitude was wonderful, but low-altitude performance left something to be desired. Fairchild-Hiller*

9

Midlands. The base consisted of three short hard-surface runways, a paved perimeter track, and Nissen huts for housing. Initially the 63rd Squadron was sent to Wittering for lack of housing.

P-47s began to arrive on January 24 and came in at a trickle until March. Zemke did his utmost to get his men oriented in British radio procedure, navigation, and even formation flying. Although the Thunderbolts had operated in string formation in the United States, it was decided that the British finger four formation would be used. This formation was composed of a flight leader and wingman plus an element leader and wingman. Their positions were staggered just like the fingers on one's hand. Three such formations made up a squadron.

Zemke did manage to get his pilots a bit of gunnery practice at Llanbedr in Wales and at Matlask up near the Wash in Norfolk before they had to go to combat. Although this was quite important, the most crucial lesson the pilots had to learn in England was bad-weather flying. With continual low ceilings and lots of fog, it was imperative that the pilots learn how to climb through the overcast and form up, plus they had to learn how to work their way down through the undercast and gloom once they returned from a mission.

At the beginning of April the group was placed on alert for combat duty. First, however, it received orders to move to Horsham St. Faith, just outside the city of Norwich. Although the field was grass, the living facilities were those of a peacetime Royal Air Force (RAF) base with permanent-type barracks and service facilities. With comfortable quarters to boost their morale, the men of the 56th felt they were ready to enter the fray with a vengeance.

Chapter 2

Becoming Operational

April 8, 1943, brought an end to the training, waiting, and tensions that had been building since the arrival of the 56th Fighter Group in England. Col. Hubert Zemke, accompanied by Maj. Dave Schilling and Capts. John E. McClure and Eugene W. O'Neill, Jr., flew their initial combat mission with

Capt. Eugene W. O'Neill, Jr. of the 62nd Fighter Squadron was another member of the 56th flight that flew the mission on April 13, 1943. E. O'Neill

the 4th Fighter Group led by Col. Chesley Peterson. The mission was what was commonly known in the theater as a "rodeo," or fighter sweep. The formation flew over Dieppe on the French coast at 30,000 feet but saw no enemy fighters and didn't even see a burst of flak.

The same four pilots remained at Debden, England, for a few days, and inclement weather prevented another mission until April 13. On that morning they flew on another 4th Group sweep, this time over Pas de Calais, France. Some consternation flared when enemy fighters were called out from a lower flight in the formation, but nothing came of it.

Late the same afternoon two flights from the 56th joined Zemke's flight of four to accompany the 4th Group on another sweep. Zemke was forced to leave the formation with oxygen system trouble, and Schilling took over. The Thunderbolts flew a course at 31,000 feet that took them over St. Omer and on to Dunkirk, both in France, but sighted no enemy aircraft and were opposed by only a few bursts of inaccurate flak.

Capt. Roger Dyar experienced engine failure on the mission but fortunately was able to glide to the English coast, where he made a forced landing at Deal. Some excitement accompanied his arrival: when Dyar passed over the coast, the antiaircraft battery fired a warning shot, and then when Dyar bellied in, they thought they had shot him down.

Another three rodeos saw no action, but on April 29 the 56th Group had its first encounter with enemy aircraft.

Maj. Dave Schilling led the group, which consisted of three squadrons of twelve aircraft each, on a sweep that took them over The Hague–Woendrecht–Blankenberg area in Holland. The for-

Squadron insignia of the 61st Fighter Squadron. USAAF

Squadron insignia of the 62nd Fighter Squadron. R. Gill

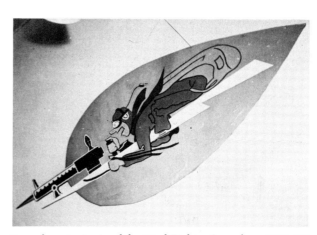

Squadron insignia of the 63rd Fighter Squadron. USAAF

mation of Thunderbolts arrived at Blankenberg a few minutes ahead of schedule and at 28,000 feet. When the formation was about 10 minutes into the second leg of the course, Schilling discovered that his radio was out.

Immediately afterwards two enemy aircraft were sighted at eight o'clock and slightly above. Schilling had no way to send a flight to meet them, so he turned the entire formation into them. Undaunted, the German pilots entered a shallow dive and went right through the formation of Thunderbolts without firing. At this moment two Me 109s attacked out of the sun on the right flank of the starboard flight. The starboard flight broke into the attack. The leader of the 63rd Squadron was then attacked out of the sun by two enemy fighters, which were engaged, and several shots were fired without effect.

As the formation of P-47s headed for the coast, another five to seven enemy craft attacked from astern. Once more several bursts were exchanged but no claims were made. Schilling tried to catch an Me 109 that had lost its initial speed, but the enemy immediately went into a dive and Schilling broke off combat. Now low on fuel, the 56th Group formation turned for home.

During the engagements, the group lost its first two pilots to combat operations. Lt. Winston Garth was hit early in the combat and was forced to bail out. He came down in the sea and was picked up by a

German boat. Capt. John McClure also went down on this mission and, like Garth, became a prisoner of war.

The group's first "ramrod," or escort, mission was flown on May 4. Thirty-six P-47s went out to meet the B-17 Flying Fortresses returning from their bombing mission. Col. Hubert Zemke had to return early with radio troubles, and Maj. Loren McCollom took over. When the bombers were reached over Walcheren Island in Holland, they were under heavy attack from up to thirty FW 190s. Lt. Walker M. ("Bud") Mahurin sighted a Spitfire under attack from four FW 190s and dove down to the rescue. He overshot the enemy fighters and took a hit in his wing on the breakaway but succeeded in thwarting the attack on the Spitfire.

A line-up of P-47Cs in which the 56th Fighter Group entered combat in the spring of 1943. P. Conger

The 56th then flew a couple of uneventful missions before May 14, when it made its first claims for enemy aircraft. The Thunderbolts had made a sweep over the bombers as they were making their run on Antwerp, Belgium. As Zemke turned the formation to head for home, four FW 190s, in string, were sighted below. Zemke immediately attacked the number 3 man in the enemy formation, which was obviously unaware of the P-47s' presence, as it made no attempt at evasive action. Zemke missed with the first burst, but the second scored hits in the area of a canopy. The 190 rolled over and went down. This brought it right in line with Zemke's guns. Another burst got hits in the left wing and fuselage. At this point four more 190s came in on Zemke's rear. Zemke turned into the attack, and a burst into the closing target showed no results. The P-47s broke for home.

Zemke's second flight, led by Capt. Merle Eby, saw four FW 190s coming in on the bombers and dove on them. Eby fired at the number 4 man in the enemy formation but saw no hits. During the attack, the number 4 man in the Thunderbolt formation was left arrears of his flight owing to the tight turn, but as he leveled out he sighted a lone FW 190 at one

o'clock that was attacking the number 2 man from his flight, Lt. Milton Anderson. At this time Lt. Albert Bailes pulled directly astern of the 190 and opened fire, closing to 300 yards. During a long burst, he saw black smoke emitting from the FW 190. The enemy craft went into a shallow, sliding turn going down. Bailes then joined up with the number 2 and number 3 men from his flight.

In addition to Lieutenant Bailes being credited with a probably destroyed and Colonel Zemke with a damaged, both Lt. Gerald W. Johnson and Lieutenant Anderson were credited with aircraft damaged in the combat.

It must be remembered that on these early missions, the Thunderbolts had no drop tanks, and their endurance was only 2 hours' flying time. The only support they could give the bombers was to escort them a short distance over the Continent and then pick them up on their return in order to try to save as many of the cripples as possible. Scoring was restricted not only by range, but also by the fighters' orders to stay with the bombers during their escort time and not to go off chasing enemy fighters. For this reason many combats were broken off at a point where a confirmed victory might have been possible. Gunnery was another important factor. Most of the pilots had had very little air-to-air gunnery training and were not schooled in the art of deflection shooting. Even on good astern shots many of the pilots developed what hunters call "buck fever" and opened fire far out of range. All of these shortcomings had to be overcome before the American fighters could become dominant in the skies over Europe.

The balance of the month of May was largely uneventful, as was early June. On June 12, forty-eight P-47s, sixteen from each squadron, led by Maj. Loren McCollom, took off to sweep the Blankenberg, Tarhout, Poperinge, and Calais areas in France. In the vicinity of Ypres, Belgium, the group sighted a formation of FW 190s, flying northeast and climbing. Maj. Dave Schilling dove to attack, but as he closed, he noted more FW 190s approaching to the rear of the flight he was attacking. Knowing that if he continued his attack, he would expose his own rear,

he slowed but continued to close. When he was 1,000 yards away, the 190s began to make a 180-degree turn.

Meanwhile, Capt. Walter V. Cook and his flight were up above and saw the FW 190s make their 180-degree turn. This placed them below and in front of him. Cook brought his flight down out of the sun from 20,000 to 5,000 feet and put himself directly astern one of the FW 190s. He opened fire at 300 yards and closed to 200 yards still firing. As Cook reported:

> I could plainly see pieces flying off the right side of [the enemy's] fuselage, and as my guns raked his ship, pieces from the left wing were also visible. One large piece broke off, and it is my belief that it was part of his aileron. Suddenly a big ball of fire appeared on his left wing and then black smoke poured out. . . . He rolled to the left, went over on his back in a gentle roll, and then went into a violent spin, with smoke pouring out from the fuselage and wing. At no time did the pilot take evasive action, and I believe he was killed.

The following day Colonel Zemke led the group on a sweep over the Gravelines, Bailleul, Aeltre in France and Knocke, Belgium, areas. Shortly after the P-47s made landfall, he observed fifteen or twenty

Maj. Loren McCollom was commander of the 61st Fighter Squadron until he departed to command the 353rd Fighter Group. USAAF

Capt. Walter V. Cook of the 62nd Fighter Squadron scored the first 56th Group victory on June 12, 1943, when he downed an FW 190. USAAF

aircraft at eleven o'clock about 15 to 20 miles ahead. These enemy aircraft were flying about 5,000 feet below the P-47s and coming toward them and to the left. Zemke took the first section of the 61st Squadron down from 27,000 feet in a diving left turn to attack a flight of four FW 190s that was above and to the rear of the rest of the enemy flights. Apparently the enemy pilots were watching the 63rd Squadron, which was clearly visible and above and ahead of its formation, and did not see the 61st Squadron, which had launched its attack from a thin layer of cirrus cloud.

Zemke reported:

As I approached the last of the four enemy aircraft, directly astern, I noted that the tail-end aircraft had white stripes around the horizontal stabilizer and elevators. This made me hesitate, for I thought these aircraft might have been P-47s coming out of France. Perhaps the hesitation helped me, for I closed to 150 to 200 yards before firing. There was no doubt in my mind then. To destroy the aircraft was a mere matter of putting the dot on the fuselage and pulling the trigger. A second after firing, the fuselage burst into flames and pieces of the right wing came off. I immediately went down to the right, leaving the number 3 plane of the four aircraft just ahead.

This plane for some reason must have been weaving, so that I had to give it deflection. The deflection proved to be a bit excessive, and I noted

Lt. Robert S. Johnson and Halfpint, *the aircraft in which he was almost shot down.* USAAF

Capt. Gerald W. Johnson of the 61st Fighter Squadron was a crack shot. He got the 56th Group's first multiple kill on August 17, 1943, when he downed two Me 109s and shared another. USAAF

Lt. Ralph Johnson also had a very rough mission on June 26, 1943. He was credited with the first group bailout. USAAF

strikes out on the right wing tip. The plane, being in a right bank, went down, placing me directly in back of plane number 2 of the string, which sat in the gun sight as one would imagine for the ideal shot. Again, when the trigger was pulled this aircraft exploded with a long sheet of flame and smoke.

Lt. Robert S. Johnson, who became a top ace in the 8th Air Force, was in the attacking flight and lined up on the leader of the string of four FW 190s. Johnson closed in to 200 yards, pulled the trigger, and hit the enemy with a 2-second burst. The FW began to emit black smoke. It then pulled up, turned over on its back, and exploded.

Six rodeos were uneventful, and then came a ramrod on June 26 that proved to be not only exciting, but also costly to the 56th. The 8th Air Force bombers went to attack Paris, and it was the assignment of the 56th to provide withdrawal support. Maj. Loren McCollum led the group and rendezvoused with the bombers in the vicinity of Forges, France. From that point until about halfway across the English Channel the Thunderbolts fought repeated determined battles with anywhere from forty to sixty enemy fighters.

No greater tribute could be paid to the P-47 than to see Lt. Robert S. Johnson's aircraft, which took this punishment and came home. USAAF

Lt. Gerald W. Johnson was leading the second flight of the second section in the 61st Squadron when he observed a dozen enemy fighters flying at his altitude in the opposite direction and to the right of the bombers. When they were well ahead of the bombers, they went into a 180-degree turn left—half of them to position themselves for a head-on attack on the Fortresses and the other half to attack the rear of Johnson's flight.

Just when he thought the 190s were in firing range, Johnson called for his flight to break left. Four of the enemy aircraft followed the P-47s through the 180 before the Germans broke away. Johnson then climbed and circled and began to look for the rest of his flight. It was not present, so he started back for the coast, looking for someone to join.

He sighted four aircraft flying to the north and above him, so he climbed and crossed over to them. The lead aircraft was a P-47, and it rocked its wings in recognition. As Johnson crossed over, he noted that the second aircraft was an FW 190 and it was lining up on the Thunderbolt. The FW got in a short burst on the P-47 before Johnson arrived, at which time it ceased firing and broke to the right. Johnson latched onto it and opened fire at 200 yards, observing strikes from the engine cowling to behind the canopy. Johnson continued to fire until the enemy burst into flames and started spinning down.

Lt. Ralph A. Johnson returned to base badly damaged and with one gear up and one down. Col. Hubert Zemke went up to observe the damage and advised him to bail out. Zemke led Johnson out over the North Sea while calling air-sea rescue to set up the recovery. Johnson bailed out from 10,000 feet and landed successfully in the water. About 20 minutes later an air-sea rescue Walrus set down on the sea and picked him up. Other than being sick from swallowing seawater Johnson was none the worse for wear.

Another Johnson, Robert S., had a terrible day. But for the rugged construction of the P-47 he would have been missing in action on the rolls of the 56th Fighter Group that day. His aircraft had been severely damaged shortly after rendezvous, and the engine quit. As the cockpit filled with smoke, Johnson tried to open the canopy to bail out. After the canopy opened only partially, he stepped on the dashboard and gave another heave, but it would not open fully. He then gave a mayday call on the radio and went back to work on the canopy, but to no avail.

Johnson tried to remove the few remaining pieces of glass so as to reach the emergency release, but this didn't work either. As he gazed around, he sighted several FW 190s in the area and out of pure frustration gave a few bursts in their general direc-

tion; he could in no way see forward, as his windshield was covered with oil.

Johnson finally turned his Thunderbolt inland to get away from the coast of France, for he felt that to go down there would certainly mean capture. When he pulled back on the throttle, he discovered that his engine would run at low speeds. This gave him hope, and he turned the aircraft and headed for England.

As Johnson headed for home, he underwent an experience that is classic in the annals of 56th Fighter Group and Thunderbolt history and is best described in his own words:

I was [at] about seven or eight thousand feet about 10 miles south of Dieppe and about the same distance inland when a single FW 190 jumped me. The FW 190 was colored a deep sky blue and had a yellow nose. When I first saw him, he was coming in at my level [8,000 feet] from four o'clock. I flew straight ahead, wondering what he was going to do. I supposed he was going to watch me go in the drink, so I just kept going downwards. He came up to within 50 yards and still did not fire, so I kicked it around into him. He pulled up, got on my tail, and peppered away. I wanted to get to England, or as close as possible, so I applied right and then left rudder alternately and kept heading north. He came past me, going much faster than I was, and I fired in his direction. I was only gliding at 180mph. He came up alongside me and flew for several minutes.

Another view of Lieutenant Johnson's badly damaged aircraft. The steel armor plate behind the seat saved his life. USAAF

I waved, and he returned the wave. Then he pulled up, fired another short burst, and then left me. I was about 4,000 feet about 5 miles northwest of Dieppe at that time. I . . . climbed up to 8,000 feet and called, "Mayday."

The distance to England was more than I had imagined, so I called for a homing. They brought me to the south coast of England. The hydraulic fluid was a half inch deep on the floor and kept flying up into my eyes, so I flew with my eyes closed half of the time. I landed at Manston. I had no brakes or flaps, couldn't see ahead, and had my wheels down, so I ground-looped to stop the plane.

Damage to the pilot was listed as a burn over the left eye, a cut on the nose, and a few steel slivers in the hands. Regardless, the Thunderbolt had brought him home to fight another day.

On the loss side, Capts. Merle Eby, Robert Wetherbee, and Roger Dyar as well as Lt. Louis Barron all were killed in action in the fights.

Following the tragic loss of these pilots and the narrow escapes of the others, it was perhaps fortunate that most of the month of July brought little action to the group. A number of rodeos and ramrods were flown, but no enemy opposition was encountered until the thirtieth of the month, when the Thunderbolts were given the task of providing withdrawal support to the bombers returning from Kassel, Germany.

The bombers were met over Holland and were under attack from approximately sixty enemy fighters. The pilots of the 56th went into action immediately and broke up the attacks by intercepting the Germans as they made their head-on approaches. This caused the enemy pilots to have to increase their angle of attack, and they were forced to break under the bombers rather than complete their head-on runs.

Capt. Robert A. Lamb in Jackie. *Lamb scored his first victory on August 19, 1943, over Breda. Note the 55-gallon drop tank. USAAF*

Lt. Joseph H. Powers was one of the pilots who scored, although he experienced some difficulty. As he started down, he found that his gun sight was out, and when he tried to put in his spare bulb, he dropped it. Nevertheless, he continued his attack on an Me 109, got in a burst at close range, and then had to pull over as he overshot his target. As he pulled up into the sun, he looked back and saw the pilot of the aircraft that he had just fired on bail out.

As Powers circled above the combat, he sighted a P-47 with three FW 190s on its tail. He called for the pilot to break and fired at one of the 190s even though he was out of range. The P-47 pilot heeded the warning and zoomed up, giving Powers a shot at a 190. Powers fired the rest of his ammunition but was only able to damage the craft.

Capt. Leroy A. Schreiber followed his flight leader down in an attack on a bevy of Me 109s but overshot and pulled up to make a second run. He sighted three Me 109s that were still in a rather close V-formation and taking no evasive action. Schreiber opened fire on the number 3 aircraft after the other two broke down and to the right. Then the number 3 aircraft started to break, and Schreiber latched onto its tail, firing from 350 to 250 yards. Pieces began to fly off the 109, and then a cloud of white glycol began to stream back. The aircraft was last seen going down spinning.

Schreiber pulled up to escape an FW 190 that was after him. As he leveled off at 20,000 feet, he sighted another P-47 down at 15,000 feet under attack from an FW 190. He called for the P-47 pilot to break, but evidently the other pilot didn't hear him. The FW fired and continued on down in a dive. Schreiber called the same P-47 pilot again and told him to take a shot at the 190 that had latched onto Schreiber's own tail as he zoomed up in front of it, but the two aircraft passed in front too swiftly for the P-47 pilot to take a shot.

Schreiber sighted three Me 109s maneuvering to make an attack on the P-47. Once more he called for the P-47 to break. Then he glanced back at his own tail, found that he was now clear, and so initiated an attack on the three Me 109s. Two of the 109s broke, so Schreiber came in astern of the aircraft that was still on the tail of the P-47. The Me 109 continued to attack the Thunderbolt, but its range was extreme and it did no damage. Schreiber pulled to within 150 yards of the enemy craft and fired. The 109 blew up in a splash of oil and flame.

In addition to Captain Schreiber's two victories and Lieutenant Powers' one, the 56th Group pilots were credited with two probably destroyed and one damaged. On the other side of the ledger, however,

Lt. Wilfred A. Van Abel of the 63rd Fighter Squadron.
Note the yellow band around the national insignia on the
fuselage. USAAF

Two aircraft from the 61st Fighter Squadron ready for
takeoff. At this time all U.S. aircraft had the white nose
and white tail stripes for identification. USAAF

they lost Lts. Jack Horton and Robert Stover in the action.

August 12 marked the first mission on which the 56th Group carried belly tanks. To protect the bombers, it was essential that something be done to increase the range of the fighters, and 8th Fighter Command had worked hard to come up with something suitable. The first tanks used by the 56th were 200-gallon pressed paper units that were fitted to the fuselage by a four-point suspension. They proved to be totally unsuitable. They didn't fit properly, they had to be patched, and worst of all they drastically affected the rate of climb of the Thunderbolts.

August 17 marked the 8th Air Force's dramatic missions to Schweinfurt and Regensburg in Germany, which resulted in dire losses to the bomber forces. Owing to weather, the two missions did not get off at proper intervals, causing the Schweinfurt mission to begin far behind schedule. This gave the Luftwaffe plenty of time to complete its attacks on the first formations of bombers, return to base to refuel and rearm, and be ready when the second force penetrated its territory.

The 56th Fighter Group flew two missions that day. It was airborne at 0924 hours and provided support to the bombers' escort to Eupen, Belgium, where it was forced to turn back owing to lack of range. A number of German fighters were sighted, but they were reluctant to do combat. They knew the

range of the P-47s and realized that as soon as the fighters were forced to break off the escort, the bombers would be at their mercy.

The second mission, led by Col. Hubert Zemke, took off at 1520 hours laden with drop tanks. The Thunderbolts climbed to 27,000 feet and penetrated to about 15 miles east of Eupen, which would normally be beyond their range. Colonel Zemke was doing his utmost to get to the bombers as quickly as he could, however, and chose to penetrate to the utmost. The P-47s experienced no trouble finding the bombers and positioned themselves on top, with one squadron covering the first box of bombers and the other two squadrons covering the rear.

The Luftwaffe forces queuing up for further attacks on the American bomber forces came primarily from Jagdgeschwader (JG) 1 and JG 26 and included a small contingent of Me 110s from I/NGJ, a night fighter unit operating out of Holland. The Thunderbolts hit the German fighters out of the east, a point at which they were unexpected, and the surprise contributed greatly in breaking up the attacks on the bombers.

Capt. Glen D. Schlitz, Jr., 63rd Fighter Squadron ace, liked to get his kills in bunches. Twice he got three on one mission. USAAF

All fighter units apparently had pets. Here is Capt. Frank McCauley and friend belonging to the 61st Fighter Squadron. F. Klibbe

Colonel Zemke reported that shortly after he had led a section of eight Thunderbolts to the front of the B-17 formation, he sighted a twin-engined Me 110 flying directly below him. Zemke made a 360-degree diving turn, which brought him down on the rear of the enemy aircraft. He closed to 300 yards before opening fire and saw immediate strikes on both engines, the fuselage, and the wings. Another burst sent pieces flying off the aircraft, and both engines began smoking profusely. The 110 went down to about 10,000 feet in a shallow dive and leveled off, but then the right engine caught fire and the craft continued in a steep dive until it crashed into the ground.

Capt. Gerald Johnson led a flight of Thunderbolts into position on the left side of the last box of bombers. As they proceeded to the vicinity of Liege, Belgium, he sighted a light gray Me 110 passing across in front of the B-17s and about 1,000 feet above them. Johnson rolled over, dived down astern and about 30 degrees to one side, and opened fire at 150 yards. A second burst exploded the aircraft. It was later discovered, on examining gun camera film, that Lt. Frank E. McCauley had fired at the same aircraft at about the same time, so the victory was split between the two pilots.

Johnson went back up into the sun at about 23,000 feet, and on leveling out he sighted a single Me 109 heading for the bombers. Johnson dived down and opened fire at 200 yards. Hits and flashes appeared on the fuselage, and as the enemy aircraft went into a left turn, it took a full burst between the cockpit and engine. A large flash erupted and smoke began to pour from the engine. As Johnson pulled up, he saw the enemy pilot go over the side and bail out.

As he pulled back up over the bombers, Johnson saw another Me 109 coming in on the Fortresses from a ten o'clock position. Obviously unobserved, he easily pulled in on the tail of the 109 and hit it with a 3-second burst. The enemy plane burst into flames and rolled over to the left and went straight down. Johnson found himself alone, as his number 2 man and the second element of his flight had to drive two Me 109s off their leader's tail. Now low on fuel the Thunderbolt leader headed for home.

Lt. Glen D. Schlitz, Jr., accompanied by one of his wingmen, Lt. John H. Truluck, Jr., went down to attack some FW 190s that were after the bombers. On the way down they made head-on passes at two FW 190s, with no observed strikes. Schlitz broke to the right and came upon four FW 190s in a string. He went after the first two aircraft in the string, fired, and hit the number 2 aircraft and then moved over to the leader. A solid burst on this 190 cut its wing

Compressibility

At the beginning of World War II little was known about aircraft and the speed of sound, what effect a power dive would have on the controls of a fighter aircraft the size of the P-47. In October of 1942 the 56th Fighter Group was based at Bridgeport, Connecticut, and the pilots of the unit were still putting their new aircraft through its paces.

On this particular day Lts. Harold Comstock and Roger Dyar were assigned the task of testing the capability of a new upright type of radio antenna mounted aft of the cockpit of the Thunderbolt. A raked antenna had been used, and it proved to be unsatisfactory. The pilots were to climb to altitude in stages, making 3-minute high-speed runs at each level before climbing.

The two pilots took off as assigned and did not see each other until they were back on the ground. Lieutenant Comstock put his aircraft through its paces and steadily climbed from one level to another until he had reached an altitude of 49,600 feet. He had hoped to push the P-47 up to 50,000 feet, but the controls had begun to get sloppy, and Comstock feared that the aircraft would fall off in a spin if he tried to push it any higher. He had been in a spin in the Thunderbolt before and didn't relish the idea of bringing the aircraft out of one on this occasion.

Comstock noted that his warning light was on to indicate that his fuel was down to 35 gallons and it was time to head for home. He dropped the nose and went down 200 or 300 feet and then rolled the aircraft over. He was now almost on his back, and the speed began to build up. At 40,000 feet he was hitting 300mph to 350mph and he found that he had absolutely no controls. Suddenly he hit what felt like a bump. He tried mightily to move the stick, but it was solid as a rock and the aircraft continued its downward plunge.

Rationalizing his situation, he immediately turned to his primary alternative. He rolled the trim tab all the way back. By this time he was down to 30,000 feet and the aircraft finally began to pull out. Comstock began to roll the trim tab forward, and by the time he was at 20,000 to 25,000 feet, he regained stick control and completed his pullout.

After landing Comstock went in and related what had happened to his operations officer, and they in turn went in to talk to the Republic Aircraft tech representative. He took Comstock's statement and passed it along to the Republic people. A few days later a delegation from Republic, including Thunderbolt designer Alexander Kartveli, came out and questioned Comstock at great length, with Kartveli making calculations all the time.

Two days later a news item broke stating that Comstock had approached the speed of sound in the Thunderbolt. Following this release, the 56th Fighter Group received a teletypewriter exchange from Gen. Henry ("Hap") Arnold stating that there would be absolutely no more talk about the dive, and so the story was put to rest. This was, however, probably one of the first recorded instances of a fighter pilot meeting the compressibility problem that would be experienced by many World War II fliers in combat situations.

Lofty, *the aircraft of Capt. Lyle Adrianse, in the hangar for repairs after absorbing a bit of battle damage. USAAF*

Lt. Frank McCauley of the 61st Fighter Squadron was an early scorer and would become a 5.5-victory ace. He is shown here in his aircraft Rat Racer. *USAAF*

off at the halfway mark. At the same time Truluck was downing another of the 190s.

As Schlitz broke to the right after his combat, another 190 passed in front of him, and he fired at it from 300 yards. Strikes appeared all over the Focke Wulf, which then burst into flames and went down in a spin.

Schlitz pulled up once more, and this time he sighted a twin-engined fighter, which he damaged with the little ammunition that he had remaining.

Capt. Walker Mahurin of the 63rd Squadron downed two FW 190s attacking the bombers—the pilot of one of those 190s being Oberleutnant Wilhelm "Wutz" Galland—but when Lt. Harold E. ("Bunny") Comstock of the same squadron sighted two Me 109s passing in front of his flight, he was told to let them go. These same two Me 109s proceeded to attack a Thunderbolt, and contrary to what he had been told, Comstock went after them. In the diving attack, Comstock's first burst went astray, but the second burst hit the 109 in the wing. As Comstock pulled up, he saw the wing break off of the aircraft, and down went the 109. Ironically, Comstock was fined on his return to base for breaking formation, even though the delay in his attack cost the life of Lt. Arthur Sugas.

The final score for the 56th Fighter Group that day was sixteen enemy aircraft destroyed, one probably destroyed, and nine damaged. In addition to Lieutenant Sugas, Lts. Voorhis Day and Robert Stultz were killed in action.

Two days later the 56th set out on another mission to escort the Fortresses attacking targets at Gilze-Rijen in Holland. Capt. Gerald Johnson had his flight up above the bombers at 25,000 feet when he sighted three Me 109s to the rear and about 2,000 feet below. He waited until the enemy fighters were about 1,000 yards behind and then took his flight down in a tight 360-degree turn to come out on their tail. As the Thunderbolts closed, the leader of the 109s did a neat slow roll and continued on. Johnson lined up on the number 3 man in the formation and began firing at about 250 yards. This pilot rolled over and went straight down. By this time Johnson found himself directly behind the leading 109, which was only about 100 yards away. This pilot went into all sorts of evasive action but took hits on the fuselage, and soon he went down trailing smoke. Johnson pulled up to gather his flight, but one of the pilots in the second section saw the Me 109 continue its dive into the ground.

Lt. Joe Powers and his flight came under attack from four Me 109s. The Thunderbolts broke down, and then Powers made a very steep climbing turn to the left that brought him up to 29,000 feet. Here he joined with Lt. Frank McCauley. The two immediately went down to hit some Me 109s at 22,000 feet that were attacking the bombers. These aircraft broke, so the two P-47s went back up. Another Me 109 headed toward the Thunderbolts, so McCauley attacked it head-on. As they closed, both pilots opened fire. Powers observed that as the 109 passed McCauley and came under him, it did a violent snap roll and started spinning. It continued down until it crashed.

The two P-47 pilots rejoined and made another attack on an Me 109 that was some 3,000 feet below them. McCauley made this closure without problem, and once strikes had appeared all over the enemy aircraft, it spiraled down until it hit the ground.

The score for the day was nine enemy fighters destroyed by the pilots of the 56th for the loss of one pilot: Lt. Glen Hodges was forced to bail out owing to engine failure.

Chapter 3

Victory and Frustration

The men of the 56th Group were great ones for nose art. This is the left side of Lt. Anthony Carcione's aircraft, which depicts a Dogpatch character. USAAF

The first of a number of staff changes took place on August 21, 1943. Maj. Loren G. McCollom left the 56th Group to take command of the 353rd Fighter Group. Maj. David Schilling moved up to deputy group commander of the 56th and was replaced as 62nd Fighter Squadron commander by Maj. Horace C. ("Pappy") Craig.

Col. Hubert Zemke led the group flying top cover for the bombers going to Villacoublay, France, on August 24. A number of FW 190s were sighted en route to the target, but few combats took place. Maj. Francis S. ("Gabby") Gabreski, leading the 61st Squadron, encountered seven 190s attempting to get through to the bombers in the vicinity of Dreux, France. As the enemy fighters maneuvered around to get in position for a head-on pass at the Big Friends, Gabreski took his P-47s in a right-hand orbit and came in behind them. Diving down, he came in on the tail of one of the 190s and opened fire. Holding the trigger button down until he almost overran the enemy craft, he noted pieces flying off and smoke emitting. He zoomed up and watched the 190 as it continued in its dive to destruction.

Two more 190s were destroyed by the 56th's Thunderbolts, which suffered no losses for the day.

The 56th did well to escape an attack by thirty enemy fighters from II/JG 26 on September 2. Col. Hubert Zemke led the P-47s escorting the bombers to Brussels, Belgium. Upon arrival the target was found clouded over, and although the bombers made two orbits, they did not drop their bombs, but headed for home.

As the Thunderbolts headed for England amid a thin cloud layer, they were bounced from above by the enemy fighters. As Zemke reported:

Just as we arrived at this position [over the back box of bombers], a call was given over the radio to break left, as we were being attacked by enemy aircraft from above. I broke left to see at least fifteen enemy aircraft firing at us from a 45-degree dive out of the cloud.

One short burst was given head-on into [an] FW 190, which passed directly over me. I suddenly heard a loud "ping," as if a bell had been struck, and my ailerons became extremely heavy. The original turn continued, and four more FWs were noted slightly below and directly ahead [of] me. A three-ringed deflection was taken on one of these aircraft, and I held the trigger down until he passed through this fire before I broke off in a dive for the deck. . . . Four other enemy aircraft followed me down for a

time but broke off combat before I hit the deck. It was then that I found that my supercharger had been hit, limiting the amount of manifold pressure I could draw. I continued home at reduced speed.

Lt. John W. Vogt, Jr., was wounded in the attack when fragments of a 20mm shell imbedded themselves in his leg. He was able to evade only by violently sliding and slipping and hedgehopping until he ran his pursuer low on fuel and forced him to give up the chase.

Lts. Wilfred A. Van Abel and Walter T. Hannigan did not return from the mission. Van Abel was later reported to be a prisoner of war, but Hannigan was killed in the combat.

The following morning Zemke was once more in the lead when the 56th ventured out as general bomber support to Morny, France. A total of about twenty enemy fighters were seen. Zemke spotted a

The right side of Lt. Anthony Carcione's aircraft goes more for feminine decoration. Unfortunately, the popular pilot was killed in action in March 1944. USAAF

Lt. Ralph Johnson survived his bailout and got on the scoreboard with an Me 109 to his credit on September 7, 1943. USAAF

Capt. John W. Vogt became an ace with the 56th Fighter Group and then went on to score further victories with the 356th Fighter Group. He retired from the USAF as a full four-star general. USAAF

Lt. Hiram O. Bevens was shot down over France on September 3, 1943. Following his capture, German officers came out to examine the P-47. USAAF

flight of four FW 190s headed for the bombers and went down to attack. As he closed on his prey, he noted tracers going past his right wing. He assumed that this was his wingman firing at the targets ahead and continued to press his attack. In fact, another flight of four FW 190s had fallen in behind him and his wingman.

Fortunately, Capt. Don M. Goodfleisch and his wingman had fallen in behind on this second flight and opened fire on the enemy fighters. Goodfleisch pulled in and fired from 400 yards, then closed to 100 yards, and the FW 190s went down in flames. Unaware of the danger to his own tail, Zemke pressed on with his attack, and he, too, sent his victim down streaming smoke and flames.

A few minutes later Maj. Francis Gabreski spotted a lone FW 190 flying below the bombers. Gabreski took his flight down in a shallow turn and came in right on the tail of the 190 which he hosed down with over 900 rounds of .50-caliber ammunition. The enemy plane went into a spin from which it did not recover.

On September 7 the group escorted B-24 Liberator bombers for the first time. Their target was to have been Leeuwarden, Holland, but owing to cloud cover, the bombers carried their loads out to sea and attacked two enemy ship convoys. While the fighters were covering the bombers attacking ships off Tessel Island, Me 109s were encountered. Lts. Ralph A. Johnson and Anthony R. Carcione attacked and shot down two of them.

It was back to France again on September 9, but the only member of the 56th able to score that day was Capt. Walker Mahurin. A flight of FW 190s was sighted queuing up on the bombers in the vicinity of Beauvais, but the Thunderbolts broke up the attack. Mahurin managed to catch two of the 190s 1,000 feet below and in front of him. He hung onto the 190 that split to the left while the other enemy craft split off to the right. An initial deflection shot missed, but then Mahurin straightened out and let the enemy fly through his fire from 100 yards. The 190 began to break up from the impact, the canopy flew off, and the pilot went over the side.

Mahurin then had to rescue one of his flight from a determined 190 that continued to hang on despite the efforts of the whole flight of Thunderbolts. As the turning match continued, things really could have gotten tedious when ten more 190s appeared on the scene. Twenty P-47s also arrived, however, and the show was over.

The old adage Beware of the Enemy in the Sun proved true for the Luftwaffe on September 16. Maj. Dave Schilling led the 56th to France, where some fifty FW 190s and Me 109s were seen approaching the bombers in the vicinity of Fougeres. This formation was immediately attacked and split up. The escort continued, and as the bombers started their bomb run, a flight of three Me 109s was sighted by a flight from the 62nd Fighter Squadron. These Thunderbolts dived down from out of the sun and broke up the attack, but not before the 109s turned into them.

The P-47s outzoomed the enemy fighters when they pulled up and came back down on the 109s. Lt. George G. Goldstein went back down on the tail of one of the enemy craft and managed to get strikes all along the fuselage and wing roots. The 109 went down spinning and smoking.

German personnel stand on the wing of Lt. Hiram O. Bevens' Thunderbolt down in France. USAAF

Capt. Gerald Johnson taxis out for takeoff in his Thunderbolt In the Mood. Note the centerline drop tank. USAAF

Thunderbolts of the 56th make a low-level pass over their base. The dedicated ground crews got a thrill out of seeing their charges in the air. USAAF

Capt. John Truluck's Lady Jane. USAAF

Lt. Robert B. Taylor was leading Yellow Flight of the 62nd Squadron when they sighted two FW 190s approaching the bombers. Once more an out-of-the-sun attack proved successful. Taylor split-essed and came down on his victim. A burst from 500 yards did not register, but one from 250 yards immediately affected the craft; pieces broke off and flames began to stream as it screamed down in a fatal dive.

September 27 brought about a ramrod to Emden, Germany, where the bombers went after the enemy submarine base. Maj. Dave Schilling led a maximum effort from the 56th, which consisted of fifty-one P-47s. As the Thunderbolts approached the bombers near Borkum Island, Germany, they sighted a number of enemy fighters. The 63rd Squadron led the way to the attack and found itself involved in a heated battle. Lt. John Truluck exploded one FW 190 and then went into a Lufbery circle with an Me 109. Both planes were close to stalling out when the 109 decided to break out. That was all Truluck needed. He opened fire, and at once the Messerschmitt began to disintegrate.

Lt. John E. Coenen downed two FW 190s, and Lt. Wayne J. O'Connor scored over an Me 109. One loss occurred on the mission. Lt. Harry P. Dugas was last seen engaged with enemy fighters and apparently was killed in the fight.

Another administrative change took place on September 30 when Maj. Philip Tukey left for 8th Fighter Command. He was replaced as commander of the 63rd Squadron by Maj. Sylvester V. Burke, Jr.

Lt. Robert Rankin's aircraft. Wicked Wacker was a P-47, and Weegie was Rankin's wife, Louise. USAAF

Another early scorer and ace of the 56th was Lt. Glen D. Schlitz, Jr. He scored his first three victories in this Thunderbolt. USAAF

October 2 brought another ramrod to Emden, which was led by Colonel Zemke. While flying along at 27,000 feet to the rear of the second box of bombers, Zemke spotted a lone FW 190 that was several thousand feet below and well back of the bomber formation. After delaying for some time owing to the difference in altitudes and distance from the bomber stream, Zemke finally decided to dive down after the enemy.

When Zemke was about 500 yards away, the 190 began to turn to the right. Zemke laid on deflection and fired, scoring strikes on the aircraft, which wavered and then straightened out. Another burst from 400 yards set the craft on fire. Still closing, Zemke fired again, and the 190 went into a shallow dive. The left gear of the plane dropped down and more smoke emitted as the 190 went into a vertical dive.

This made Zemke the first ace of the 56th Fighter Group. Although it has always been thought that Maj. Gerald Johnson was the first 56th ace, official records show that his supposed fourth victory of August 17, 1943, was split with Lt. Frank E. McCauley.

Maj. Dave Schilling was credited with two victories on the mission. Both were scored using the diving speed of the Thunderbolt. He caught an Me 109 as it attempted to climb up to bomber altitude and shot an FW 190 out of a formation of five on a diving attack.

October 4 brought the first real big day to the 56th Fighter Group. Fifteen German aircraft fell to the group's guns, and two pilots—Capt. Walker Mahurin and Lt. Vance P. Ludwig—pulled the hat trick: three victories each on one mission.

Major Schilling led the group as escort to the bombers that journeyed to Frankfurt, Germany. This also marked the first time that the P-47s had carried the new 108-gallon paper drop tanks, which enabled them to penetrate more deeply with the Big Friends. In the vicinity of Duren, Germany, a large formation of Me 110s was sighted as they formed up to the rear of the bomber formation. These twin-engined aircraft, armed with rockets, were readying themselves for a concentrated attack on the bombers while out of the range of the P-47s' .50-caliber guns.

The Thunderbolts of the 56th were ready. As Lieutenant Ludwig related the combat:

> We saw approximately twenty Me 110s at six o'clock to the bombers 5,000 feet below. Major Schilling peeled off sharply. I followed and fired at a blue-green Me 110 ending up dead astern. His right

Lt. Vance Ludwig got the group's first triple victory and won the first Distinguished Service Cross. USAAF

First ace of the 63rd Fighter Squadron and destined to be a top ace of the group was Capt. Walker M. ("Bud") Mahurin. USAAF

engine smoked, burst into flames, and he entered a slight diving turn to the right.

I pulled up sharply to the left into the sun; picked out a second, darker-colored Me 110; . . . throttle[d] completely back; [and] dove on him, closing slowly from dead astern to 150 yards. He broke sharp right, but I was able to pull one and a half rings' deflection on him. His right engine burst into flames; he rolled onto his back and dove straight down. I followed and fired a second burst, observing further hits.

I was at 15,000 feet, close to the bombers, and broke sharply to the left up into the sun. I saw two Me 110s flying straight and level, parallel to the left of the bombers. I throttled and closed slowly on the right one, directing Lt. [Adam J.] Wisniewski to fire on the left one. I experienced return fire above me and dropped lower so that the rear gunner could not depress his guns to follow me. I fired approximately 3 seconds from dead astern and observed strikes over the fuselage and right wing, and the right engine caught fire. The plane snapped viciously onto its back and went straight down burning. I pulled up to the left and observed a P-47 firing on [an] Me 110.

Captain Mahurin had joined Lt. John Vogt in going down to attack an Me 110, but en route he sighted another, so he left Vogt to continue on his own. Mahurin throttled back and bounced down-sun and opened fire from 300 yards. Strikes were noted all over the aircraft, and as Mahurin pulled up, the right engine was blazing and the 110 was headed down.

Capt. Don Goodfleisch and his Thunderbolt Li'l Goody. Goodfleisch became a commanding officer of the 63rd Fighter Squadron. USAAF

Capt. Leroy Schreiber came to the 62nd Fighter Squadron as a replacement in August 1943 and immediately became one of the hunters. Schreiber had 12 victories in the air and two on the ground when he was killed strafing on April 15, 1944. USAAF

The second 110 that Mahurin attacked was hit and rolled over on its back. Mahurin hung right with it and continued to fire. Mahurin broke off from the combat at 18,000 feet, but the enemy craft was observed by others to continue down in flames.

As Mahurin climbed back up to the bomber stream, he sighted a third Me 110 headed away from the combat zone. Mahurin closed to 300 yards and opened fire. This time strikes appeared all over the engine, and as he pulled up and looked back, Mahurin could see that the right engine was on fire and the plane was shedding pieces all over the sky.

Capt. Don Goodfleisch also got one of the Me 110s, and pressed his attack so close that he almost downed himself. As he pulled up from his attack, he noted dark smoke pouring out the right side of his engine and that his windshield was covered with

oil. On his arrival in England, it was found that pieces from the enemy plane had pierced his cowling and broken a pushrod on his engine. Goodfleisch also had to depend on his flight members to lead him home because he was unable to see through his fouled windshield.

Maj. Dave Schilling led the group once more on October 8 when the P-47s provided withdrawal escort for the bombers returning from Bremen, Germany. As the Thunderbolts joined up with the bombers, two straggling Big Friends were sighted under attack at the rear of the formation. Immediately the escort went into action. Schilling sighted an FW 190 positioning itself to make an attack on one of the stragglers and dived down to the attack. All it took was a burst closing from 400 to 250 yards to send the enemy craft down in flames.

Another early scorer in the 63rd Fighter Squadron was Lt. Harold E. ("Bunny") Comstock. Comstock would fly two tours with the 63rd Squadron, the second as commanding officer of the unit. USAAF

Capt. Leroy Schreiber also sighted a straggling bomber that was being followed by an FW 190 and went to the rescue. Apparently the tail gunner on the Big Friend was wounded or dead, for the enemy fighter pulled right up level with the bomber, firing repeatedly, and received no return fire. Schreiber pulled in behind the 190 and closed to pointblank range before opening fire. Pieces began to fly off his victim, and a flame began to trail back after a second burst was delivered. No doubt the pilot had been hit, for he took no evasive action as his plane began its downward journey. Schreiber noted that the aircraft was marked with a large V behind the cockpit, which would denote that it was flown by a Luftwaffe group leader.

Schreiber and his wingman, Lt. Harry Coronois, then sighted another FW 190 and positioned themselves astern of the aircraft. This time Schreiber provided cover while Coronois slowly closed and downed the enemy fighter.

Capt. Ray Dauphin went to the assistance of a straggling B-17, directed his fire at the attacking FW 190, and latched on as the enemy craft broke hard to the right. Dauphin fired, using about 20 degrees' deflection, and noted good strikes on the aircraft when suddenly his instrument panel exploded. His Thunderbolt had taken three 20mm hits from another enemy aircraft. Dauphin suffered cuts on his arms and his left leg and momentarily lost track of events. Fortunately, he recovered at about 18,000 feet with no enemy on his tail.

Undaunted by his wounds, Dauphin pulled up into the sun and re-formed his flight. Two FW 190s were sighted, and Dauphin hastened to intercept, but his attack was prevented owing to excessive engine vibration when he opened his throttle to move in. With this the P-47 pilot headed for home.

October 10 was marked by the pitched air battle between the men of the Flying Fortresses and the Luftwaffe as the Americans attacked targets at Munster, Germany. The 56th Group was assigned as withdrawal escort for the heavies. When Maj. Dave Schilling and the Thunderbolts had threaded their way through bad weather to the rendezvous, they found the bombers under heavy attack.

As Major Schilling saw it:

As we approached, I observed about sixty to seventy-five enemy aircraft making frontal, side, and rear attacks, and rocket bombs were also being employed. As we came in on the right side of the bombers, I saw six to eight enemy aircraft making a frontal attack on the lead box. I figured that we would be too late if we attempted to head them off, so I made a sharp 180-degree turn and picked them up as they finished their pass. One of the 190s broke left as he came out at 16,000 feet, and I dove on him.

I opened fire at 400 to 500 yards, dead astern, and could see flashes on his wings and fuselage but could not retain him in my sights long enough to hold a steady stream of fire on him until I had closed to about 300 yards.

At that point there was a sudden explosion in his left wing. Smoke began to come from the wing, the wing tip, and around the cockpit, and as I was forced to pull up over him, there was a huge flash.

Capt. Gerald Johnson was leading Blue Flight of the 61st Fighter Squadron. He reported that he sighted some twelve to fifteen enemy fighters to the rear of and above the second box of bombers that he had rendezvoused with. Johnson sighted an Me 110 closing on a B-17 that had fallen back from its information. He related:

As I neared the Me 110, I could see large bulges under each wing just outside the engines, which were probably rocket installations. I opened fire at about 300 yards and saw strikes on the fuselage and starboard engine, which started smoking. By this time we were within 200 yards of the B-17, and the enemy aircraft went under the B-17 very close. Since I was attacking from slightly above, I had to pull up hard to miss the Fort and went over the top. I

Lt. Fred Christensen was another of the early replacements of 1943 who was destined to become a top ace in the 56th Fighter Group. USAAF

then half-rolled and came out on the tail of the Me 110 again. At about 250 yards I opened fire, and the port engine started burning. There were strikes near the cockpit and along the fuselage. The pieces started flying off around the tail, and the enemy aircraft fell off to the left in a spin.

Johnson pulled back up, sighted an Me 210 twin-engined fighter, and closed in. As he fired at the enemy craft, he began to receive return fire from the rear gunner, but as he closed to pointblank range, the fire ceased and the 210 began to shed pieces and the port engine began to burn. At this point one man went parachuting over the side while the aircraft continued downwards.

Lt. Robert S. Johnson was in Captain Johnson's flight that day and became an ace by downing his fourth and fifth enemy aircraft but also had another narrow escape. As the P-47s attacked the enemy aircraft that had the B-17s under fire, Lieutenant Johnson selected an FW 190, but this aircraft broke hard and escaped. He then lined up on an Me 110 and ran right up its tail, firing all the way. The enemy

craft broke up under the massive firepower, and the lieutenant had to fly through the debris.

The Thunderbolt pilot then sighted three FW 190s in a V-formation and made a head-on attack. Johnson stated:

The one on the right pulled up to the right and started firing at me. Again I missed, so I gave more lead on the center FW 190. I saw strikes about the engine and cockpit, and then I had my left rudder cable severed by the FW 190 who was firing at me. I pulled up and around and saw the FW 190 that I had fired on burning and the pilot bailing out. I never saw his chute open. I was trying to find out how to fly my ship with no left rudder. Finally I found I could fly it with the trim tab, so I headed home.

Lt. James M. Jones, Jr., of the 62nd Squadron had quite an experience that day and was most elated to get home in one piece. Jones had been in on the initial attack of some of the Luftwaffe fighters but lost his target. As he orbited, he sighted two P-47s getting ready to attack an Me 210. As the P-47s closed on the enemy craft, Jones sighted a third fighter, which he initially took to be another Thun-

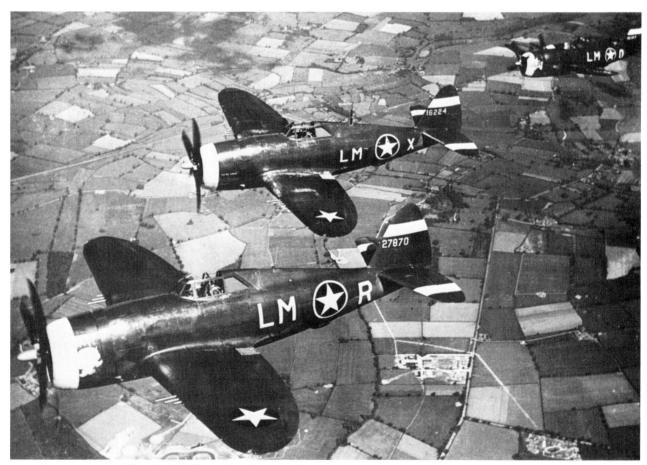

Capt. Horace Craig of the 62nd Fighter Squadron leads his flight in a beautiful formation. Note the glistening waxed fuselages and wings of the aircraft. USAAF

derbolt joining the attack. Then, as the aircraft passed below him, he saw that it was an FW 190 going after the P-47s. Jones let the FW pass, kicked hard rudder, and made a diving, dead-astern attack on the 190. The enemy pilot sighted the P-47 and broke to the right. As he straightened out, Jones closed on him, firing. The enemy pilot started a barrel roll, but as he rolled over on his back, smoke began to pour out and the aircraft started down in a violent spin. The pilot bailed out.

Jones was now alone, and as he climbed to set course for home, he was attacked from nine o'clock by two FW 190s. He called for help. When no one came, he initially went into a Lufbery circle. He did not seem to be gaining on the FW 190 he was chasing, and the other 190 chose to orbit above, waiting for him to break out. Jones then shoved everything forward and dived for the deck. At 10,000 feet he began to ease off and continued down to treetop level. One FW 190 hung on, and as it closed to about 1,000 yards, it began to take occasional shots at Jones. The P-47 pilot continued on his westerly course at full throttle pulling 60 inches

of manifold pressure. About 15 miles northeast of Antwerp, the German pilot finally gave up the chase.

Jones continued right on the deck, for he was not certain that the enemy had left him for good. As his fuel supply dwindled, he decided he might as well climb, and if the enemy was still present, he would have to fight it out. But on climbing to 1,500 feet no enemy appeared, so he set course for England.

Owing to the fog, Jones was unable to know when he reached England but was able to get a fix by radio and was directed to an airfield. He let down from 600 to 100 feet and still could see nothing. Thinking that he might as well climb and bail out, he slowly made it up to 800 feet. At this point he found a break in the murk and sighted an airfield that was still under construction. Jones immediately dropped his gear and began to let down. Several trucks were present, but he felt sure they would get out of the way. He picked out a runway and set down. He had rolled about 150 yards when he sighted a truck coming across his path. He immediately hit his right brake in an attempt to ground-loop but veered to the right and hit a tractor. A large

Another formation led by Capt. Horace Craig. These photos were taken from a B-24 Liberator, and its tail is visible here. USAAF

flash lit the cockpit, and Jones was temporarily stunned. He learned later that when he hit the tractor, fuel from it sprayed on his aircraft and ignited. Two medics from an engineering outfit leapt onto the wing and dragged him to safety.

Unbelievably, the 56th had struggled and fought its way out of the conflict with a total of ten victories while losing none of its own.

Eighth Bomber Command returned to the ball bearing factories at Schweinfurt again on October 14. The mission itself cost sixty bombers, and other bombers were write-offs on return owing to heavy damage sustained in the big air battle that became known as Black Thursday. The 56th was assigned penetration escort for the mission, but the Luftwaffe did not choose to attack the bombers while the Thunderbolts were on station.

The P-47s did encounter a few enemy aircraft as they turned for home. Capt. Gerald Johnson sighted two FW 190s 2,000 feet below him and shot one of them down in a diving attack. Fifteen Me 110s were sighted about the same time. Maj. James C.

Two 56th Group Thunderbolts in a rat race above the clouds. Such high-speed flying has always been a fighter pilot favorite. USAAF

Lt. James M. Jones of the 62nd Fighter Squadron and his aircraft A'hm Available, named after a comic strip character. USAAF

Lt. Col. James C. Stewart chalked up 11.5 aerial kills with the 56th Group and led many of the group missions. USAAF

*Col. Hubert ("Hub") Zemke, commander of the 56th
Fighter Group. H. Zemke*

When Col. Robert Landry had the 56th Group, he flew Louisiana Pirate. USAAF

Stewart led his flight down even though he knew that they only had time for a quick pass. The attack proved to be successful, however, not only in breaking up the enemy formation before it could get to the bombers, but also in seeing Lts. Frank McCauley and Norman E. Brooks each down one of the twin-engined fighters.

Colonel Zemke led the group on an escort to Duren on October 18. The Thunderbolts made the rendezvous point, but because of bad weather, the bombers never arrived. As the P-47s winged homeward, two enemy aircraft were sighted. The Thunderbolt pilots singled out one of the Me 210s, and a combination of six pilots took turns firing until the enemy went down.

The mission to Duren was repeated on October 20, and this time the bombers went to the target. Zemke took the escort up to 30,000 feet above the bombers to get out of the clouds. All total, some fifteen to twenty enemy fighters were encountered in the target area, but clouds prevented any amount of contact. Zemke managed to chase an FW 190 in and out of cloud formations and to down it, though he had to utilize all of his ammunition to do so. Lt.

John Vogt also caught an FW 190 and got it in a diving attack.

The 56th did not see further combat during the month of October, but a momentous event took place on the thirtieth of the month. Col. Hubert Zemke was recalled to the United States to brief the powers that be in Washington on the accomplishments and future needs of the 8th Air Force. He was replaced by Col. Robert H. Landry.

Live Bait

Lt. Ralph A. Johnson of the 62nd Fighter Squadron was leading a flight on the mission of September 7, 1943. Lt. Anthony Carcione was flying his wing, and Lt. John Eaves was leading the element. The 56th was escorting B-24s for the first time, and their target was the submarine pens at Leeuwarden. The takeoff and climb out had been normal. The Thunderbolts were scheduled to meet the Liberators about 30 miles inland and north of the Zuider Zee.

Flying in and out of the clouds, the P-47s lost sight of the B-24s. The group leader announced that the mission had been recalled and that the group would return to base. While flying back Johnson's flight entered a clear area, and there, to their amazement, were two Me 109s flying in formation.

The 109s were slightly below and off to one side. Carcione became very excited and reported the 109s about three times. Johnson told him to hold his place and that they would be in position to attack shortly. By now the lead 109 was just ahead and Carcione could wait no longer. He swung in behind the lead, and the second 109 pulled in behind him. Johnson fell in on its tail, and a real rat race was going. Fortunately, the 109 in front of Johnson made a slight turn to the right, which enabled Johnson to open fire. He hit the right wing root, and the wing came flying back to add to the excitement.

By this time the lead 109 was on its way to the deck. The pilot of the wingless 109 bailed out, and the American flight flew by to inspect him. The B-24s dropped their bombs on a coastal convoy but only splashed water on the ships.

On return Carcione stated, "All's well that ends well, but next time I don't want to be the bait."

Chapter 4

Carrying the Fight to Germany

The first ramrod of November 1943 was flown on the third when the bombers went to Wilhelmshaven, Germany. As the Thunderbolts approached the bombers, the American pilots noticed P-38 Lightnings all over the sky, most of them on the left side of the bomber formation. Capt. Walker Mahurin went after an Me 109 that was stalking four P-38s and whose pilot couldn't seem to make up his mind which one to attack. Mahurin came in on the 109's tail apparently unseen and opened fire from 400 yards. Strikes were registered, and Mahurin pulled out to the side. As the 109 headed for the clouds, Lt. Wayne O'Connor positioned himself behind the

The star of Capt. Walker ("Bud") Mahurin continued to rise in the fall of 1943 as he scored a further four victories in November. USAAF

Capt. Donovan Smith and Ole Cock. USAAF

enemy aircraft and opened fire. Mahurin also sprayed the 109 a couple of times, and the plane burst into flames.

Mahurin took off to catch up to the bomber stream. As he came up on the rear of a B-24 formation, he noticed that it was under attack from an Me 110. When Mahurin reached the enemy craft, it had positioned itself to begin putting rockets into the B-24 formation. Mahurin described the next events:

I came up directly astern of [the Me 110] and opened fire at about 400 yards. Again I saw many hits on both engines and the fuselage. I passed about 20 feet away from the enemy aircraft, and just as I looked into his cockpit, my wingman opened fire. At that time both the rear gunner and the pilot were looking at me. The rear gunner twirled around, grabbed his gun, and started to aim just as my wingman's bullets hit the 110. His shots hit the left wing and the rear gunner at the same time. I peeled up and around and started to deliver a second attack. By this time the 110 was smoking from both engines and was heading for the clouds. . . . I opened fire from about 400 yards, closing to pointblank. This time I saw a maze of flashes. The enemy aircraft belched black smoke, and my ship was covered with oil from the 110. As I broke up and away, I noticed the right engine was in flames from the prop spinner back.

I believe the reason I had to make two passes at each enemy aircraft was because three of my guns had malfunctioned and did not fire.

Lt. Robert S. Johnson caught an Me 109 ducking in and out of the contrails behind the bombers and shot its left elevator off. The enemy went down in a vertical spiral. The pilot never came out.

Even though he had departed as commander of the 56th Fighter Group, Col. Hubert Zemke returned on the morning of November 5 and led the penetration support. Using his proven methods of bomber protection, Zemke left the 62nd Squadron to protect the rear of the B-24 formation while the 61st and 63rd Squadrons moved up north in the direction

More of the 56th Fighter Group nose art. Lt. Joseph P. Walker and Little Eva. *USAAF*

Capt. Francis S. ("Gabby") Gabreski joined the 56th Group in England and became an outstanding ace and leader. USAAF

where the enemy fighters were assembling for their attack. The 63rd Squadron engaged, with Colonel Zemke downing one FW 190 and Lt. John D. Wilson another. Lt. George F. Hall knocked down an Me 210.

Maj. Francis Gabreski brought the 61st Squadron up and spotted twenty FW 190s well out ahead, making a run on the bombers from eleven o'clock above. The P-47s were between the enemy fighters and the bombers at 23,000 feet, so Gabreski decided to make a head-on attack. As Gabreski told it:

> At that moment it is assumed that the leader of the enemy formation spotted us, as he decided to make a 180-degree turn to the left, losing altitude and diving away from us. I followed in pursuit, overtook about the fourth fighter from the left, and opened fire at 500 yards and closed to 200 yards. I observed hits on the right side of the fuselage and right wing. The plane burst into flames from the inner portion of the wing, rolled over, and spun.
>
> Breaking off to the left, I picked up another FW 190 making a gentle left turn. I closed to about 350 yards [and] observed a few hits, but the plane continued to orbit. I broke off the attack as I ran out of ammunition.

Following the disastrous mission to Schweinfurt in October, 8th Bomber Command made no further attempt to penetrate deep into Germany. Every effort was being made to come up with a solution that would enable the fighters to go all the way to the target. The Thunderbolt groups, including the 56th, were using 75-gallon drop tanks and then moved up to 108-gallon tanks in an attempt to increase their range. With the use of the latter tanks, endurance increased to 3 hours or perhaps 3 hours and 15 minutes if proper throttle and turbo settings were used.

Two major improvements had been made to the Thunderbolt. The engine had been modified to accommodate water injection, which would give a pilot in trouble an immediate but short-lived increase in power. More important and welcomed was the installation of wide-blade propellers, which did

Another of the 1943 aces was Capt. Joe Powers. He scored 14.5 aerial victories while flying with the Wolfpack. USAAF

Lt. Wayne A. Brainard had the comic strip character Alley Oop fitted with an Uncle Sam top hat on the nose of his P-47. USAAF

wonders for the rate of climb of the P-47. With the "paddle-blade" propellers the rate of climb was increased about 600 feet per minute at low altitude and speed was increased some 10 miles per hour.

Escort tactics had improved greatly, and the fighters made rendezvous with the bombers along their routes. Certain groups would provide penetration escort, if possible over the target. As the bombers came off target, they would be picked up by fresh fighter units that would stay with them on the way home. This minimized losses greatly and made the Luftwaffe's job more difficult. Many targets lay beyond the range of the Thunderbolt, however, and therein lay a problem.

The arrival of the Lockheed P-38 was welcomed by 8th Fighter Command, as its staff felt that this was the aircraft that would fill the long-range bill. Although the P-38 was able to stay with the bombers, the weather of northern Europe did not agree with its performance—nor did it sit well with the Lightning pilots, who nearly froze thanks to inadequate heating in their cockpits.

Maj. Francis Gabreski led the group on a withdrawal mission from Munster on November 11. Capt. Walter Cook was leading White Flight of the 62nd Squadron and was letting down through the overcast from 28,000 to 23,000 feet as rendezvous

Lt. Joe Icard of the 62nd Fighter Squadron became an ace on the Berlin mission on March 6, 1944. USAAF

was made with the bombers. As Cook let down to within 2,000 feet to the right of the bombers, he sighted four FW 190s below to his right. This set up a perfect bounce for Blue Flight. Cook stated:

[As the bounce was made,] I saw only the leader escape. I then turned left and with my number 2 man and number 4 man started along the bombers, but we were attacked a number of times from the rear by sixteen enemy fighters and had a running fight for about 40 or 50 miles when I decided to run for home and stop breaking into the enemy. With our throttles wide open we approached the bombers when I saw an FW 190 above and to my right flying 90 degrees to me, towards the bombers. As he crossed my nose, I turned left, pulled my sight through him, and opened fire at about 500 yards. He broke left, jettisoning his belly tank, and half-rolled down. I followed him in the roll, still firing, and saw many strikes in the vicinity of the cockpit. I saw his canopy fly off after I hit him, but I believe it was due to my fire, because I believe the pilot was dead.

. . . I was then flying west beside the bombers when I saw my wingman being attacked from the rear and an FW 190 ahead of me was turning left into me. The 190 was about 500 feet below me and 800 yards away. I pushed my nose down and pushed my sight through his line of flight and fired a short burst. I saw an explosion on his right wing about 3 feet from his cockpit. Apparently I hit his ammunition. Then I pulled up, looked back, and the FW 190 was going down to the right. I could not watch him because I was being bounced from behind by another FW 190. I broke, and the FW 190 climbed into the clouds.

Leading Blue Flight of the 62nd Squadron was Capt. Eugene O'Neill. When O'Neill sighted the flight of four FW 190s shortly after rendezvous, he took his four P-47s down to the rear and right of the bombers, directly astern of the enemy fighters. He opened fire early, but closed to 200 yards firing all the way. Large pieces came flying off the FWs, and when O'Neill broke combat, the enemy was seen going down.

At the same time two other members of O'Neill's flight were getting in their licks. Both Lt. George Goldstein and F/O Joseph W. Icard closed rapidly, firing and watching as their victims shed parts. The pilot of Goldstein's 190 bailed out but apparently hit the tail of his aircraft as he went back.

O'Neill had to get a 190 off the tail of his wingman following the first combat. Both O'Neill's aircraft and the FW 190 went into a high-speed dive that reached 550mph indicated, and O'Neill was able to get strikes damaging the 190 before he broke combat.

The ordeal of Lt. Melvin C. Wood on this mission was another outstanding tribute to the ruggedness of the Thunderbolt. Wood and his flight leader were attacked by enemy fighters as they let down through the overcast to get to the bombers. Wood was hit by a 20mm shell that came from an FW 190 and that exploded in the engine and caused it to cut out. He then took another 20mm hit from dead astern that struck the right horizontal stabilizer. Two more hits from the same burst made contact with two blades of his propeller. One shell made a clean hole through the blade, but the other left a torn and jagged edge about 10 inches long. The unbalanced propeller caused the P-47 to jump and buck, and then the engine stopped. Wood was in a vertical dive, and he finally got the engine running again.

The Thunderbolt pilot pulled out of his dive at about 17,000 feet, but he immediately ran into another four FW 190s. He was forced to hit the deck slightly south of Enschede, Holland; from there he headed out over the English Channel.

As Wood flew over the Channel, the engine continued to cut out, and as he decreased his rpm and manifold pressure, it grew much worse. When he finally cut back to 1400rpm and 23 inches of mercury, things got so rough that it was impossible to read the instrument panel. About 10 miles from the English coast the engine stopped completely. Wood finally got it started again by priming, turning the emergency booster pump on, and hitting the starter. By this time he was down to 2,000 feet and was preparing to bail out, when the engine finally kicked over. Wood managed to get home and land just before his fuel supply was exhausted. Another save by the P-47.

Not all were as lucky as Wood. Lts. Wayne J. O'Connor and Malcolm Van Meter were killed in the day's action.

November 25 marked the first bombing raid to be carried out by Thunderbolts of the 8th Air Force. P-47s of the 353rd Fighter Group dive-bombed airfields at St. Omer while the 56th Group did level bombing from 24,000 feet. Lt. Col. Dave Schilling led fifty-three Thunderbolts, each laden with a 500-pound bomb, to the target. A B-24 Liberator had been assigned to act as bombardier. The P-47s encountered flak over the entire route and got a taste of what the bomber crews had to experience on every mission. On arrival at the target the release mechanism on the B-24 didn't work properly, which

Col. Robert H. Landry took command of the 56th in the fall of 1943 while Col. Hubert Zemke was back in the United States. USAAF

Lt. Stanley Morrill became a rising star of the 62nd Fighter Squadron in November 1943. He was an ace with nine kills before he was killed in action. USAAF

caused the bombardier to release late. On his release the Thunderbolts dropped their 500 pounders. Rather than laying a good pattern over the target area, most of the bombs from the P-47s fell wide of the airfield. Following this failure, the 56th did very little level bombing from that date forward.

November 26 was a maximum effort for 8th Bomber Command. It dispatched a record number of bombers, primarily for targets at Bremen. The Luftwaffe saw fit to oppose its bombing strenuously and presented the opportunity for the 56th Fighter Group to set a new record in the number of enemy

Capt. Walter V. Cook became an early ace of the 56th when he downed two Me 110s on November 26, 1943. USAAF

aircraft destroyed. Twenty-six German fighters fell to the guns of the Thunderbolts.

Rendezvous was made with the bombers just west of the target shortly after noon. Capt. Walter Cook reported that as he arrived, flying at 33,000 feet, he sighted many Me 110s and Me 210s attacking the rear of the bombers. Cook and his wingman, F/O Irvin E. Valenta, went down to attack the twin-engined fighters. Both American pilots opened fire on an Me 110, and Cook was rewarded with the sight of pieces flying off his victim, which began to blaze. As he looked around, he noted that the Me 110 that Valenta had attacked was also flaming.

Cook then went after the leader of the Me 110 formation, opening fire from about 400 yards and closing to 150 yards. He broke off his attack with the twin-engined fighter going down in flames. Valenta had closed in on another Me 110 and almost collided with it. This enemy craft also went down smoking.

Valenta made another pass on an Me 110 flying away from the bombers, but as he opened up on it from 500 yards, it split-essed and went for the deck. He then latched onto another Me 110 that was busy lobbing its rockets at the bombers. Valenta closed on this aircraft and got good hits on it before breaking off the combat.

Lt. Col. Dave Schilling, who was leading the group, sighted a lone FW 190 some 10 miles west of the bomber formation. Schilling did a slight turn left and went down to get on the tail of the enemy aircraft. By this time the enemy had sighted the P-47 and went into a flick roll followed by a split-ess. At this point Schilling was some 800 yards behind the FW. Schilling then broke off the combat and headed for rendezvous with the bombers. Unseen by Schilling, but observed by three other pilots in his formation, was a red parachute, which appeared after Schilling broke the chase.

As the Thunderbolts neared the bombers, several enemy fighters were sighted and attacks were made upon them. During these passes, Schilling lost his wingman and wound up alone. At this time he sighted an FW 190 in a shallow dive making a run on the bombers. Schilling made his move and closed on the enemy fighter. As he opened fire and began to close, he noted a heavy concentration of strikes and the 190 went down vertically, smoking.

Maj. Francis Gabreski, leading Blue Flight of the 61st Squadron, went after a pair of Me 110s as soon as he reached the rendezvous. He dived down on the stern enemy aircraft, and as he closed to 200 yards, he noted that both of the Me's engines were burning and pieces were beginning to fly off. His closure was faster than he had anticipated, and he

Capt. John H. Truluck was an ace with the 63rd Fighter
Squadron and also won a Distinguished Service Cross.
USAAF

A 61st Fighter Squadron aircraft is mired down after a
takeoff accident. Maj. Francis Gabreski got three of his
early victories flying this aircraft. USAAF

Lt. Gene Barnum of the 61st Fighter Squadron touches Pistol Packin Mama for luck. P. Conger

had to dump the stick to avoid a collision. Smoke and soot covered the Thunderbolt, and oil covered the leading edge of the wing. What Grabeski didn't know was that the leading edge of his right wing was crushed and his left wing was torn.

The Thunderbolt pilot formed up with his wingman, Lt. Eugene E. Barnum, and headed for another Me 110 that was trying to get into position on the rear of the bombers. As Gabreski approached, the 110 started a low diving turn. The Thunderbolt went in hot pursuit, and the enemy pilot had the twin-engined fighter going all-out. Gabreski opened fire from 600 yards and hit the 110 just before it rolled over and went down vertically. It never pulled out of its dive.

Capt. Walker Mahurin was leading Blue Flight of the 63rd Squadron. As they approached the bombers, they, too, sighted myriad Me 110s on the rear of the bomber formation. Mahurin wasted no time as he swiftly closed in on the closest enemy fighter and opened fire. His first target broke away,

A famous photo of the pilots who set an early kill record in the European theater of operations. These pilots were credited with 23 enemy aircraft on November 26, 1943: left to right, Capt. Walter V. Cook, Lt. Stanley B. Morrill, Lt. John P. Bryant, Lt. John H. Truluck, Capt. Walker Mahurin, Lt. Harold E. Comstock, Lt. Col. Dave Schilling, Maj. Francis S. Gabreski, Capt. Ralph Johnson, Maj. James C. Stewart, Lt. Frank W. Klibbe, Lt. Jack D. Brown, Lt. Eugene O'Neill, Lt. Raymond Pety, Lt. Irvin F. Valento, and Lt. Anthony Carcione. USAAF

so he cut in behind a second Me 110. This one was firing rockets into the bomber formation, as flashes could be seen in and around the Big Friends. Mahurin opened fire and moved in to pointblank range. Pieces flew off the enemy fighter, and as Mahurin closed to within 20 yards of the craft, he could see that the rear gunner was dead. The 110 was now burning, and the pilot went over the side and opened his parachute.

Mahurin moved right in on another of the twin-engined fighters and opened fire. It, too, immediately began to blaze and went down spinning. Mahurin went off for another target at full throttle and approached a third Me 110. As he closed to 400 yards, he was cut out by a flight of Thunderbolts that went roaring in between him and his target.

An Me 109 was sighted, but as Mahurin maneuvered to get into position to fire, the enemy pilot split-essed and went straight down. Mahurin did not follow. At this time the group commander called for the P-47s to assemble and head for home. As Mahurin set course on the right side of the bombers,

he spied an Me 110 heading down. Diving down to 14,000 feet, Mahurin called for two P-47s to cover his tail while he attacked. He pulled in astern of the enemy fighter and hit the trigger. The full impact of the .50 calibers hit the fuselage of the Me 110, and then the 110's engines began to burn. The aircraft nosed down, burning fiercely. In his report, Mahurin paid tribute to the Thunderbolt for bringing him home even though he had flown the aircraft in combat at full boost for at least 30 minutes. Although the engine overheated and ran rough, the journey home was accomplished uneventfully.

The only 56th Group pilot lost on the mission was Lt. Byron L. Morrill, who went down to become a prisoner of war.

On November 29 the 56th provided penetration support to Bremen. En route to the target two FW 190s were encountered. They were attacked by Lt. Col. Dave Schilling and Lt. Felix D. ("Willie") Williamson. One of them was destroyed by the combined firepower of the two Americans.

Maj. Francis Gabreski was leading White Flight of the 61st Fighter Squadron. As the squadron

Lt. Charles Reed in Princess Pat *flies off the wing of a B-17. Nothing was more popular with the men of the Big Friends than the sight of an escort fighter. USAAF*

approached the target area with the bombers, it was bounced by enemy fighters. This split up the P-47s, and Gabreski was left alone with his wingman, Lt. Joe Powers. These two Thunderbolts went off to investigate some contrails out to the side and ahead of the bombers. The trails turned out to represent forty-plus enemy fighters.

Gabreski and Powers bounced the first eight Me 109s, which were at 28,000 feet heading for the bombers. Powers then called for a break, as they were being attacked from astern. Gabreski recalled:

I broke off my attack and pointed my nose up in a 45-degree climb. Outclimbing my pursuers two or three times, Lieutenant Powers and I made a determined effort to close on eight Me 109s just below us at 28,000 feet. Having the advantage of altitude and with full throttle, I pointed my nose towards the formation, picked out a straggler, closed to 600 yards, and fired. I observed hits on the fuselage and belly tank. The belly tank broke into pieces. I pressed my attack, closed to 200 yards, when I observed gray smoke pouring from the engine, along with a very little flame. The plane fell off to the left, went into a spin, and was last seen going into the clouds.

A few seconds elapsed, and I swung over to the right, picked out another 109 [flight] of four, opened fire at 700 yards, and closed to 200 [yards] from dead astern. The belly tank blew up, and strikes were seen centered on the fuselage and wings. Smoke and glycol poured out of the engine while the plane went into a slight dive and flew straight for about 10 seconds. At 24,000 feet the 109 fell off slowly to the left, rolled over, and went straight down.

While Gabreski was attacking his second victim, Powers sighted another 109 coming in on his leader. He swiftly turned into the 109 and hit it with a short burst. At this, the 109 reversed its turn, which caused it to mush into Powers' line of fire. The P-47 pilot then hit the 109 with a long burst, from which the enemy aircraft rolled over and exploded.

Lt. Harold Comstock was flying in Capt. Walker Mahurin's flight when, over Papenburg, Germany, Lt. John Wilson called in a break. Comstock broke to the right and saw Wilson with an Me 109 shooting at him. Wilson had been hit in the left leg and was doing his utmost to get away. Comstock stated:

The work of the ground crews was unsurpassed. Here mechanics and armorers get Maximum Goose ready for a combat mission. via Sam Sox

Lieutenant Wilson had to reverse his turn. The P-47 roll was slightly faster than the Me 109 [roll], but our climb and turn were very inferior to his. I turned to drive him off Lieutenant Wilson's tail, and my first two passes were from about 400 yards. I hit him in the left and then the right wing. On my third pass I raked him from the engine to behind the canopy and on both wing roots. He fell off to the right in a spin, smoking badly.

The 56th accounted for six German fighters for the day but lost Lt. Frederick Windmayer of the 63rd Squadron. He was heard stating that he was low on fuel and thought that he was going to bail out over the Channel. Nothing further was ever heard from him.

Maj. Francis Gabreski led the group on a penetration escort on December 1. This was not a good day for the 56th; although by and large combat was limited, that which took place was sharp and vicious.

A number of vapor trails were present upon arrival in the target area. Gabreski went off in search of the enemy, but his first two attacks were quickly broken off by enemy aircraft that refused to do combat.

He attacked for the third time, going after a Ju 88 that snapped and rolled to the right and headed for the clouds at full throttle as soon as Gabreski opened fire. At this moment Gabreski felt his engine lose power and oil splattered over the windshield. He immediately zoomed up to 12,000 feet and leveled off. Smoke was now coming out the side of the engine cowling, and Gabreski began warily to contemplate bailing out over Cologne, Germany. He decided to try to stay with the aircraft as long as possible, but the cylinder head temperature was climbing and the oil pressure began to drop. To worsen the situation he noted contrails from Me 109s ahead.

Gabreski's wingman, Lt. Norm Brooks, told him that if he was going to try to make it home, Brooks would stick with him. The hits that Gabreski had taken from the rear gunner of the Ju 88 were troubling but not fatal. Gabreski set course for home with an engine that was running rough, at about 150mph with 17,000 feet of altitude.

Slowly but surely Gabreski began to climb at about 300 feet per minute. He finally got up to 24,000 feet. All the while his faithful wingman was weaving back and forth across his tail, giving him protection. As he flew out over the North Sea, he heard a distress call over the radio. A Thunderbolt had a propeller stuck in high pitch and was heading inland. Gabreski turned and to his amazement saw that the malfunctioning aircraft was piloted by Brooks, who was doing the 180. Gabreski limped

into England, made a successful landing, and hurried to operations to learn what had happened to Brooks. Fortunately, Brooks had managed to decrease his pitch a bit after getting to lower altitude and had made it back to England.

Gabreski and Brooks were two of the fortunate pilots who made it home that day after unfortunate experiences. Several Thunderbolts ran into combat with a scattering of Me 109s and FW 190s. Three of the enemy aircraft were downed by the pilots of the 56th, but the American fighters lost three of their own. Lts. Vance Ludwig and Harry M. Pruden, Jr.,

Lt. Donovan Smith of the 61st Fighter Squadron had a good day on the ramrod to Emden on December 11, 1943. He shot down two Me 110s and shared an FW 190. USAAF

were killed in action, and Lt. Cleve M. Brown, Jr., was shot down and taken prisoner.

Lt. Col. Dave Schilling led fifty Thunderbolts out on December 11 to furnish penetration and initial withdrawal to the bombers striking at targets in Emden. Rendezvous was made, and it was observed that the Big Friends were already under attack. Some twenty-plus single-engined fighters were seen to make passes on the bombers from eleven o'clock, and then forty-plus twin-engined fighters were sighted down below, assembling for their onslaught from the rear.

The 61st Squadron began to maneuver into position to go after the twin-engined attackers. Maj. Francis Gabreski made a sharp turn to get after six Me 110s and at that time saw a huge explosion. He assumed that this was probably a bomber getting hit, but it turned out that two 61st Squadron P-47s had collided during a crossover to get at the enemy. Lts. Edward J. Kruer and Lawrence R. Strand did not survive the mishap.

Lt. Paul A. Conger, leading Yellow Flight of the 61st Squadron, quickly positioned himself on the six o'clock position of the Me 110s. He put a short burst into the fuselage of one Me 110 and then lined up on the leader of the formation. Conger proceeded to spray the 110 from 500 yards down to 150 yards. A small explosion was observed, and black smoke poured back from the right engine. The aircraft went into a spin, and another pilot in the fight later saw it hit the ground.

Conger then came in on the rear of a Ju 88 flying with an Me 110 at 23,000 feet. These aircraft headed down, with the Thunderbolt in hot pursuit. The Ju and Me were traveling at a good 400mph, and closure was slow. At 10,000 feet Conger began to fire on the rear plane from 500 yards. As he closed to 100 yards, the right engine exploded and burned. As he passed underneath the plane, he saw the leading enemy aircraft hit the water. Conger zoomed up and saw the rear enemy craft hit the water in flames.

Capt. Robert A. Lamb was flying White One on the mission. When the twin-engined enemy fighters

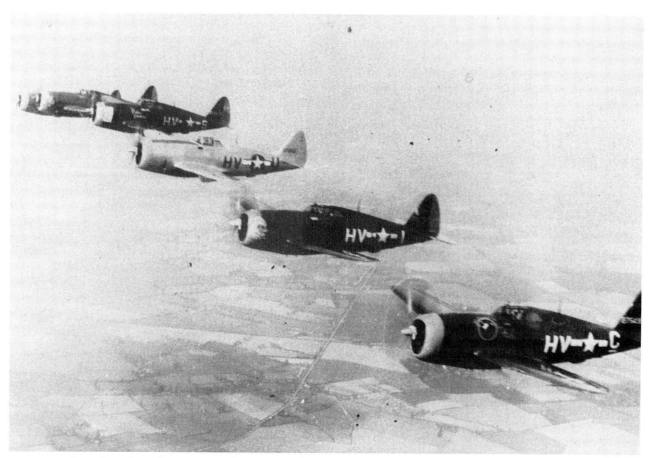

A 61st Fighter Squadron formation with Capt. Paul Conger's Hollywood Highhatter *in the foreground.* USAAF

were sighted, he dived down from 34,000 feet to 26,000 feet and went to work. He lined up on an Me 110 and hit it with a long burst. Two figures went over the side to parachute. Lamb then went after a Ju 88, which fired its rockets at the P-47 as Lamb pulled by it.

Lamb next pulled in behind six Me 110s flying at 23,000 feet. As he closed astern, the formation dived away to the left. Lamb followed the 110s down to 15,000 feet and attacked while they were all flying abreast. He closed on the third craft from the left and hit the trigger, and the eight .50 calibers did their job. The right wing collapsed and one man bailed out. While Lamb was firing at this enemy aircraft, the one to the right pulled into a sharp left break and both men aboard bailed out.

Meanwhile, Major Gabreski had flown several attacks on enemy aircraft following the midair collision of the two 61st Squadron Thunderbolts and had downed an Me 110. As he recovered altitude from his victorious combat, he sighted a formation of six aircraft that he took to be P-47s and went over to join them. Much to his surprise he gazed down on black crosses as he flew over the formation. He gave his Thunderbolt full throttle and headed for home.

As Gabreski was leaving the Emden area, he sighted a lone Me 109 approaching from his two o'clock position and well beneath him. Initially, he thought that the German pilot went his merry way and he continued to head for home. The 109 pilot began to make an effort to do combat, however. By this time Gabreski was low on fuel and in no position to do battle.

The 109 kept closing, so Gabreski turned into it in the hope that it would break off. They went two or three rounds at full throttle and with no decision in sight, then the P-47 pilot decided to climb and head for the bombers. As he ascended through 27,000 feet, Gabreski noticed that the 109 went into a shallow dive, picked up speed, and then pulled up in a stalling climb pointing his nose at the Thunderbolt. Gabreski broke hard right, stalled the plane, and while in the stall was hit. A 20mm shell pierced the skin of the aircraft, nicked Gabreski's boot, and struck the right rudder, where it exploded. The P-47 lost all power and went into a spin. Gabreski grabbed the canopy, opened it, and was ready to bail out when the aircraft came out of its spin.

Gabreski went into a dive with the canopy still open, all the while looking to the rear for his pursuer. He finally found shelter in the clouds at 1,000 feet. Gabreski continued to bob in and out of the clouds until he reached the Dutch coast, at

Maj. Robert A. Lamb was an early ace and leader in the 61st Fighter Squadron. USAAF

Lt. George C. Goldstein's Thunderbolt expressed Goldstein's opinion of the Nazis. He was shot down in December 1943 and survived to become a prisoner of war. USAAF

51

which point the Me 109 gave up the chase. The Thunderbolt pilot struck out over the North Sea with only 50 gallons of fuel left, but with a helpful controller guiding him in he made it back to base with a few gallons to spare.

Seventeen German fighters had fallen to the Thunderbolts, and the 56th's only losses were the two pilots who were victims of the midair collision.

December marked a momentous event in the strategic bombing of Germany. The initial P-51 Mustang group, the 354th, although assigned to the tactical 9th Air Force, began flying escort missions with the 8th Air Force. The range of this aircraft made it possible for fighters to go all the way to any target in Germany with the Big Friends. Once its capabilities became known, most of the fighter units in 8th Fighter Command put in their bids for the aircraft. The 56th, however, which had trained on the Thunderbolt and was happy with the aircraft, voted to keep its trusty mount.

The first experience the 56th had with the Mustangs came on a ramrod mission to Bremen on December 20. Just as the Thunderbolts of the 63rd Squadron were reaching the target, a group of Mustangs was seen coming out head-on at 25,000 feet. Immediately following them at 28,000 to 31,000 feet were fifteen Me 109s, which attacked by flights. The 109s were initially identified as P-51s, which caused some confusion. As one flight was attacked by six Me 109s, the P-47s turned into them. Trailing the 109s was a lone FW 190. Following the crossover, the 190 turned away from the 109s and got on the tail of F/O Walter E. Frederick. Lt. Charles Clamp turned onto the tail of the 190 and opened fire on it from 300 yards. The 190 rolled over to the left and went down smoking, apparently out of control.

Lts. Charles W. Reed and Harold Comstock went after two ME 109s that nosed down and then pulled up in a sharp climb and came in behind them. The 109s were able to outclimb and outturn the P-47s at 31,000 feet. Lieutenant Comstock was able to lose his opponent only by flying through the B-24 formation.

Lt. Joe Powers also had a lot of trouble with one of the 109s. He chased one of the enemy aircraft coming off its attack on the bombers. Although Powers cut him off, the enemy pilot outclimbed and outturned the Thunderbolt. Finally, by pulling into a stall turn, Powers was able to fire a burst at the 109 from about 300 yards with a nearly 60-degree deflection shot. Some hits were observed as he turned back the other way. The 109 then did a violent snap roll and started to spin. As the 109 pulled out

and rolled over on its back, Powers was able to hit it again. This time the enemy pilot flipped over and bailed out.

As Powers was forming up to go home, he sighted another Me 109 chasing three P-51s. He ran after the 109 and managed to get a few hits before the Mustangs reversed their course and came back. Powers broke off and left the Mustangs chasing the 109.

Even with the confusion the 56th Group was credited with five enemy aircraft destroyed for the day but lost Lt. Robert Taylor of the 62nd Squadron, who was not seen again after ditching his aircraft.

Capt. Walker Mahurin scored his twelfth and thirteenth victories on December 22 on a ramrod to Osnabruck, Germany. The escort was slightly west of the target when two Me 109s were observed lining up on the rear Liberators. Mahurin went down after the 109s. The enemy aircraft went down through a small cloud, and only one of them came out on the other side. Mahurin closed on the aircraft and noted that it had a large fuel tank under one wing and rocket containers under each wing. The Thunderbolt pilot closed to 100 yards and let go a long burst that hit the fuel tank. The 109 exploded.

As he broke off combat after flying through debris and flames, Mahurin sighted another 109 climbing up to the level of the bombers at 26,000 feet. Apparently the 109 pilot did not see the Thunderbolt behind him, as he took no evasive action. Mahurin was looking right into the sun and couldn't see through his gun sight, so he closed rapidly and just fired short squirts into the sun. Finally the nose of the enemy aircraft dropped, and it was obvious that it had been hit hard, as it was smoking. Another burst was sufficient to send parts flying off the aircraft, and it went into a vertical dive.

Two other enemy fighters were downed on the mission, with Lt. Robert S. Johnson scoring his seventh victory.

Limited action was seen for the balance of the month of December. Lt. Robert S. Johnson scored his eighth victory on the thirtieth when he finally downed an FW 190 after a high-speed dive, and then on the thirty-first he scored two more victories near St. Gilles, France. A half dozen FW 190s attempted to attack the bombers, and Johnson chased two of them down to 4,000 feet, where they sought refuge in the clouds. On both occasions Johnson fired from long range to prevent the escape of the 190s, and on both tries he got good strikes that resulted in the destruction of the enemy aircraft.

The mission of January 4, 1944, gave the pilots of the 56th Fighter Group a new lease on life. On this mission the P-47s were all outfitted with paddle-

The *wolf* was another popular item for fighter nose art.
This one graces the nose of Lt. Wayne O'Connor's aircraft.
USAAF

Lt. Joe Egan's *Holy Joe*. Egan became one of the aces of the
63rd Fighter Squadron. USAAF

Lt. Robert Taylor and his Thunderbolt Taylor Maid. He was killed on an escort mission to Bremen on December 20, 1943. USAAF

blade props, which did wonders to the performance of the Thunderbolts. The task was to provide penetration and withdrawal support to the B-17s attacking Munster. Some fifty enemy fighters were reported flying head-on to the bombers north of Munster, but when the Thunderbolts arrived and attacked, the enemy dispersed and attempted to get through to the bombers in small numbers. Most of these were driven off by the escort without claims.

The only claim for the day was made by Lt. Michael J. Quirk. He was leading a flight from the 62nd Fighter Squadron when he sighted a straggling Fortress under attack by some FW 190s. The P-47s made a 180-degree reversal and sighted two

flights of P-47s that were orbiting the B-17 that was under attack but were doing nothing to assist it. Quirk saw one of the 190s make its pass and get strikes on the Big Friend, which went into a gentle dive.

Quirk was still in a dive and had to follow the 190 for several thousand feet before he could get in a good firing position. As he closed to 250 yards, he hit the trigger but saw no results. He moved in closer and fired once more. This time large flashes were seen and the leading edge of Quirk's right wing was hit by pieces flying off the enemy aircraft. When last seen the 190 was in a high-speed, tight spiral, going down and smoking badly.

The mission of January 5 was led by Lt. Col. Dave Schilling as the Thunderbolts gave escort to the B-17s attacking ball bearing plants at Elberfeld, Germany. Enemy fighters in formations of twelve to twenty appeared in the target area, but most chose to avoid combat in the hope that they could pursue their interception of the bombers once the escort had departed. The Thunderbolts of the 56th mixed it up in several sharp actions and downed four single-engined fighters.

Maj. Dave Schilling's first P-47, whose nose was adorned by Dogpatch character Hairless Joe, came to grief in a crash-landing. USAAF

Chapter 5

Winter Doldrums and Big Week

The New Year brought about another great change to the 56th. Beginning in late 1943, the aircraft complement for the group had been increased from seventy-five P-47s to 108 P-47s. Slowly, additional pilots and ground crewmen had been assigned to

Lt. Thaddeus Buszko and his aircraft Flak Sack, *of the 62nd Fighter Squadron. USAAF*

the unit to bring it up to a full personnel complement that could put the increased number of aircraft in operation. When this had been accomplished, it became possible to operate two group formations, A Group and B Group. This plan was inaugurated on January 11.

The bombers' target was the FW 190 assembly plant at Oschersleben, Germany, and its defense brought about one of the largest air battles since the Schweinfurt mission in October 1943. Strangely, B Group escorted the bombers to an area west of Hanover, Germany, and did not encounter enemy opposition. For A Group it was a different story. On rendezvous the 61st Squadron positioned itself out in front of the Fortresses, the 62nd Squadron took up its post over the third box of bombers, and the 63rd Squadron formed up out at three o'clock to the bombers.

The 61st Squadron, led by Col. Dave Schilling, was hit by twenty-five Me 109s and ten FW 190s from 3,000 or 4,000 feet above. This created a large dogfight, and angry fighters attacked each other all over the sky. Capt. James R. Carter was in Schilling's squadron. When the Me 109s had been met head-on, he broke to the left and climbed up above the fight. A 109 appeared in front of him, and he dived on it, going straight down. Hits were observed, but too much action was occurring to follow it down. Carter and his wingman broke off combat and climbed back up to the bombers. Eight enemy fighters were seen climbing up to the bomber formation, and Carter and his wingman made a head-on pass, which caused the enemy to dive for the deck.

About this time Carter received a distress call regarding a straggling bomber. The Big Friend was sighted, and it had six enemy fighters going after it.

Carter and his wingman got on the sun side and bounced an FW 190 that was flying parallel with the bomber. As they approached, an Me 109 made a pass at the Fortress and broke over in front of the 190 and turned to the right. Carter immediately latched onto it and closed to 200 yards before he began to fire. Several bursts took their toll on the 109, and the pilot jettisoned his canopy and bailed out.

After the initial onslaught Schilling climbed back up to the bombers and caught sight of two FW 190s blasting away at a straggling Fortress that was on its way down. He fell in behind one of the 190s and sent one down in flames. He then picked up the other 190 and went after it as it entered a dive. Strikes were scored in the dive, but the enemy pilot managed to find sanctuary in the clouds, so Schilling began to gather his forces to return to base.

Lt. Glen D. Schlitz of the 63rd Squadron managed to repeat an earlier feat and performed what the RAF pilots called "the hat trick" by downing three enemy aircraft. As Schlitz told the story:

The first batch of Germans I saw included about seventy-five FW 190s and Me 109s. I led my flight of P-47s at the first group of about twenty Me 109s. They were flying tight, but we got in and I shot the leader off first. He nosed over, I gave him a burst in the belly tank, and he blew up like a firecracker. The fool who was flying his wing just sat there watching, so I gave him a few bursts, too, and he blew up.

A stalwart and dependable leader of the 61st Fighter Squadron was Capt. James R. Carter. USAAF

Lt. Hillyar S. Godfrey and everybody's favorite Bugs Bunny, Thumbs Up Doc. USAAF

Col. Hubert ("Hub") Zemke and one of his first P-47s with
the wheel painted on the nose and My Friend spelled out
in Russian. USAAF

Lt. Joseph P. Walker and Miss Box. Walker flew his tour
with the 62nd Fighter Squadron. USAAF

Capt. Bob Lamb's Jackie, in which he scored his early
victories. USAAF

I guess there were more Germans in one spot that day than I've seen since starting my combat operations in April. After we broke up the Me 109 crowd below, I saw a single attacking a struggling Fort, so I went down and he repeated what the others did. I guess good old caliber .50s affect them all the same way. When my bullets hit this fellow, he nosed up, exposing his belly tank, so I gave him a few there and he blew up.

January 19 brought about important staff changes to the 56th. First and foremost, Col. Hubert Zemke returned from the United States and took command of the group from Col. Robert Landry. The following day Zemke appointed Maj. Francis Gabreski deputy executive flying officer and operations officer of the group. Maj. James C. Stewart took over command of the 61st Fighter Squadron.

On January 21 the 56th A Group was assigned a support mission over the Pas de Calais area, where the heavy bombers struck at a number of V-weapons sites. Thunderbolts from the 61st Squadron sighted

This piece of flak may not have had the pilot's name on it, but it sure came close to getting his name on his crew plate. USAAF

Lt. Frank Klibbe ran out of fuel in one tank while the water injection switch was accidentally turned out. Result: fouled plugs, no air start, crash-landing. F. Klibbe

four FW 190s climbing up to attack a formation of eight B-17s. Red Flight went down after the enemy aircraft, and Blue Flight followed it down. Lt. Robert S. Johnson saw the enemy craft pull up to position themselves to attack Red Flight and called for Red Flight to break, but apparently Red Flight didn't hear the call. One of the FW 190s began to line up on Lt. Allen Dimmick as Johnson dived to his rescue.

Johnson stated:

I rolled over on my back, diving straight down from about 13,000 feet, yelling for Red Two to break or pull out. I opened fire at extreme range, hoping to scare the FW off. Red Two didn't seem to hear me. I saw heavy strikes on Red Two's left wing root. I was then about 5,000 [feet] and hitting the Focke Wulf. He pulled from side to side, making a difficult target. I felt pretty bad, as I had been just a fraction too late to save Red Two, so I was definitely determined to get a kill. I hit him at different times in my dive, and finally at about 1,000 feet I closed to 100 yards and saw strikes all over the canopy and wing roots and evidently hit his guns, for [they] all went off. I last saw him at 800 feet on his back in a dive at 475mph.

Johnson's victory was the only one for the day and the only recompense for the death of Dimmick.

January 29 saw both A and B Groups providing withdrawal support to the bombers that attacked targets at Frankfurt. Lt. Col. Francis Gabreski led B Group. A number of enemy aircraft were sighted shortly after rendezvous, but the P-47s encountered primarily those attacking straggling Fortresses. Gabreski went down out of the sun to close on an Me 110 that was lining up a B-17. He opened fire and closed to 100 yards, at which time glycol began to stream back from the twin-engined German fighter. As Gabreski pulled off, the 110 was seen to spiral downward with smoke and flames pouring from the right engine.

Capt. Joseph H. Bennett was flying with Gabreski, and he, too, sighted a B-17 under attack. Five Me 110s were ganging up on this aircraft when Bennett took his flight in to do battle. As he lined up on one of the Me 110s and opened fire, he noted two other P-47s from his flight also closing on his target. Bennett moved over to the next enemy aircraft on the right and opened fire. Both Bennett and his wingman, Lt. Praeger Neyland, fired on this aircraft, and it went down with its left engine burning. Bennett then moved over to a third target. He opened fire on this aircraft from slightly above and closed from 400 to 50 yards. As he passed under the Me 110, one of its propellers was windmilling, and as he pulled up, he saw the aircraft nose over in a vertical dive.

All total, B Group accounted for four twin-engined fighters, with no losses.

A Group was led by Lt. Col. Dave Schilling. After rendezvousing with the bombers he discovered that they were not a part of his task force, so he flew north to look for his charges. Some 15 miles south of Bonn, Germany, he sighted an Me 109 at 25,000 feet with one wheel down. Schilling immediately pulled in on the stern of this aircraft, opened fire at 200 yards, and sent it down in flames.

On the way out Lts. Harold Comstock and Kenneth Lewis were bounced by two FW 190s from out of the sun over Knocke. Lieutenant Lewis was shot down and killed, and Lieutenant Comstock managed to damage the enemy aircraft that had downed Lewis.

The 8th Air Force put up over 800 bombers on January 30 to attack German aircraft assembly plants at Brunswick, Germany. Both A and B Groups of the 56th were assigned as withdrawal support for the Big Friends. A Group was led by Schilling. Although combats could be seen in the distance, the P-47s engaged in no action until they encountered ten to twelve enemy fighters in the vicinity of Almelo, Holland, on the way home. Lt. Michael Quirk came in on the tail of one Me 109 and damaged it, and then closed on another 109. This one he closed on until he left it a ball of flame.

B Group, under Lt. Col. Francis Gabreski, sighted enemy aircraft 8 minutes before the group made rendezvous with the bombers. Ten-plus twin-engined fighters were seen flying in close formation at 12,000 feet in the vicinity of Lingen, Germany. The P-47s broke up this enemy formation, but Gabreski and his wingman, Lt. Frank W. Klibbe, didn't even fire at these. As they pulled up at 12,000 feet, a lone Me 210 was sighted. Gabreski attacked this aircraft and got numerous strikes on it before he left it with its right engine on fire and trailing gray smoke.

Some 10 minutes later Gabreski and Klibbe found two Me 109s well below them as they cruised along at 13,000 feet. Gabreski took the enemy craft on the right, and Klibbe took the 109 on the left. Both pilots waited until close range before they opened fire. Multiple hits were made on both of the Me 109s. Gabreski's target went down streaming smoke, with its propeller windmilling. Klibbe's victim went into a verticle dive, streaming smoke.

Lt. George Hall and his wingman, Lt. Lloyd M. Langdon, became separated from this flight, which had bounced a formation of Ju 88s. They set up escort for a formation of B-24s when they saw fifteen Me 109s below and heading northeast. The two Thunderbolts split-essed and came in on the rear of the Luftwaffe formation. Hall fired at four of the Me 109s, damaging two of them and sending two of them down in flames.

Langdon pulled up alongside Hall on the rear of the Me 109s and began firing. His target took hits, and an explosion occurred in the left wing root. Shortly thereafter Langdon's fire took its toll on another enemy fighter, whose pilot was seen to bail out.

Capt. Walker Mahurin of the 63rd Squadron sighted a formation of sixteen Ju 88s at the time of rendezvous and led his flight after them. He picked out the tail-end Charlie and scored several hits around the tail of the aircraft and on its right engine. Mahurin claimed only a probable on this Ju 88. "By this time," Mahurin related,

The enemy aircraft were in a turn to the left, evidently trying to get into a Lufbery circle. I picked out one [of] the Ju 88s in the middle of the bunch and began to fire at it. At first I noticed several hits in various places, but when my tracers started coming out, I was able to get a considerable burst into the cockpit and right engine. The Ju 88 then rolled over on its back and went straight down from 6,000 feet. I claim it as destroyed.

By this time there were several more Thunderbolts in the fracas, and my memory of the following incidents is rather jambled. I started after another enemy aircraft and began to fire at it. I am not sure whether or not I hit him, but during this time I ran out of ammunition. At this time I was within 50 feet of him. I tried several times to ram him, but each time I would get into his prop wash and miss him. He finally straightened out and headed for the cloud

layer. As I tried to ram him for the final time, he rolled and disappeared into the cloud.

Lt. Robert S. Johnson scored his thirteenth and fourteenth victories on the mission. His first was an Me 210 that was downed after his squadron had broken up its formation shortly after rendezvous. The second was an Me 109 that he caught as it pulled out of a dogfight and headed south just on top of the cloud cover.

B Group was credited with thirteen enemy aircraft for the day and lost none of its own.

February 3 saw the Thunderbolts provide penetration support for bombers whose targets were the U-boat and shipbuilding facilities at Wilhelmshaven. The 63rd Squadron of B Group was the only one to see any action, and it was limited. Capt. Walker Mahurin and Lt. Charles Reed downed Me 109s near the rendezvous point. This marked the fifteenth victory for Captain Mahurin.

On the way home Captain Mahurin's supercharger regulator went out and he was forced to drop down to approximately 10,000 feet. Lt. Joseph L. Egan, Jr., with his wingman, Lt. Lloyd Langdon, dropped below the clouds to protect Mahurin on his way home. As they did so, they sighted six Me 109s and two FW 190s start attacks on Mahurin and his wingman, Lt. Russell B. Westfall. When the six Me 109s sighted the two Thunderbolts, they rolled over and went down through the next-lower overcast. The FW 190s, however, decided to proceed with their attack on Westfall. Egan and Langdon were

Another crash-landing, this time on the English sea coast by a 62nd Fighter Squadron Thunderbolt. USAAF

As the endurance of the P-47s was extended, so was the length of time the pilots had to sit on the hard parachute and life raft packs. Capt. Mike Quirk had the resultant red rear depicted on the Donald Duck on his aircraft. S. Sox

then forced to fight for some time and drive the enemy fighters away.

By this time both pilots were very short of fuel and still some 200 miles from home. They both felt they could still make it, so they set out on what they believed was the shortest route home. Unfortunately, Langdon's plane ran out of fuel 40 miles from the English coast. Egan circled above, radioing the position to air-sea rescue. After doing all that he could do, Egan had to go on. He, too, ran out of fuel before he reached the coast but was able to glide to shore and crash-land on the beach. Langdon was never found.

The 56th escorted the bombers back from Frankfurt on February 4. Although no great opposition was encountered, the 62nd Squadron of B Group mixed it up with twenty-five FW 190s near Charleroi, Belgium. Lt. Fred J. Christensen attacked a 190 that was on the tail of a P-47. He pressed his

Two Thunderbolts from the 63rd Fighter Squadron out over the English Channel. The aircraft in the foreground was that of Lt. Robert B. Campbell, Jr. USAAF

attack from 250 yards to pointblank range, at which time the enemy aircraft exploded.

Lt. Michael Quirk downed another FW 190 that was flying with a wingman who deserted it as soon as the P-47 opened fire. On the way out Quirk encountered a twin-engined aircraft near St. Omer. As he approached, a man was seen to parachute from it. The premature action so astonished Quirk that he watched the parachute all the way to the ground. When he began to look for the aircraft from which the man had exited, he was unable to sight it either in the air or on the ground.

Lt. James E. Fields had destroyed an FW 190 in the initial attack and was on his way home when he was jumped by eight Me 109s in the vicinity of Lille, France. To escape he dived to the deck and flew so low that when he looked up he "saw a tree." Fields struck the tree, damaging the propeller and the wings. During the action, one 20mm shell hit the hydraulic line in the left wing, so it became

necessary for Fields to belly-land when he came in at Manston, England.

The 56th provided area cover for the bombers attacking targets in the Pas de Calais area on February 6. Thunderbolts of B Group encountered enemy fighters in limited numbers and managed to down five of them. Capt. Robert A. Lamb, leading White Flight of the 61st Squadron, went after six Me 109s in the Beauvais area. He went down on the enemy aircraft as the lead 109 pulled up to attack the bombers. The attacking 109 then turned south, with the P-47s right behind. Lamb swiftly closed on the

Lt. Joseph Egan was one of the original members and early aces of the 63rd Fighter Squadron. USAAF

Capt. Mike Quirk of the 62nd Squadron became one of its top aces and also commanded the unit before he was downed by flak and became a prisoner of war. USAAF

initial flight of two and opened fire from 200 yards. One of the enemy aircraft began to fly apart, and the pilot went over the side.

As he closed on his target, Lamb became the target of two 109s coming in from his rear. Lt. Robert J. ("Shorty") Rankin, doing the good wingman's duty, made a feint into them, and they broke away. Some minutes later Lamb and Rankin went after four Me 109s, but as Lamb broke up-sun, three Thunderbolts came racing through between them and Rankin was forced to break hard right, leaving Rankin all alone. It was then that Rankin spotted two Me 109s down at 8,000 feet and went after them. The P-47 pilot began firing from 600 yards, but his deflection was off, so he hung on the tail of one of the 109s until he had closed to 200 yards at 5,000 feet. A long burst from this distance gave instant results, and the 109 went down in a vertical dive until it exploded on the ground.

Capt. Eugene O'Neill was leading Red Flight of the 62nd Squadron when he sighted a straggling B-17 under attack in the vicinity of Paris. Two FW 109s dived from 18,000 feet to intercept the Fortress, which was at 11,000 feet. O'Neill and his flight went after the second 190, and O'Neill opened fire from

Lt. Robert ("Shorty") Rankin, an early replacement pilot who became an ace in the 61st Fighter Squadron. USAAF

Full profile of Capt. Eugene O'Neill's L'il Abner, the Dogpatch comic strip character. USAAF

500 yards but saw no strikes. As he closed the distance, he gave the enemy a long burst, which sent it spiraling down, smoking fiercely.

During this period of February, two significant additions were made to the 56th Fighter Group. Before he joined the 56th, Lt. Col. Francis Gabreski had been in England flying with the Polish No. 315 Fighter Squadron of the RAF. From time to time Gabreski continued to visit his Polish friends. As the 56th Group became more involved in combat, some of the Polish pilots begged him to see if they could join the American unit. Gabreski went to Colonel Zemke, who took the matter up with 8th Fighter Command. The move was approved, so a half dozen Polish pilots, including ace B. Michael Gladych, were assigned to the group.

The second addition to the group was squadron markings. Zemke had been requesting that he be allowed to use some sort of squadron marking so that he could more easily identify the group's aircraft in the air. Permission was granted, and the cowlings of the 56th Group's P-47s were painted as follows: 61st, red; 62nd, yellow; and 63rd, pale blue.

The group went back to Frankfurt on February 8 but saw little action. Lt. Joe W. Icard of the 62nd Squadron's Red Flight was attacked head-on by four

These markings were below Captain O'Neill's cockpit: the four-leaf clover, and Jessie-O for his wife. USAAF

This aircraft from the 63rd Fighter Squadron is another example of how the Thunderbolt could take a beating and still make it home. USAAF

Several pilots from the Polish Air Force came to fly with the 56th Fighter Group. They are shown here with Maj. Francis S. Gabreski: left to right, S/Ldr. B. Mike Gladych, F/Lt. Sawicz, Gabreski, F/Lt. Janicki, F/Lt. Tadeusz Andersz, and F/Lt. Withold Lanowski. USAAF

Thunderbolts from the 56th peel off to come in for a landing. USAAF

Me 109s near Cambrai, France. As the enemy aircraft completed their pass, one of the 109s racked around to attack Icard, who turned into it. When the 109 broke, Icard got on its tail and hosed it down in a high-speed dive.

On February 3 Maj. Horace Craig, commanding officer of the 62nd Fighter Squadron, became the first member of the 56th Group to complete a combat tour, and on the ninth he was replaced as commanding officer by Maj. Leroy A. Schreiber.

A momentous order was passed down from 8th Fighter Command Headquarters in early February. With the departure of Brig. Gen. Frank O'D. Hunter as commander, his replacement, Maj. Gen. William E. Kepner, gave the pilots a new lease on life. They were instructed as follows: "If bombers are not being attacked, groups will detach one or two squadrons to range out, searching for enemy aircraft. Upon withdrawal, if endurance permits, groups will search for and destroy enemy aircraft in the air and on the ground."

Lt. Frank Klibbe's Little Chief at rest. It has a centerline drop tank hung, so a mission must be forthcoming. F. Klibbe

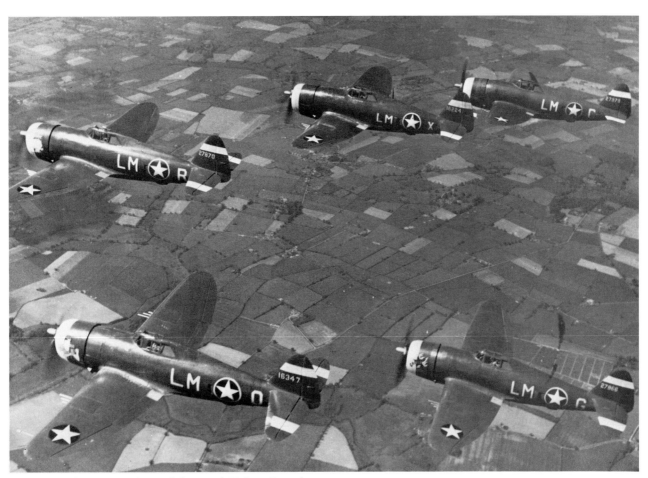

A beautiful formation photo of the 62nd Fighter Squadron over England. Note how well the white identification stripes show up in the air. USAAF

A typical rainy day in England. Lt. Tony Carcione's aircraft glistens in the moisture. Note the drop tanks over on the edge of the hardstand. USAAF

Capt. Donovan Smith and his aircraft Old Cock were well known in the 56th. Smith became an early ace and leader in the 61st Fighter Squadron. USAAF

The 56th Group wasted no time getting on the scoreboard with ground kills, which were now being credited to the pilots in the same fashion as air kills in order to encourage the pilots to get down to earth for victories. The group was escorting the bombers to Frankfurt when four Me 109s were sighted in the vicinity of Liege. Colonel Zemke left the 63rd Squadron with the bombers and took off after the fighters. The 109s were dispersed, and Lt. Joe Icard was credited with downing one of them.

Colonel Zemke then attempted to catch up to the bomber stream but could not. He gave the order to turn back. On the route home the P-47s passed over an enemy airfield identified as Juvincourt, France, where a number of parked planes were seen. Zemke led the two squadrons in a single strafing pass and destroyed an Me 109 on the ground for the group's first ground kill.

Maj. Sy Burke led B Group that day, and it encountered a few enemy fighters on the way out. Some Me 109s and FW 190s were intercepted making halfhearted passes at the bombers, and four of them were downed by Thunderbolts from the 56th.

Another administrative change took place in the 56th on February 19. Maj. Gerald W. Johnson, who had been a 56th ace before he went over to the 356th Fighter Group, returned to take command of the 63rd Fighter Squadron. This move delighted the men of the 63rd, who knew that they would no longer suffer from "see-no-evil, hear-no-evil" leadership.

For some weeks 8th Air Force had wanted to get Operation Pointblank underway. This operation would be directed at destroying the Luftwaffe in the air and on the ground. Massive air assaults would be flown against aircraft assembly plants and airframe factories in Germany. Not only the heavy bombers of the 8th Air Force, but the strategic bombers of the 15th Air Force from Italy would join in the attacks on the targets. It was felt that this would surely bring the Luftwaffe up to do battle in the air, where it could suffer further destruction.

The operation had been on hold for some weeks owing to weather, but finally the weather people forecast a period of clear skies over the Continent and all stops were pulled to get maximum efforts into the air beginning on February 20. The period February 20 through February 25 would become known as Big Week.

The Thunderbolts of the 56th were fitted with 150-gallon drop tanks for the mission of February 20. These tanks were made from sheet metal and manufactured in England. The additional fuel would keep the P-47s in the air for an extra 15 minutes, or enable them to have a range of 350 miles.

A Group rendezvoused with the bombers and passed up the line to the front box west of Dummer Lake, Germany. No opposition was encountered until the P-47s were about ready to break escort in the vicinity of Hanover. At that time Lt. Justus D. Foster called Lt. Col. Francis Gabreski and reported a formation of twin-engined fighters below at seven o'clock. He suggested that Gabreski lead the squadron in a 180-degree turn to the left that would put the Thunderbolts in an excellent position for the bounce.

This was soon accomplished, and the ensuing battle was described by Lt. Donovan F. Smith:

Upon completion of our turn we were up-sun and directly behind [the enemy]. We started our pass at 23,000 feet. Colonel Gabreski identified them as thirteen Me 110s flying in two sections of six and seven respectively. Colonel Gabreski led the entire 61st Squadron into one of the most coordinated and surprising attacks I have ever seen. He was about 500 yards in front of me. He opened fire, and an Me 110 on my left fell to pieces. His tail came off, and flaps and pieces of wings, et cetera, flew all over the sky. Then I closed up on the one on the extreme right, and he started a slight turn to the right. I was very close and hauled up about three-quarters of a ring deflection at 175 yards and hit him all over. He fell out of control, and his right engine started burning fiercely.

I kept on flying straight ahead and fired at two or three others, as were several other fellows in the flight, observing several hits. I flew through the whole mess. P-47s were shooting all around me and Lt. [Claude E.] Mussey on my left fired at a 110 and I saw several pieces fly off his engine and he then flipped over on his back.

I continued on up to the first bunch, which up to now were unmolested and evidently more completely unaware of their coming fate. Another P-47 and I made a simultaneous attack, he taking one of the middle ones and I taking the one [on] the extreme right. I saw Lieutenant Foster get very good hits all over his, and right after that mine exploded in the port gas tank and flew to bits.

The 61st Squadron downed seven of the Me 110s, with Colonel Gabreski getting his twelfth and thirteenth victories and Lt. Robert S. Johnson getting his fifteenth and sixteenth victories.

Lt. Col. Dave Schilling led B Group, which did not encounter any enemy fighters until it got ready to break escort. At that time Capt. Leroy Schreiber observed an Me 109 at 15,000 feet positioning itself to make a stern attack on a B-24. Schreiber made a pass at the 109, which broke for the deck as soon as it came under fire.

Schreiber then sighted a flight of four Me 109s that had made an unsuccessful attack on the Liberators. As they swung around for a stern attack, the

P-47 pilot went down after them. Schreiber reported:

> Opening fire on the number 4 man from 300 yards, at 10,000 feet, I saw strikes all over the wing roots and engine and learned later that his engine dropped out.
>
> I then slid over behind the number 3 man, waggled my wings, and opened fire at 275 yards. There was a heavy concentration of strikes around the cockpit, engine, and wing roots, and I believe the pilot was killed immediately.
>
> I then waggled my wings at the number 2 man and opened up on him from 250 to 300 yards. He also was hit around the engine and cockpit, and I believe that he, too, was killed. The plane went down, out of control, with the engine burning badly.
>
> I waggled my wings at the leader, but [he] broke immediately. As he did so, I fired about thirty rounds at him and saw some hits. I had fired with insufficient deflection, however, and did not follow him down because my ammunition was nearly gone.

En route home Schreiber sighted a Dornier Do 217 bomber letting down to land at Wuntsdorf, Germany. Schreiber closed and fired his remaining ammunition but did not do sufficient damage to down the 217. This aircraft he turned over to Lts. Fred Christensen and Stanley B. Morrill, who finished it off. In addition to sharing the Do 217, Morrill made a strafing pass on a line-up of six Me 110s that were getting ready to take off from the airfield.

The pilots of B Group had added another six victories to the scoreboard for February 20, which made it a most satisfactory initiation to Big Week.

The following day Col. Hubert Zemke led A Group providing withdrawal escort for the bombers that attacked Brunswick. Although fighter opposition was experienced in numbers, in some areas A Group saw very few German fighters. Its only score

for the day was an Me 110 that Capt. John Vogt downed north of Munster when it attempted a lone wolf attack on the bombers.

B Group, which was led by Capt. Leroy Schreiber, became much more involved. Maj. Gerald Johnson was leading the 61st Squadron when it rendezvoused with the B-17s near Osnabruck. The withdrawal was going without incident until the squadron reached the Zuider Zee, in Holland, where five enemy fighters were queuing up on a straggling Fortress. As the Thunderbolts came roaring down, the FWs broke off—save one that pressed its attack, but it was shot down by a gunner on the bomber.

Johnson tacked onto an FW 190 that broke to the left, and at about 10,000 feet he had closed to 250 yards. A long burst from dead astern caused large pieces to fly off the enemy craft, and it went down in a slow spiral. This was Johnson's first victory since returning to the 56th and pushed his score to 9.5.

Also flying with the 61st Squadron that day was Capt. Mike Gladych. He went down with the rest of the P-47s to drive the FWs off the B-17. He pulled up and came under attack from two Me 109s flying abreast. He evaded by turning into the attack and then going into a dive. The 109s split and turned in opposite directions. He chose the one that broke to the left and managed to get on its tail. Gladych opened fire at 400 yards, and the 109 went into a dive and crashed in the Zuider Zee.

As Gladych climbed back to altitude, he sighted another Me 109 above him in a climb. Gladych pushed the throttle wide open and hit the water injection in order to overtake the enemy. As he closed, the 109 flicked over to the right. The P-47 pilot fired and saw the 109 go into a dive. He followed it but pulled out when he saw the Me enter the mist at 1,500 feet, still in a vertical dive.

Most of the fighters that were downed by B Group were 109s and 190s that were attempting to get to stragglers. The pilots of the 56th downed eleven of them.

Another mascot seen here with Lt. Fred Christensen is a proverbial black cat. USAAF

Lucky Little Devil *was the name painted on the side of Capt. John Vogt's aircraft. USAAF*

The weather turned foul on February 22. The B-17s of the 3rd Bomb Division canceled their missions, and the B-24s of the 2nd Air Division were recalled. The Fortresses of the 1st Air Division plodded on, however, and the escort went with them. A Group, led by Lt. Col. Francis Gabreski, saw the bombers being engaged south of Munster. Fifteen enemy fighters had just made a pass at the bombers, and they recovered to the left side of the bomber stream. This put Gabreski and his Thunderbolts directly astern at 23,000 feet.

The P-47s immediately attacked, and Gabreski sent an FW 190 down in flames. Among the attackers was F/O Evan D. McMinn, who saw two of the FW 190s positioning themselves to get on the tails of two Thunderbolts. He went after them and fired from dead astern. One of the 190s rolled over and went straight down, and McMinn went after him. With the dive rate of the Thunderbolt he stayed right on the tail of the enemy, and whenever he could get lined up he fired. Pieces of the enemy craft came flying back and cracked the windshield of the P-47, which in turn broke McMinn's sunglasses. He was forced to pull up, but Capt. Praeger Neyland saw the German pilot bail out.

Capt. Leslie C. Smith had downed an FW 190 on the initial attack of the enemy formation. As he broke off the combat, he sighted another 190 getting ready to attack Gabreski and his wingman. Smith went after the 190, and just as he was ready to fire, the FW split-essed for the deck. The two fighters

Capt. Leslie C. Smith receives the Distinguished Flying Cross from Brig. Gen. Jesse Auton. Smith was an early ace and leader of the 61st Fighter Squadron. F. Klibbe

Capt. Leroy Schreiber scored a number of his victories flying this 62nd Fighter Squadron aircraft. USAAF

hurtled down, nearly getting into compressibility before the enemy fighter finally pulled out at 6,000 or 7,000 feet. When the German pilot saw that Smith and his wingman were still with him, he went into another dive. Smith slowly continued to gain on the 190, and at about 3,000 feet he was very close. At this time Smith opened fire. Pieces flew off the 190, particularly from the control surfaces, and the left wing seemed to sag a bit. The plane seemed to go out of control and rushed earthwards as Smith pulled out at 1,000 feet.

Lt. Joseph Egan shot down an Me 109 on the initial attack against the fighters that were making runs on the bombers. Following this combat, he and his wingman pulled back up to 23,000 feet, where he sighted thirty enemy fighters that were working a figure eight pattern and going down after the bombers in twos and threes. Egan singled out two FW 190s and came in astern, but when he hit the trigger, his electrical gun sight went out. Undaunted, Egan tried to make do with the old ring-and-post sight but still didn't get any hits. Finally, by pumping the stick he was able to score a few hits, but he had to pass underneath his target to avoid ramming. Egan's wingman lined up on the same 190, and then his guns refused to fire. The two frustrated Thunderbolt pilots headed for home.

Regardless, it had not been a bad day for A Group. It was credited with downing ten enemy fighters.

Maj. James Stewart led B Group. As they escorted the Liberators on withdrawal, the 61st and 62nd Squadrons sighted very few enemy aircraft. Major Stewart did spot two Me 109s in the area southwest of Munster. He went down and destroyed one of them in a high-speed dive.

The 63rd Squadron caught ten to fifteen Me 110s attacking a box of bombers shortly after rendezvous, and Capt. John Vogt led them in to attack. The Thunderbolts not only broke up the formation, but shot down four of the 110s and probably destroyed another.

Heavy weather over the Continent grounded all aerial activity on February 23, but on the twenty-fourth the bombers headed for aircraft targets once more. The 56th A and B Groups were dispatched to escort the Big Friends to Schweinfurt.

Col. Hubert Zemke led A Group, which encountered sporadic attacks by small formations of enemy fighters. Maj. James Stewart downed an FW 190 in the vicinity of Kassel, and other pilots of the group destroyed four other enemy fighters. One loss occurred on the mission: Lt. Wilbur N. Kelly.

Capt. Leroy Schreiber led B Group, which met with scattered opposition from Dummer Lake to Holzminden, Germany. Maj. Gerald Johnson spotted three FW 190s in the vicinity of Minden, Germany, which were at eleven o'clock climbing toward the bombers. As Johnson went down, one of the 190s

Little Chief's Lufbery

The escort mission of February 22, 1944, would be forever welded in the mind of Lt. Frank Klibbe, who, with his Thunderbolt *Little Chief*, would be engaged in a 12-minute struggle for life or death. The mission for the 56th was to provide penetration support for the bombers en route to Bernburg, Germany.

The 56th A Group was being led by Lt. Col. Francis Gabreski, and they encountered enemy fighters south of Munster that were attacking B-17s. Lieutenant Klibbe was flying wing to Capt. Donovan Smith, who sighted an FW 190 and went down to attack. As the 190 peppered away at a Fortress, Smith pressed his attack until the enemy fighter became enveloped in flames and had a wing break off.

Now it was to be Klibbe's turn. Smith let him take the lead, and shortly thereafter Klibbe spotted an Me 109 down about 6,000 feet. Klibbe planned to dive down and level out and then close on the enemy aircraft. All was going well until, as he began to set his sights on the 109, a P-38 Lightning flashed into view right between Klibbe and his target. Having been denied his chance at this aircraft, Klibbe began to climb for altitude.

As he climbed through 8,000 feet, under the impression that Captain Smith was still with him, Klibbe suddenly discovered that the aircraft that he had seen behind him was not a P-47 but an FW 190, and the twinkle of lights in the leading edge of its wing told him he was being fired at. Klibbe immediately went into a Lufbery circle.

Klibbe pulled the stick into his belly and did his utmost to tighten his turn. The engine was wide open with full supercharger on, and the G-forces began to build up. *Little Chief* was straining and giving Klibbe its best. The Luftwaffe pilot was firing whenever he thought he had his nose pulled through, and Klibbe kept ducking whenever he would look back and see the guns firing.

Two Thunderbolts passed Klibbe down on the deck, and Klibbe called for help, but the call went unanswered. He continued to pull in tighter and hope that he could find some solution to escape the trap he was in. Soon four more P-47s were sighted passing overhead, but Klibbe was unable to make them understand where he was.

Klibbe had now resigned himself to his fate and knew that he and *Little Chief* could only escape through the ability of both of them to outperform the German pilot. Slowly Klibbe managed to get more distance between his P-47 and the FW 190, and soon he managed to secure a 180-degree position from the German fighter. Klibbe had just about made up his mind to make a break for it when the FW 190 rolled over and went into a dive.

It was over! He and *Little Chief* had performed to their utmost and bested the German for some 12 minutes, which must have been something of a record.

A tired Thunderbolt pilot who was now low on fuel and exhausted from his ordeal happily headed for home.

Eyes of the Eagle

On the morning of February 29, 1944, Maj. Gerald W. Johnson was leading the 63rd Fighter Squadron escorting B-17s. The Thunderbolts were flying at 24,000 feet, and all was very quiet. As the P-47s crossed the east side of the Zuider Zee, Johnson sighted a bogey down at about 5,000 feet, flying north. As no other activity was in the area, Johnson advised his charges that he was taking his flight down after the unidentified aircraft and told the balance of the Thunderbolts to stay with the bombers.

As Johnson descended, his speed began to build up and it was obvious that he would overshoot the bogey, which he identified as a Ju 52. Now certain that he could not make the strike, Johnson called his number 3 and told him to down the enemy craft.

Johnson pulled up in a tight turn and looked back, expecting to become a witness to his number 3 pilot downing an enemy aircraft. To his amazement he observed not three but seven Thunderbolts behind him in a tight turn, all hot on his tail.

Well, how nice, thought Johnson. *They wanted to save the kill for me.* He then came around and easily shot the enemy aircraft down. As soon as it was hit, it burst into flames and went down in a fireball.

When the pilots returned to base, Johnson learned that no one had seen the enemy aircraft until he set it on fire. Also, his call about his flight going down had been garbled, and for that reason two flights had followed him down. Strangely, the Ju 52 was the only enemy aircraft seen by the 8th Air Force that day, and but for the keen sight of Gerald Johnson the score for leap year day, February 29, would have been zilch.

Capt. Mike Gladych of the Polish Air Force wasted no time in showing his skills. Gladych had considerable combat experience before coming to the 56th. He scored an additional 10 aerial victories with the group. USAAF

turned 180 degrees, giving him a perfect shot from astern. Johnson closed from 300 yards to point-blank, and the 190 went down in flames.

Capt. Mike Gladych was flying with the 61st Squadron and had several interesting experiences. He was forced to drop down to 10,000 feet owing to difficulties with his oxygen system. He sighted an FW 190 with a P-47 on its tail and followed them down in a dive. They wound up right on the deck, and finally the P-47 gave up, apparently having expended its ammunition without result. Gladych then took up the pursuit, and the Luftwaffe pilot led him on a merry chase. The 190 stayed so low that Gladych had to concentrate on his flying rather than his firing, and he, too, ran out of ammunition and was forced to climb back up to altitude without result.

Back up at 10,000 feet Gladych found no Thunderbolts to join, so he set course for home. He was getting low on fuel so he leaned his mixture out and started for England. He was soon spotted by three FW 190s. As they attacked from astern, the only evasive action that Gladych could afford was to turn 90 degrees without increasing his rpm or manifold pressure. The Polish pilot stated that the German pilots must have been very inexperienced, as they attacked singly, always leaving two overhead. Each time Gladych thought an enemy pilot was ready to fire, he would close his throttle and the fire would pass in front of him. Finally the Germans came at him from astern, all three abreast. As they opened fire Gladych kicked rudder and went into a spin.

He recovered on the deck. Apparently the trick worked, for two of the FW 190s were gone. The lone enemy aircraft remaining made a few passes without firing and left. Gladych climbed back up and gave a mayday, as he thought he would have to ditch, but fortunately he landed in England with dry tanks.

The following day was the last day of Big Week, and the 56th Group's two formations furnished withdrawal support from Regensburg. By the time the 56th picked up the bombers, opposition was not great, and only three enemy fighters were downed by the group's aircraft that day. Capt. Michael Quirk chased an FW 190 over hill and dale before he finally got it. Capt. Robert Lamb really got in a rat race. He pursued an Me 109 that took him not only down on the deck, but through gorges, around cities, and over all sorts of obstacles before Lamb finally got some telling hits.

During Big Week, the 56th downed fifty-nine enemy fighters and the 61st Squadron became the first fighter squadron in the European theater of operations to reach the 100 victories mark.

Both groups went back out on February 29, but "leap year day" produced nothing in the way of enemy opposition coming back from Brunswick. One Ju 52 was sighted crossing the east coast of the Zuider Zee, and Maj. Gerald Johnson shot it down.

The "office" of a P-47 Thunderbolt. For a fighter it had a spacious cockpit. S. Sox

Lt. Charles Clamp, Jr.'s, P-47 on a rainy English day. The weather seemed to bother the pilots more than the enemy did. USAAF

Chapter 6

Momentous March 1944

The Thunderbolts took the bombers to Frankfurt once more on March 2, 1944. Aerial action was scarce, and for the 56th it was almost nil. The only victory scored was by Maj. Gerald Johnson, whose sharp eyes found a lone Me 109 nosing around the bombers in the vicinity of Aachen, Germany. John-

Capt. Jerry Johnson went to the 356th Fighter Group for a short while before he returned to the 56th to command the 63rd Fighter Squadron. USAAF

son went down and destroyed the 109 before its pilot knew what hit him. The enemy pilot bailed out.

The group lost one P-47 and its pilot on the mission. Lt. Edward N. Rougeau went down to become a prisoner of war.

For several months the question that had been on the mind of most members of the 8th Air Force was, when were they going to attack Berlin, Germany? With the arrival of the P-51 Mustang it was certainly possible to escort all the way to the target. As a matter of fact, the installation of shackles on the wings permitted the Thunderbolts to carry a 100-gallon drop tank under each wing, which further increased their range.

The initial attempt at Berlin came on March 3, but the weather prevented its being carried out. The following day the bombers ventured out again. Most of them aborted the mission, but a few got through to the Berlin area. The 56th was airborne and was forced to skirt a number of fronts but encountered no enemy opposition. Unfortunately, a veteran pilot was lost on the mission: Lt. Irvin Valenta was last seen entering a cloud formation over The Hague. It was presumed he fell victim to turbulence.

On March 6 the 8th Air Force launched over 700 bombers escorted by over 800 fighters to attack targets at Berlin. This time the industrial targets in the suburbs of the capital city of the Third Reich had no escape. The strike came in force and resulted in what was probably the largest air battle of the war. The 8th lost sixty-nine bombers and eleven fighters, and many aircraft returned so badly damaged that they were only good for salvage.

Col. Hubert Zemke led the 56th A Group, which put up thirty-five Thunderbolts. Zemke reported:

As group commander I disposed of the squadrons of my group over the five combat wings of the 1st Bomber Division so that I led well ahead of the front combat wing while the 62nd Squadron took a combat wing just to the rear and a bit south. The 61st Squadron was placed on the northern flank and on a combat wing further back. These positions were held for nearly a half hour, with the fighters patrolling at 23,000 and 25,000 feet in and about the bombers.

After passing Dummer Lake, still no direct enemy action had been seen, but it was known that a concentrated force was just ahead and could be expected. This information had been received from the ground and relay system back in England.

Up leading the 61st Squadron was Maj. James Stewart, who reported:

Maj. James Stewart's aircraft. Stewart was group operations officer but flew most of his missions with the 61st Fighter Squadron. USAAF

Lt. William P. Gordon's Barbara Ann II *of the 62nd Fighter Squadron. S. Sox*

Adorning the nose of Gordon's aircraft was another personal marking, Maximum Goose. *S. Sox*

We rendezvoused with the front combat wing of bombers near Lingen about 1125. Our position was on the left side of the bombers, so when I noticed another combat wing 3 or 4 miles to our north flying line abreast, I headed toward them, getting north of them. We continued on course with these bombers, making an occasional orbit, when due to radio transmitter trouble I turned the squadron over to Lt. Robert Johnson and turned my flight over to Lt. [Melvin] Wood. About 1140, when our two flights were a little ahead of the bombers and we made a 180-degree turn to the left to pass back by them, we saw what I thought was a full group of friendly fighters coming in at us from two o'clock and heading to the bombers from about seven thirty. We went right through the first box of about forty enemy aircraft and saw that they were FW 190s. We also noticed a box of twenty to forty enemy aircraft giving [the first box] high cover at about 30,000 feet. Half of the first box made head-on attacks on the bombers. At least twelve of them crossed in front of the bombers and made a tight turn on [the bombers'] right, coming in on them from three or four o'clock.

I took my wingman in front of the bombers and tacked onto the last of the FW 190s making these three or four o'clock attacks. I saw four blazing bombers as I passed . . . less than 1,000 feet [under them]. About this time I lined up on the rear FW 190 and saw a lot of hits on the wings and fuselage. The enemy aircraft rolled over and down vertically into the clouds, which were about 3,000 feet.

I then closed on the next enemy aircraft, and he noticed me on his tail and took evasive action. I finally closed up to 400 yards and hit him first on the right wing, then on the fuselage, and finally in the cockpit. His canopy blew off, and he rolled over to the right and dove vertically down through the clouds. I am sure in both cases that the enemy pilots were dead and that it was impossible for the enemy aircraft to have pulled out of their dives had they only been stunned.

When the 61st Squadron encountered the large enemy formation, Lieutenant Johnson radioed to Colonel Zemke for assistance and Zemke led his charges up at full throttle. His P-47s were some 15 to 20 miles away, and it took them a good 10 minutes to arrive on the scene. By this time all that was to be seen were several parachutes and burning aircraft falling still farther back.

Zemke spotted a lone FW 190 flying 3,000 feet below, however, and went down after it. The Luftwaffe pilot had lined up on a Fortress and was shooting at it when Zemke closed. The 190 went into a left-hand turn, which allowed Zemke to cut across and tag on its tail. When the Thunderbolt closed to 300 yards, Zemke opened up and saw immediate strikes. The burst was held until a collision was imminent. The 190 was last seen going down in a dive, trailing over a mile of smoke.

Zemke then sighted an Me 109 at some distance to the south. This one he chased down, and they went into a turning match. After one turn at full throttle Zemke was able to fire from 300 yards with 20 degrees of deflection. Hits finally showed up on the 109's wing, and the Luftwaffe pilot went into a dive. Down went the Thunderbolt now, blasting him all over. Smoke, flames, and pieces began to stream back as the 109 fell earthwards.

Zemke re-formed his flight, and they climbed up to 20,000 feet. At that time a lone Me 109 was sighted at the same altitude but some distance away. The enemy aircraft continued to circle, and the P-47s headed for it. When they were within a mile or so, the enemy aircraft went into a dive toward them. As the 109 continued in its dive, it suddenly broke into flames and went tumbling in a vicious spin. No ammunition had been fired, but the aircraft was totally consumed by flames before it struck the ground. Many years later Zemke was to learn that this aircraft had been fatally damaged by a P-47 from another group and that, unbelievably, the pilot had managed to bail out at a lower altitude.

Zemke pulled back up to 20,000 feet and headed west. At that time he sighted an FW 190 just above scattered clouds. He went into a long circular dive and opened fire before the enemy aircraft escaped. Some hits were scored before Zemke ran out of ammunition. His target was last seen diving into a cloud.

All total, Zemke's group downed eight enemy fighters but lost Lt. Andrew B. Stauss.

B Group was led by Maj. Gerald Johnson. It had to wait for the bombers, which were late making it to the rendezvous point. Lt. Fred Christensen sighted an Me 109 north of Dummer Lake, but when he attacked, the aircraft fled into a cloud bank, and although he waited, he never saw the 109 come out.

As he pulled back up, he sighted an FW 190 heading for a straggling Fortress that was about 5,000 feet below. Christensen attacked from up-sun and dived underneath the enemy aircraft. As he opened fire, he saw a large explosion, which was probably the 190's belly tank. More strikes were seen around the wing roots, and the aircraft went into a sloppy left turn. Hits were scored in the 190's left wing. Christensen was now down to 2,000 feet and dead astern. Another burst brought hits and flashes all over the 190. Christensen was forced to fly through all sorts of debris, and he observed the enemy pilot bail out as he did so.

Capt. Walker Mahurin stated that he was not really aware that the bombers they met with were under attack until he began to see flashes of 20mm bursts around them. The Thunderbolts sped to the rescue, but by the time they arrived, the concentrated attack had been dispersed. Following an abortive attack on an Me 109, Mahurin sighted an FW 190 at nine o'clock and went after it as it headed for the deck. This aircraft sought refuge in a cloud, but the density of the cloud was not enough to hide it. Mahurin was able to pepper the 190 down, but he finally lost it in another cloud. This time he was unable to find it again.

As Mahurin and his flight pulled back up toward the bombers, he spied a Thunderbolt in a turning circle with an FW 190 on its tail. As Mahurin attacked, the 190 broke off its attack on the P-47 and began to turn left. Mahurin used his water injection and was able to outturn the 190, get within 150 yards of it, and stay there. After a few more turns in the circle the 190 pulled up in a steep climb. Mahurin went up after it. The Thunderbolt pilot related what happened next:

As [the 190 pilot] fell off, he rolled over in order to pull the old standby of the Luftwaffe—the split-ess. I followed this also, gaining on him in the dive. When he pulled out of the dive, he headed straight for the clouds in the same manner as the other Jerry had. I was able to pepper him soundly, seeing many hits on both wings and fuselage. The Jerry appeared to be having difficulty in flying his ship. He made a

This is the Thunderbolt in which Capt. Paul Conger was painfully wounded on the March 6, 1944, mission to Berlin. P. Conger

180-degree turn to the left, and as I pulled up, I saw his canopy fly off and saw him jump over the side.

The limited action seen by B Group resulted in only two confirmed aerial victories. Capt. Mike Gladych destroyed an Me 109 on the ground when one flight strafed Vechta Airdrome in Germany. The only casualty was Capt. Paul Conger, who was painfully wounded in the shoulder and side from flak.

On March 8 the A and B Groups of the 56th were dispatched to furnish penetration support for over 400 B-17s and 200 B-24s assigned to bomb the VKF Ball Bearing Works at Berlin. This mission resulted in a big and successful air battle.

A Group, under the leadership of Lt. Col. Dave Schilling, made rendezvous with the bombers in the vicinity of Dummer Lake at 1242 hours. A few minutes later the first of three bunches of twenty-plus enemy fighters were sighted approaching the Fortresses from the southeast and slightly below. Maj. Gerald Johnson led the 63rd Squadron in after a flight of ten Me 109s trying to work their way

around to the rear of a B-17 formation. Upon interception the enemy formation broke up and Johnson got in a fleeting burst at a 109 without result.

He then pulled in on the tail of another 109, and as he closed, his fire took a heavy toll on the aircraft. As Johnson pulled up over the 109, he could see that most of the canopy was gone, the engine cowling was flying off, and the pilot was slumped over on the right side of the cockpit.

Johnson and his wingman were still together, so they started back to the bomber formation. Then they sighted a gaggle of thirty to forty enemy fighters diving down on the Fortresses from above in flights of four to six aircraft. As the Germans pulled out, they would attack any straggler that they had knocked out of the formation. Johnson and his wingman were not in time to break up the enemy formation, but they did drive off two attacks that were made on the stragglers.

As they started back to the main formation, Johnson got on the tail of an Me 109 that had just

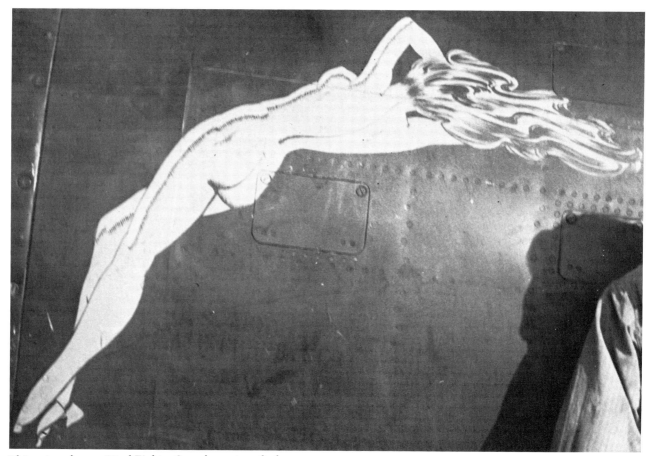

This artwork on a 62nd Fighter Squadron aircraft shows the influence of the Vargas-type pin-up art that was popular during World War II. S. Sox

come through the bomber formation. In a high-speed chase that reached 450mph the Thunderbolt pilot finally closed to 300 yards and opened fire. Strikes were seen, but Johnson had no idea he had put telling shots into the craft until he did an orbit at 6,000 feet and saw the 109 continue its downward course and crash.

Capt. Joseph Bennett and his wingman provided top cover for another flight from the 61st Squadron that dropped down to attack some FW 190s that went after the bombers. As he orbited and sank to about 12,000 feet, he noted a single FW 190 descending. When no Thunderbolts below went after the enemy, Bennett decided he would. He had to kill some speed going down, and when he finally leveled off, he saw that the 190 had its wheels and flaps down as it prepared to land at Wunstdorf airfield. Bennett opened fire from 400 yards and peppered the craft profusely before he broke away to the right to keep from flying over the airfield and testing its defenses. When he looked back, he saw the 190 burning about 200 yards short of the runway.

Bennett climbed back up looking for his wingman but instead encountered two FW 190s. This meeting resulted in a head-on approach, but the 190s broke off without a fight. Bennett climbed back up to 2,000 feet, where he encountered two Me 109s firing at him from 30 degrees and 200 yards. He broke into them and did a snap roll to the left. Bennett was of the opinion that they thought they had downed him, for when he leveled off, one of them was 100 yards ahead of him. The P-47 pilot immediately looked for the second 109, but it was not to be seen. Opening fire from about 15 degrees, Bennett saw the 109 break as if to chandelle, but instead it rolled over and went straight to the ground.

As Bennett climbed, he came under attack once more, this time from two Me 109s that broke off the encounter when he turned into them. Next came two FW 190s, one of which took a shot at him before he put his nose down and headed west at full boost. About 3 miles east of Steinhuder Lake, Germany, Bennett spied an Me 109 flying at about 2,000 feet that had been damaged and was apparently looking for an airfield. Bennett pulled up to about 300 yards and gave it a short burst. When last seen the pilot

One of Lt. Col. Dave Schilling's aircraft in the winter of 1943–44. Note the drop tank mounted on the centerline. USAAF

was crawling up over the side of the cockpit to bail out.

Bennett closed out a successful day by shooting up a train on the way home.

Maj. James Stewart flew with the 61st Squadron as a spare. Following the initial interception of enemy fighters, he was able to get on the tail of an FW 190, which he drove all the way to the deck before it crashed on the edge of a patch of woods.

On the route home Stewart observed ten parachutes, apparently from a downed American bomber, that were being circled by a twin-engined Me 110. Stewart went down immediately to thwart the threat. As soon as the enemy aircraft sighted him, it made an attempt to get away from the Thunderbolt. Stewart pushed the throttle open and shortly had the 110 in range and opened fire. His first burst hit in the cockpit area and sent pieces flying. A second squirt hit the right engine. As Stewart used up the remainder of his ammunition, he overran the enemy aircraft. As he and his wingman pulled up and looked back, a large fire was observed on the edge of a woodland.

Capt. Leroy Schreiber scored his ninth and tenth victories on the mission, downing an FW 190 from one of the initial attacking enemy formations and then shooting down an Me 109 while he was furnishing top cover for a flight of P-47s strafing an airfield on the way home.

Lt. John Truluck, Jr., of the 63rd Squadron, was involved in a high-speed-dive pursuit of an Me 109 that wound up down on the deck. As Truluck related it:

I followed him to the deck and continued to fire at various intervals. He led me across two airdromes, between trees, et cetera. At 0 feet I finally got a number of hits on him, and he began smoking. I saw him jettison his belly tank and canopy. I was overshooting and pulled up, thinking he was going in. My wingman called and said [the 109] was still flying, so I pulled out to the side and went down on him again. He was getting ready to belly in when I began firing again. He hit the ground throwing dirt, trash, and pieces of his plane up in front of me.

Afterwards Truluck and his wingman, Lt. John C. Marcotte, pulled back up to 10,000 feet, where they saw two P-47s in combat with two Me 109s being covered by two other Thunderbolts. Truluck described the subsequent events:

I let down to 4,000 feet and saw quite a bit of firing by the P-47s—they were striking ground ahead of the 109s. Two of the P-47s were at about 500 to 1,000 feet, cover[ing] the other two. Then I noticed the 109s getting in on the tails of the P-47s. The top two went down, but they couldn't do any good.
Since I was out of ammunition, I told my wingman to go down and help. I saw him make one pass

and overshoot. I then saw both 109s firing—one was hitting his P-47 all over. I called my wingman to get in on the scrap and went down on the 109. I closed to about 150 yards and pulled the trigger but had no ammunition. Then I tried to ram him. Then the P-47 exploded. I had dropped about 15 degrees of flaps but needed more so dropped about 25 to 30 degrees, rammed [the] throttle forward, and made a pass at him, trying to clip him with my wing. I missed by about 10 feet.
As I pulled up, the other 109 was coming at me from about 30 degrees [head-on], so I went for him, hoping to make him break and stall out. He was firing but not accurately. Then the first one was coming in on my tail, so I began a Lufbery at about 25 feet and look[ed] for help.
The other P-47s had disappeared, and the 109s were getting inside me, so I gave [the engine] water injection, pulled up into a straight climb, and left them. When I got to 20,000 feet, my wingman called and said he was heading out at 11,000 feet but was having supercharger trouble.

Shortly thereafter Marcotte was heard to say, "I'm bailing out." He descended to become a prisoner of war.

A Group scored a total of fifteen aerial victories for the day and had one more destroyed on the ground. Besides Lieutenant Marcotte, it lost Lts. Joe Icard and Frederick L. Roy, both of whom were killed in action.

B Group was up in full strength under the command of Lt. Col. Francis Gabreski. It, too, ran into stubborn and determined resistance in large numbers from Dummer Lake up until the point it broke escort. Lt. Robert S. Johnson of the 61st Squadron went after three Me 109s attacking a single Fortress. One of the 109s disappeared, and Johnson remained in pursuit of the other two.

As usual, the enemy fighters headed for the deck, and Johnson finally caught up to one of them at 3,000 feet. There he scored with a solid burst that sent the 109 crashing into the ground.

Johnson pulled up over an airdrome where he sighted several Thunderbolts making strafing passes. He climbed back up to 11,000 feet and sighted another P-47 with an FW 190 on its tail. Johnson called for the other Thunderbolt to climb and turn, and as it did, Johnson dived on the enemy aircraft, which broke combat and fled.

As he climbed back up, Johnson's number 2 and 3 aircraft came under attack from an Me 109. He called for them to break left, and when they did, the 109 broke right, so Johnson made a head-on attack on it, scoring a few hits. Johnson got on its tail and followed it down in a dive, scoring more hits. When he pulled out at 2,000 feet, the 109 continued downward in a vertical dive.

These two victories marked Johnson's eighteenth and nineteenth scores.

The first silver Thunderbolt to arrive on the scene. Capt. Paul Conger is in the foreground. This aircraft arrived in March 1944. P. Conger

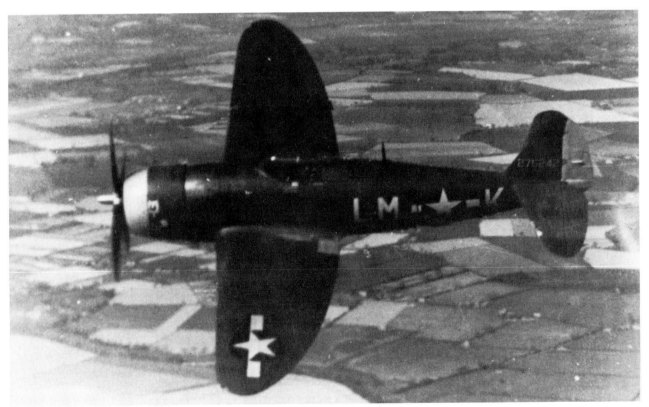

Capt. Mike Quirk banks into the camera to give a good profile of his aircraft. The rudder on this aircraft is yellow. USAAF

At about the same time Capt. Michael Quirk became involved in combat with an FW 190. Quirk had moved in so close to the enemy aircraft and hit it so hard that he couldn't figure out why it wouldn't fall. He finally ran out of ammunition and pulled up alongside the German aircraft and flew formation with it. The 190's left aileron was gone, huge holes gaped in its left wing and tail surfaces, and many other holes decorated the fuselage.

The Luftwaffe pilot chopped his throttle in order to get a stern attack on Quirk, but Quirk pulled up above him. Quirk then called in his wingman, Lt. John B. Eaves, to finish the 190 off. Eaves scored many more hits on the enemy aircraft, which crash-landed in a large field.

Capt. Walker Mahurin, leading the 63rd Squadron, thought that he was going to have to depart his escort mission before he had a chance to fire his guns in anger. As time began to run out, he looked over the side and saw an airdrome. One FW 190 was circling the field to the left. Mahurin stated:

I called the flight, and we started to attack. . . . The Jerry, now aware of our presence, passed down the runway from west to east and started straight off at treetop height. I dropped down behind him and began to fire. At first my shooting was rotten and I missed [but then I] got close enough to him to score a few hits on his fuselage [before] the 190 disappeared into the trees. I pulled up to make another pass at him, but he had crashed into the trees.

As we pulled up from this attack, we started to climb up while heading west. We again passed over the same airdrome. This time we spotted an Me 110 which had taken off and made a 90-degree turn into the traffic pattern.

I immediately made a left turn and started after him. I passed right over him and noticed the occupants looking at me. When I turned around to make another pass, I saw my number 3 man, Lt. Bernard [R.] Smith, come in behind it and hit it severely. When he broke off, the Me 110 did one more left turn and bellied into a field. . . .

. . . I noticed a Ju 88 that had just taken off, so I pulled up and went down on it, closing very fast. This time I fired and hit the enemy quite hard from about 200 yards to pointblank. As I broke up, I passed over the nose of the ship and saw at least four men in the cockpit. Its right engine caught on fire—the ship then let down in a nearby field and exploded.

For the fourth and last time we again went over the airdrome. At 6,000 feet we saw another gray 190 circling the field for a landing. Again we bounced. By this time everyone in the vicinity of the airdrome was fully aware of our presence. When the pilot of the 190 saw us coming, he started off to the south right at treetop level. I put on the water and began to close on him. I fired and fired but could observe no hits because my windshield was covered with oil. The Jerry would beetle along the treetops, and whenever he came to a field, he would

drop down on the field again, pulling up to go over the trees. Finally, he pulled up to avoid some high-tension wires and I was able to get in a good burst. By this time the Jerry was smoking badly. When I had expended all my ammunition, I pulled up and broke off the attack. Lt. Harold [L.] Matthews, my number 4 man, saw him continue in a roll, go over on his back, and plow into a forest.

The three victories for the day made Captain Mahurin the top ace of the 8th Air Force with 19.5 victories to his credit.

Polish ace Capt. Mike Gladych tangled with three FW 190s on the mission and downed one of them but was hit and boxed in by the other two. He was not aware that the pilot who chose to box him in rather than shoot him down that day was Capt. Georg Peter Eder, a top Luftwaffe fighter leader and ace. The two 190s that survived Gladych's attack guided him over a Luftwaffe field to force him to land, but as they came in very low, Gladych opened fire on a line of FW 190s. When the field defenses opened up, his 190 escort broke away and gave Gladych the opportunity to escape. He managed to get back to England but had to bail out when he ran out of fuel over a solid overcast.

B Group was credited with downing thirteen German fighters for the day plus destroying another on the ground. Its losses were Lt. Caleb L. Reeder, who was hit by flak and forced to bail out and become a prisoner of war, and Lt. Anthony Carcione, who was killed in action.

The 56th enjoyed another big day on March 15, when it provided penetration support for some 350 bombers attacking two targets at Brunswick. Lt. Col. Francis Gabreski led the group on the mission, which encountered between seventy-five and ninety enemy fighters from Dummer Lake to Solingen, Germany. Most of the Germans were sighted at 23,000 feet coming in to the bombers from nine o'clock, and the balance of about twenty-five aircraft were flying top cover at about 33,000 feet.

Capt. Robert S. Johnson took his flight down after eight FW 190s in the lower box, and the 109s immediately broke for the deck. At that time the Me 109s that were flying top cover came down on the Thunderbolts. By this time P-47s and P-38s were all over the place and the enemy fighters were scattered about 5 miles north of the bombers.

Johnson came upon an FW 190 at about 16,000 feet and initially made a head-on pass before maneuvering his P-47 onto the tail of the enemy aircraft. He gave the 190 a short burst, following which the enemy pilot rolled the 190 over and bailed out.

Johnson soon got on the tail of another FW 190 and hit it with a couple of short bursts that blew away most of its canopy. The enemy aircraft, apparently with a dead pilot inside, twisted and turned all the way to the ground.

The P-47 pilot then climbed back up to 11,000 feet, where he sighted an Me 109 right on top of the clouds. Johnson throttled back completely and leveled out right behind the enemy fighter. When he was about 400 yards behind it, the 109 went into a cloud at 3,000 feet. Following along, Johnson was right there on top of his victim when it emerged from its cover. A short burst sent pieces flying all over the place, flames broke out, and the 109 split-essed into the clouds.

Brig. Gen. Jesse Auton, left, and Maj. Gen. Wiliam E. Kepner, right, at the decoration ceremony for Col. Hubert Zemke, center, who has just received the Distinguished Service Cross. USAAF

Capt. Stanley B. Morrill and one of his early aircraft, showing another character from the L'il Abner cartoon strip. USAAF

In the Spring of 1944 the ace race began to heat up and Capt. Walker "Bud" Mahurin and Lt. Robert S. Johnson were right in the middle of it. Here Colonel Zemke (center) poses with Johnson (left) and Mahurin (right) under the nose of Johnson's aircraft Lucky. USAAF

These three victories ran Johnson's score up to twenty-two and made him the top scoring ace in the 8th Air Force—a title that would stand for some months.

Lt. Joe Powers also went into the low formation of German fighters and became further involved when the top cover dropped down. He drove an FW 190 away from a P-47, and then he went a couple of circles with it before combat was broken when the 190 split-essed.

Powers sighted another FW 190 at his level of 10,000 feet going in his direction. Powers stated:

> I did a skidding barrel roll and came out about 200 yards behind him. I opened fire and closed to about 75 yards. I observed many hits, and he began to smoke. I overran him and pulled up to make another pass. Just as I was starting down again, I saw he was going to crash. He went straight in and exploded.
>
> I then bounced two Me 109s which were at 4,000 feet. I fired at the number 2 man, who immediately rolled on his side and bailed out. The leader was a different story. I was closing rapidly on him in a straight dive. When he pulled up, I fired, but due to mushing I fired under him. I pulled streamers off my wing roots but could not get the dot far enough above him to hit him. Just as I pulled the dot through him, he dumped the stick and I overshot, so this is the big one that got away.

Lt. Robert Rankin went after an Me 109 in a high-speed dive, and though he did some firing, he was never able to overcome the buffeting to get in a long burst. When he finally pulled out, the 109 continued downward, so he had to settle for a probably destroyed on that one. A dogfight with an FW 190 was not productive because Rankin was still carrying his auxiliary tanks.

Rankin was later much more successful when he went hunting for the many singles that were in the area. Two Me 109s fell to his guns before he headed for home.

Once more A Group was successful, with thirteen confirmed victories for the day. Its solitary loss was Lt. John Kozey, who was forced to bail out southeast of Quackenbruck, Germany, after his aircraft had been damaged by fire from enemy fighters. He became a prisoner of war.

Maj. Gerald Johnson led twenty-four Thunderbolts of B Group on this mission. Combat began west of Dummer Lake where some thirty to forty enemy fighters put in an appearance, and further formations were encountered throughout the escort. The bombers were about 15 minutes late for rendezvous. When they did appear, Johnson saw that they had already been joined by a sizable force of Thunderbolts, so he took his formation on out in front of the stream.

Capt. Michael Quirk was leading the 62nd Squadron, which was out on the right of B Group. Just south of Dummer Lake enemy aircraft were sighted, and when the Thunderbolts let down to 17,000 feet, Quirk observed some thirty to forty FW 190s and about ten Me 109s going 180 degrees to the 190s. The Focke Wulfs were climbing parallel with the bombers at 5,000 feet in a close formation, with the exception of ten that were flying abreast in a loose line.

Quirk reported:

> As we only had eight ships in Groundhog Squadron [62nd Squadron], we attacked with plenty of speed so [that] we could pull up and not get in a dogfight. I picked out [an] FW 190 leading a flight, opened fire at 300 yards, and hit him immediately. I saw many pieces and the belly tank come back. I closed to pointblank range but did not observe any more strikes as I fired. I pulled up to the left and looked back at the enemy aircraft. It was in a turn to the left, smoking badly as it fell into a spin. As [it] disappeared in the overcast at 3,000 feet, it was burning badly and spinning straight down.

Lt. Fred Christensen went down with Groundhog Squadron and mixed it up with the FW 190s. He downed two of them, one of which exploded and left black soot all over his P-47.

When Major Johnson saw that the 62nd Squadron was engaged, he turned his 63rd Squadron to the right to give it cover. After seeing that it did not need assistance he led the balance of the group on to Dummer Lake, where it orbited and made several S-turns waiting for the bombers to arrive. When they arrived, the Thunderbolts proceeded ahead of the lead box of B-17s. Shortly thereafter two boxes of enemy aircraft were sighted approaching from the northeast. These planes were in rather tight formation. Thirty to forty fighters were in the lower box, and twenty to thirty in the upper.

Johnson immediately took his P-47 in their direction and intercepted the lead flights as they began to peel off to attack the bombers. Johnson got on the tail of an Me 109 and opened fire. Initially he did not get hits, but as he closed to 150 yards, he was blinded by smoke and debris coming off the aircraft, which streamed down in flames.

Johnson described the subsequent scene:

> As we pulled up from this attack, there were dogfights going on in every direction. After dodging a few aircraft, both friendly and enemy, I managed to get on the tail of another Me 109, holding my fire until about 250 yards. He received a good solid burst over the wing roots, fuselage, and canopy. As I pulled up over him, he was going down out of control, trailing a lot of black and white smoke. A few seconds later there was a parachute open in this vicinity, which I believe was the pilot; however, I cannot be sure.

Capt. Leslie Smith was leading White Flight in the 61st Squadron when they entered the fight with the lower formation of enemy aircraft. Smith stated:

I noticed [an] Me 109 on the tail of a red-nosed P-47, so dove down and to the right to try to drive him off. The P-47, who turned out to be F/O [Evan] McMinn, was already hit and was trying to get away from the enemy. He did a two-turn spin and a snap roll later, I think. I closed very rapidly, and at about 250 yards I gave him [a] short burst. No hits, so I waited a second to adjust my aim. I closed so quickly that by the time I shot again, I was about 50 yards away. I hit the 109 with only my right guns. I saw smoke pour out of the engine and fuselage as I went by the enemy. I looked back and saw the Me 109 roll slowly over on his back and head straight down in a spiral. I saw the pilot's chute open.

Flight Officer McMinn got back in the fight following his rescue by Captain Smith and damaged an FW 190. He then flew as wingman for Lt. Robert Rankin while Rankin downed his two Me 109s. By this time McMinn's engine was running very rough, but he managed to make it home.

B Group downed a dozen enemy fighters during its heated combats, but better yet it suffered no losses and broke up the enemy attacks on the bombers.

The following day the 56th furnished penetration support as 700-plus heavy bombers attacked targets in southern Germany. Weather obscured the primary targets, so the bombers went after secondary targets at Friedrichshafen, Germany. Col. Hubert Zemke led A Group, which sighted enemy fighters shortly after rendezvous.

Lt. Joe Powers reported thirty-plus contrails at 32,000 feet up ahead of the bombers. Just as the Thunderbolts arrived at that altitude, the enemy fighters dived on the bomber formation in a steep dive. The P-47 pilots dropped their tanks and went down after them. Most of the enemy craft went on into the cloud bank below, but Powers managed to chase an Me 109 down to 3,000 feet, where he exploded the aircraft with a solid burst. Powers had to fly through debris, which damaged his prop hub.

Powers then joined two other P-47s that gave chase to an FW 190. This 190 had a bit of a head start, and try as they might, the Thunderbolts couldn't get close enough to bring it down. All three American pilots fired at it in an attempt to turn it so that guns could be brought to bear, but they were forced to give up in disgust.

Capt. Leroy Schreiber was leading the 62nd Squadron on the mission. It stayed up as top cover for the Thunderbolts that initially went down after the enemy aircraft attacking the bombers. Seeing no more of the enemy in the area, Schreiber went down through the clouds seeking the enemy. He soon found two Me 109s, which he engaged in a turning contest until one of them fled. This gave him the opportunity to latch onto the tail of the other Me 109, which he set on fire. The enemy aircraft rolled over and went into the ground, where it exploded.

Schreiber then engaged two FW 190s and got good hits on one right down on the deck. The enemy pilot pulled up, and Schreiber hit him again. At this time the canopy came off, in addition to sundry other pieces, some of which hit Schreiber's wind screen, cracking it. As the Thunderbolt pilot passed below to escape the debris, he saw his wingman, Lt. Arlington W. Canizeres, firing on the 190, getting further hits on the aircraft, which crashed near St. Dizier, France.

Lt. Col. Francis Gabreski led B Group, consisting of twenty-four aircraft, on the mission. He heard the call from A Group when it encountered the enemy fighters queuing up on the bombers, so he started climbing and heading for the fight. By the time he and his group arrived, the enemy formation was broken up. Like the pilots of A Group, Gabreski also let down through the overcast and went looking for the enemy. He sighted two lone FW 190s, which he initially took to be Thunderbolts. He closed, holding his fire, and then when he was close enough for positive identification saw that they were FW 190s. The enemy aircraft sighted him by then, and both broke in a panic.

Gabreski and his wingman, F/O Evan McMinn, went back down and found another FW 190. Gabreski got on the tail of this one and chased it back up through the clouds. When Gabreski broke out at 6,000 feet, he sighted an FW 190 that had one wheel down and was descending. Gabreski got on the tail of the aircraft, and just as he was about to fire, the 190 went into a left-hand turn. Finally, the P-47 pilot was able to pull his nose through and get strikes on the enemy aircraft. The 190 rolled over on its back and went straight down through the overcast. Gabreski went down and leveled off, and as he did so, he saw the 190 burning on the ground.

The P-47 pilots then went off looking for the airdrome. An Me 109 came in and made a pass at Gabreski but missed as Gabreski headed on back down through the overcast. Shortly Gabreski ran into four FW 190s. A quick 180 put him on the tail of one of the enemy. As Gabreski recalled:

He dove for the deck in a very shallow left turn while I tacked on and waited until I closed within range. Skimming treetops with eight barrels blazing, I found it difficult to hit my target till the tracers passed beneath him. I raised my sight a bit, and that did it. Hits all over the fuselage. I broke off. Just as I did so, the aircraft hit the trees, cartwheeled, and exploded. A few minutes later I picked off another

190 on the treetops and pursued it for 5 minutes, throttle wide open, but was unable to close within range, so I broke off and proceeded toward home alone. A good time was had by all.

Lt. Fred Christensen also went down below the overcast and found two flights of three FW 190s. He dived beneath one flight and pulled up blazing away at the number 3 man. The enemy went down in flames. He then went after the number 2 man, who proved to be more difficult to down. This one broke sharply to the right, and Christensen had to use water injection to catch him. As Christensen fired, the 190 went into three snap rolls and then went spinning straight down until it crashed in a field.

During this period, 8th Fighter Command finally decreed that all fighter units would have distinctive markings. This had been more or less pioneered by the 56th when it had painted its cowlings in squadron colors. As of mid-March 1944 it was decreed that the Thunderbolts of the 56th Fighter Group would have red cowlings. This marking they would keep until the end of the war.

Also during this period when the race for the top fighter aces was going on, the name Zemke's Wolfpack became prominent in news releases. From that point on the name Wolfpack would be associated with the pilots of the 56th Fighter Group of the 8th Air Force.

Maj. Francis Gabreski led B Group on withdrawal support from Friedrichshafen on March 18. No enemy opposition was encountered until the fighters had broken with the bombers and were on the way home. Near Cambrai, Lt. Joe Powers sighted two FW 190s flying below him. He split-essed and came down to attack one of the FW 190s, but it was already under fire from Lt. Samuel D. Hamilton, Jr. Hamilton ran out of ammunition without doing any damage, so Powers took over the attack. The P-47 and the FW 190 were skimming the ground when the Thunderbolt guns finally hit their target. The 190 flipped over on its back and went straight into the ground.

Lt. Col. Dave Schilling gets ready to taxi out with his armorer lying on the wing. Note the tape over the gun barrels to keep dust and foreign objects out. USAAF

Then came a most interesting little combat. As described by Powers:

The three of us then started home on the deck but met another FW 190 and started chasing him. I closed very nicely on him, and when I was in range, I pulled my trigger and discovered I was out of ammunition. I informed my wingman of my predicament and told him to stay behind the FW 190 and I would turn it for him. I pulled up above and abreast of the 190 and then dove on him. The FW turned into me, not realizing I was out of ammunition, but in doing so he glanced off the top of a hill. In striking the hill he tore [off] large sections of his cowling and wings. One wheel came down, and his prop was torn off. At this time Lt. Dale [E.] Stream opened fire, forcing the enemy pilot to bail out.

A penetration support mission to Frankfurt on March 20 saw little action. Maj. Gerald Johnson's B Group was the only one to encounter the enemy, and this was on the way home. Maj. James Stewart held his squadron in position until the last minute before setting course for England. When they finally turned, a squadron of enemy aircraft was sighted at about 18,000 feet. The 61st Squadron was trailing the enemy aircraft at 19,000 feet, and off ahead of the enemy aircraft was the 62nd Squadron of the 56th.

Stewart had his 61st Squadron push things along so they could overtake the German force before it came in on the tail of the 62nd Squadron. The Me 109s had just begun to attack when the P-47s of the 61st Squadron got to them. Major Stewart came in on the rear of one enemy flight and downed a 109 immediately.

As Stewart climbed to the left, he saw the remainder of the Me 109s circling, and then they began diving for a small hole in the clouds. Stewart and his Thunderbolts went down after them and caught the enemy on the deck. Stewart put telling hits into one of the 109s, and his wingman, Lt. Dale Stream, finished it off.

Stream became separated from Stewart during the combat and then encountered a number of Me 109s, which he chased in and out of the clouds before setting course for home. En route he passed right over some 200 Luftwaffe personnel in formation. As he racked around to make a pass at them, he

A mixed color formation from the 61st Fighter Squadron. HV-I is Lt. Gordon Blake, HV-U Capt. Paul Conger, HV-S Lt. Eugene Barnum, HV-W Lt. Robert Keen, and HV-G Lt. Steven Gerick. P. Conger

Another formation photo showing the 61st Squadron all formed up. USAAF

Capt. Robert S. ("Bob") Johnson with another pet, this time a bird. USAAF

came under fire from ground guns, which put a hit in his fuselage. Stream rolled out and came across the airdrome at full throttle. A twin-engined aircraft came across his sights, and he fired, scoring numerous hits, which set the plane on fire.

March 22 marked another milepost for the 56th Fighter Group when it put up not two but three groups. This was the first occasion for a C Group. The assignment for the day was to escort the bombers that were returning to Berlin. Strangely, fighter opposition was almost nil, yet it was a costly mission for the 56th. Lt. Melvin Wood was shot down by flak over Ijmuiden, Holland, and Lts. Donald M. Funcheon, Dale Stream, and Claude Massey were last seen climbing into the clouds over England. It could only be deduced that the last three pilots either collided in the clouds or spun out and crashed in the Channel. The only survivor was Lieutenant Wood, who became a prisoner of war.

On March 27 the bombers were dispatched to attack targets in western and northwestern France. The 56th A Group, under the command of Lt. Col. Francis Gabreski, was briefed to provide withdrawal support for the 2nd Air Task Force attacking installations at Bordeaux, Merignac, and Calzaux. B Group, under Lt. Col. Dave Schilling, provided target support to the 4th Air Task Force, which attacked Chartres and Tours.

Gabreski's group arrived at the rendezvous point to pick up the withdrawal support for the bombers and found that friendly fighters were all over the place. Gabreski decided to proceed to the rear of the bomber stream. After about 20 minutes he sighted three Me 109s down at 4,000 feet going after a straggling bomber. Gabreski went down in a dive and leveled out 400 yards behind one of the Me 109s. He opened fire and closed to 200 yards. The 109 suffered a slight explosion, rolled over, and went down in flames.

Gabreski then broke to the right and lined up behind a second Me 109 that was still flying along fat and happy, taking no evasive action. A solid burst from Gabreski's eight .50 calibers sent it crashing to the ground trailing smoke. These victories were numbers seventeen and eighteen for Gabreski.

Capt. Mike Gladych, flying in Gabreski's squadron, sighted a couple of Me 109s about the same time as his leader did. He dived down to the attack, and as he lined up on the enemy fighter, it pulled up and the pilot bailed out.

Maj. Gerald Johnson was leading the 63rd Fighter Squadron in A Group. When the squadron was relieved of escort, it dropped down to find some strafing targets. What transpired then was related by Lt. Archie R. Robey:

After we had dropped down to find an airport or some other target to strafe, I fired at some high-tension wires in the vicinity of Lassay, France, and saw one pole and wires fall to the ground. At 1545 hours we sighted some trucks with soldiers in them, and Major Johnson, Lt. Evert Everett, and myself went down to attack. We then strafed and severely damaged some of the trucks.

After we had made a couple of passes on different trucks, we headed out to the coast. At that time someone called in a line of trucks to our right just entering a small town. We then flew over the town of Conde, France, to see if we could sight them. As we passed over Conde at about 1,000 feet, my plane was hit by .303 and 20mm fire. I caught up with Major Johnson, and after we had gone 5 miles east, he called to say that he was hit and was crash-landing.

Lieutenant Everett and myself circled and saw him belly in an open field. Major Johnson then got out of his plane and had apparently opened his parachute in the cockpit and set it on fire, as smoke was coming from the cockpit. I called Yardstick [56th Fighter Group Commander] and said, "Postgate White 1 has landed on his belly. I think I can land. Shall I go down and pick him up?" To this Yardstick answered, "Roger, Roger." I then lowered

Maj. Walker M. ("Bud") Mahurin's successful career came to an abrupt end on March 27, 1944, when he was shot down. His final score was 20.75 in the air and 0.25 on the ground. USAAF

my wheels, but my flaps would not come down due to the battle damage my plane had received. Not being able to cut my speed I was unable to land in such a small field. However, as I was circling around, I saw Major Johnson surrounded by a group of civilians, all of whom were shaking his hand, and with his free hand he waved me on. He then started to run towards the adjoining woods, accompanied by the civilians.

Unfortunately, Johnson's reception by French civilians didn't enable him to evade the Germans who would take him prisoner.

Lieutenants Robey and Everett continued on toward the coast on the deck. As they approached Arromanches, France, both Thunderbolts were hit by ground fire. They pulled up to 2,000 feet, and at that time Everett gave a mayday and said that he was going to ditch. Robey encouraged him to bail out but heard nothing further from him. Robey then called an air-sea rescue launch site, which told him it was responding. By the time the launch reached the vicinity, no sight of Everett or his plane was seen.

Robey arrived over England and got his wheels down, but his flaps were inoperative, his propeller was in fixed pitch, and his right tire was shot up. As he came in to land, his engine quit completely and he was forced to skid off the runway to come to a stop.

B Group, under Lt. Col. Dave Schilling, also had a bad day. No opposition was encountered on the escort, and the men picked out ground targets for strafing. As they set out seeking targets of opportunity, Maj. Walker Mahurin sighted a Do 217 twin-engined bomber about 15 miles south of Chartres, flying south on the deck. He circled and closed in behind the Do, firing from 400 yards. Strikes were seen all over the bomber. As Mahurin closed on the bomber, however, he was hit by fire from the rear gunner of the enemy aircraft.

Capt. George F. Hall, leader of Blue Flight, wrote:

I saw four chutes from the enemy aircraft, and it then crashed on the edge of a town. Major Mahurin pulled up to the right and called over the [radio telephone] that he believed he was hit and would have to take it easy. He said that he was afraid his engine was heating up. A few seconds later fire was

Lt. Joe Curtis originally flew with the 61st Fighter Squadron and later came back to fly with the 63rd Fighter Squadron. USAAF

coming out of his supercharger duct and Major Mahurin bailed out quite low. His ship crashed and burned. He landed after about four swings of his parachute, approximately 1 mile east of his plane, in a large open field. There was a wooded area about ³/₄ of a mile . . . south of him, near Pouvray, France, on the road between Bonneval and Voves. I flew quite low over him. He stopped running, looked up and waved, and then ran into the woods.

Fortunately, Major Mahurin was able to evade capture, thanks to assistance from the French underground. He would arrive back in England on May 7. At the time he was downed, his score was 20.75 enemy aircraft destroyed in the air.

The 62nd Squadron lost Lt. James Fields on the mission when he was shot down strafing near Chartres. Fields joined the growing list of 56th Group pilots who had become prisoners of war.

The final aerial action for the group in the month of March took place on the twenty-ninth when it furnished withdrawal support to the heavies returning from Brunswick. Lt. Robert Rankin scored the only aerial victory for A Group when he sighted three Me 109s northeast of Nienburg, Germany. He closed on the tail-end Charlie of the group and hung onto it until he ran out of ammunition, but the 109 finally flamed and went down spinning.

Other Thunderbolts went down north of Dummer Lake and attacked trains and other targets of opportunity. Among those scoring was Lt. Archie Robey with a locomotive destroyed, and Col. Hubert Zemke destroyed an oil dump and damaged a locomotive and switching station.

B Group's only claim for the day was made by its leader, Lt. Col. Dave Schilling. He sighted a formation of twelve Me 109s above him forming up to make an astern attack on the bombers. Schilling caught up with the number 4 man in the rear formation and sent him down in flames. Immediately afterwards he got in a burst at another 109 before it broke and went down in a dive.

Tragedy struck the base of the 56th that same day when a B-24 crashed nearby. At the instant of the crash the aircraft's bomb load exploded, killing not only the crew aboard, but six members of the 56th Fighter Group. Another thirty were injured, and the station firefighters were hard pressed to control flames and destruction.

The final administrative change of March was also made at the end of the month when Maj. Robert Lamb took command of the 63rd Squadron following the loss of Maj. Gerald Johnson.

From a combat standpoint March 1944 was probably the most significant month of the war for 8th Fighter Command. Throughout Big Week in

A Thunderbolt undergoing maintenance. The deeds of the pilots were dependent on the expertise of the ground crews, and both were highly aware of this and very supportive of each other. USAAF

February, when the concentrated bombing effort was put forth to destroy the German aircraft industry, the Luftwaffe had opposed the missions vehemently. During the month of February, the German fighter force lost 17.9 percent of its pilot strength. Fighter pilots defending the Reich lost 225 of their number killed and another 141 wounded.

When the Berlin missions came during the first days of March, the Luftwaffe was up in force to counter the onslaught on the capital city of Germany and its industrial targets. The 8th Air Force suffered its highest bomber loss ever on March 6 when sixty-nine heavy bombers were downed. The Luftwaffe lost sixty-six fighters, or 12.5 percent of those that rose to combat the American forces. The Berlin mission of March 8 saw significantly less opposition, and the following day, even though they had a solid cloud cover, no Luftwaffe fighters rose against the bombers.

Despite bad weather the 8th Air Force was able to fly twenty-three missions during the month even though it lost 349 bombers. The Americans, with their growing numbers, could afford these losses and keep striking at all the strategic targets in Germany and the occupied countries of Europe. In March 1944 German fighter forces lost 22 percent of their pilot strength, with the Reich defense force losing 229 pilots killed and missing and 103 wounded. The Luftwaffe could not recover from such drastic losses as it had suffered during February and March. Although its production of fighter aircraft would recover, it could not keep pace in training pilots to operate them, nor could it in any manner compensate for the loss of the many veteran and outstanding pilots who fell in the big air battles of that period.

From this time on the Luftwaffe could only attack the bomber stream when the time was right and the opportunity presented itself. Eighth Fighter Command was able to put up a fighter escort in such numbers that if rendezvous were kept and the bombers didn't stray from course, the Luftwaffe could not attack without taking significant losses. As the Allied forces prepared for the invasion of the Continent, the fighter forces of the Luftwaffe were moved in to defend the Reich rather than being kept along the invasion coasts where they could combat the forthcoming landings.

It had been a hard and long fight for the Thunderbolt pilots who had set out in the spring of 1943 to combat the best that the Luftwaffe had to offer in order to make possible the daylight bombing offensive. They had their problems, and many times it had been thought that the Thunderbolt just would not be able to stand up to the well-trained forces of the Germans and the fighter aircraft they flew, which in some ways were much superior to the early P-47s. As the fight progressed and modifications were made, the Thunderbolts showed their full capabilities. As the pilots gained combat experience, they, too, began to excel their opponents in combat. Increasing numbers made it possible to carry the fight to the Luftwaffe and to strike at Germany's bases and the industrial centers from whence its aircraft came.

Finally, the appearance of the P-51 Mustang in December of 1943 made no targets in the Third Reich exempt from the attacks of the 8th Air Force's heavy bombers. It was, however, the Thunderbolt that had carried the fight and had significantly defeated the best combat pilots that the Luftwaffe

Capt. Donovan Smith on Hun Hunter, *which was undergoing maintenance. The 56th had an excellent mainte-* nance team that managed to keep both A and B Groups operating. USAAF

had to offer. The 56th Fighter Group had been in the forefront of these battles, and its efforts were an immeasurable quantity in the wresting of air superiority from the Luftwaffe, which had been accomplished by the end of March 1944. For the balance of the war the skies over the Continent would belong to the Allied forces.

Another photo of the well-known red-reared Donald Duck and its pilot, Capt. Mike Quirk. USAAF

Chapter 7

Sweeps and Fans

The first action in April 1944 took place on the eighth when Col. Hubert Zemke led A Group escorting the bombers to Hespe, Germany, which was attacked with excellent results. Following the bombing, one flight dropped down to strafe an airdrome, where three planes were destroyed. A

Capt. James McClure entertains the troops on his unicycle. In the background is Lt. Albert P. Knafelz's Stalag Luft III. USAAF

second flight strafed Salzbergen, Germany, where a gasoline dump was destroyed. When the fighters left, flames were leaping over 200 feet high.

The following day the bombers set out to strike aircraft factory installations in Germany and Poland. The weather turned out to be terrible, and many of the bombers turned back, but the 56th Group went right along with the force that made its way to the targets. Lt. Col. Dave Schilling, leader of A Group, and his wingman became separated from the rest of his force when a gaggle of between twenty and thirty FW 190s was sighted at 21,000 feet about 20 miles southeast of Schleswig, Germany.

As Schilling reported:

We immediately swung around to the rear of the formation and sneaked in range from underneath and the outside. I opened fire from about 300 yards with about a 10-degree deflection from above and saw strikes all over the aircraft. I continued firing until I had closed to 150 yards, when I pulled up violently to avoid a collision with particles from the aircraft, which exploded. Several pieces struck my aircraft, knocking two holes in the leading edge of my right wing and one in the blister of my canopy.

Immediately following this several of the rear-end Charlies saw my wingman and I and flick-rolled to the deck. I picked another target at about a 30-degree deflection at about 300 yards and opened fire. He saw me and turned right, rolled, and went down. I saw several strikes and followed him to 15,000 feet, where I broke off and climbed back up. I then saw my wingman diving on the tail of [an] FW 190 as I rejoined the rear end of the formation. By this time they had me spotted and split into two formations, half of them getting behind me. I flicked, hit the switch, and went down. At about 12,000 feet I overboosted the engine due to excessive rpm and blew a cylinder head, causing a lot of oil and smoke to come out of the left side of my engine.

I had no sooner hit the deck with everything cut back trying to stop the smoke, when I saw two FW 190s ahead turning to the left. I was still indicating over 400 [mph] and lined him up from about 350 yards with about a 10-degree deflection. I noticed a large concentration of strikes on the wing roots, cockpit, and canopy. As I passed over him, he pulled up steeply to the left, winged over, and went straight in and exploded, leaving a large column of smoke.

I continued on course out and happened across a lake several miles southeast of Schleswig, saw an Arado 196 on floats ahead, and fired at it from about 900 yards. I undershot but raised my sights and hit it squarely with a heavy concentration of strikes all over it. It began to smoke just as I passed over it.

After I crossed the lake, I saw a Junkers Ju W34 ahead and slightly to the right preparing to land at Schleswig airdrome. I was overeager and fired too soon and only got about five to seven hits before I ran out of ammunition. I then proceeded out on course and saw an FW 190 firing at me from about 500 yards. I figured that excessive pressure would set the accessory section on fire but took the chance.

As I did so, smoke and oil again poured out of [my] cowling and the FW 190 pulled up to my right and turned back. I waited until he was out of sight and then cut back to 1800rpm and 29 inches of mercury. The fire stopped, and I figured I might make it. Shortly after I had crossed out, I saw Helgoland [, Germany,] out ahead and to my right and turned left, but due to the haze almost flew over a large convoy led by three [enemy] destroyers. I turned right and figured I could get between them. They must have been asleep because I was past the two of them before they opened up, and then they shot everything from both places.

Capt. Robert S. Johnson and Lt. Samuel Hamilton were flying together on the way home when they sighted contrails at three o'clock to the bombers and up at about 23,000 feet. Johnson had not been able to release his belly tank but had continued on the mission. He reported that at that point he and Hamilton attacked a formation of fifteen FW 190s. He stated:

[The enemy fighters] had dived down and were coming up from the rear and beneath the bombers. We got on their tail and began tangling. Some rolled to the deck. I fired a short burst at one and broke into two FW 190s on my tail. These two went on to get on Lieutenant Hamilton's tail as I tangled with two more FW 190s. I got rid of these two and began to look for more targets. I saw Lieutenant Hamilton on the water northwest of Kiel [, Germany,] turning with two FWs on his tail.

From Lieutenant Hamilton's viewpoint:

As I started to climb, I saw two FW 190s on my tail and broke left. [I] wound up in a Lufbery at 3,000 feet with both of them on my tail. I pulled my turn as tight as I could, and they could not get deflection. Finally one stayed on my tail and the other started making head-on passes at me. When he would open fire, I would return it. Finally, I got in a fatal burst and the FW making these passes caught fire and crashed in the bay. In the meantime I had called Captain Johnson for help and he had come from 18,000 feet after ridding himself of several enemy aircraft.

As Johnson came down, he fired at the 190 making head-on passes that was downed by Hamilton. Then the other FW got on Johnson. Johnson told what happened next:

I gave throttle and outclimbed the FW 190 in a spiral to the left. He dropped his nose, so he stalled, and I rolled over and got on his tail. Lieutenant Hamilton had also hit this one in the left wing tip. The FW would break into me every time I tried to line up on him. I fired several times at him, seeing strikes twice. He turned inland, and I got on his tail again and was firing and hitting him when he bailed out.

B Group, led by Lt. Col. Francis Gabreski, had broken escort with the bombers when fighters were sighted. Maj. Leroy Schreiber, along with Lts. Arlington Canizares and John E. McClure, went after six enemy fighters, but the Germans dived for the

*The arming of the .50-caliber guns in the wing of a
Thunderbolt. USAAF*

deck before they could intercept. They then found themselves over an airdrome, which Major Schreiber went down to strafe while the other two P-47s flew top cover. Schreiber shot up three Me 109s, which left one probably destroyed and the other two damaged.

Major Schreiber related the story of the balance of the mission:

[An] Me 109 took off to give battle, and Lieutenant Canizares attacked him near the airdrome. I climbed up from the deck and came back to join the fray. Lieutenant Canizares and I both made passes at the Me 109, who was a very aggressive and able pilot. Lieutenant Canizares hit the 109 and straightened him out [to] where I could finally get in a good burst from about 250 yards. The pilot pulled up and bailed out.

We started out on the deck conserving the little gas we had left, when another 109 attacked from six o'clock. I told Lieutenant Canizares to continue on course because he was lowest on gas, but he said he would turn with the bandit. Lieutenant Canizares was well aware that any further maneuvering would reduce his gas to the point where it would be impossible to return to England. He was also aware that he was out of ammunition. His action in fighting with this last enemy aircraft was motivated by self-sacrifice.

Lieutenant J. E. McClure and I both joined in his last fight and drove off the 109. I got in a 90-degree deflection shot from about 200 yards, finally, with no visible results, after which the enemy aircraft broke off his persistent attacks and left us alone.

Lieutenant Canizares made it out over the North Sea, where he bailed out, but in doing so he struck the tail of his aircraft. He was picked up by air-sea rescue but died of his injuries.

The next aerial action came on April 13 while the fighters were providing withdrawal escort from Augsburg, Germany. A Group encountered five Me 109s, which were attacked, with one being destroyed and two damaged.

Capt. Robert S. Johnson, flying with B Group, got his twenty-fourth and twenty-fifth victories when he broke up some FW 190s attacking a straggling B-17. When he went after the first one, his guns initially wouldn't fire. Then, when the firing began, the 190 went into a cloud. Johnson pulled up just in time to see the aircraft come out of the cloud and explode.

His second victim forced Johnson to do some fancy deflection shooting. When he got behind the 190, it pulled up from the deck in a right chandelle. As Johnson related:

I followed, chopping throttle, and fired a deflection shot and hit him, seeing strikes near the engine and fuselage. I pulled up, as I was going too fast to turn with him, and then sliced toward him again as he turned left again. I saw that I had his line of flight, so I opened fire at 100 degrees. He flew through my fire. I saw three or four strikes in the cockpit where he should have been, as well as several along the engine, wings, and fuselage. I wheeled left to get another shot at him and followed him into a cloud. I pulled up again. I saw him come out of the cloud and dive into the ground from about 3,000 feet. The pilot didn't bail out.

April 15 was devoted to strafing missions by 8th Fighter Command. A Group, with twenty-four Thunderbolts, led by Col. Hubert Zemke, went after airfields in northern Germany near the Danish border. Flensburg airdrome, where fifteen He 111 bombers were found parked, was strafed. Eleven of the bombers were destroyed, and Colonel Zemke took top honors with three destroyed and one shared. The attack was not without loss, as Maj. Leroy Schreiber, commanding officer of the 62nd Squadron, was hit by flak over the airdrome and spun in from 700 feet. At the time of his death Major

Lt. Joel Popplewell and Slugger *of the 61st Fighter Squadron. S. Sox*

99

Schreiber had been officially credited with twelve victories in the air and two on the ground.

The 61st Squadron strafed Handewitt airdrome and Eggebeck Airdrome, where they destroyed four enemy aircraft on the ground. Another casualty was suffered, however, when Capt. Dick H. Mudge was shot down by flak over Eggebeck Airdrome. He was able to bail out and became a prisoner of war.

B Group, led by Lt. Col. Francis Gabreski, swept the area of Stade, Neumunster, Schleswig, and Albersdorf. It was letting down to strafe Altona airdrome when ten to twelve enemy fighters were sighted in the area. Capt. Fred Christensen led the 62nd Squadron down out of the sun. The enemy craft were flying at 5,000 feet with six planes tight abreast and one straggler off to the left flank and two to the right. Christensen dived under the one on the left and identified it as an Me 109. As he opened fire, the 109 seemed to stop in midair and an explosion took place. The 109 went into a turn to the right and then fell straight down, flaming.

Christensen then attacked an FW 190 that went down and straightened out just above the treetops. The Thunderbolt pilot went to water injection to catch it. Short bursts seemed to be hitting from time to time, but Christensen now had an FW 190 on his tail. He hung onto his target until it hit a tree and

Capt. Mark Moseley was a 6.5-victory ace with the 62nd Fighter Squadron. USAAF

went cartwheeling. He then did an orbit, with the 190 on his tail, before going on water injection and climbing. As he pulled up through 4,000 feet, the FW gave up the chase.

Three other FW 190s were destroyed by the squadron, but it lost Capt. Charles R. Harrison, who was downed by one of the FW 190s. His plane went in and exploded.

Two administrative changes came about this time. Maj. James Stewart moved up to 8th Fighter Command, and he was replaced as commanding officer of the 61st Fighter Squadron by Lt. Col. Francis Gabreski. Maj. Lucien A. ("Pete") Dade, Jr., took over the 62nd Squadron following the death of Maj. Leroy Schreiber.

It was also time for a move. The 56th Fighter Group shifted from Halesworth south to Boxted in Essex, England. The Boxted base had originally been built for bombers, but until this time it had been home to the 354th ("Pioneer Mustang") Group. It was not as remote as Halesworth and, fortunately, was not as muddy. The group lost no time settling in and continuing its operations.

The group flew area patrols on April 20 while the bombers struck at V-weapons sites. No fighter opposition appeared. The lone victory of the day went to Capt. Felix Williamson, who found a lone Ju 88 stooging around in the Paris area and shot it down.

The Thunderbolts had escorted the bombers attacking targets in Ruhr, Germany, on April 24 and were on the way home when B Group, led by Capt. John Truluck, broke escort 70 miles east of Strausburg, Germany. They flew north and were going down to attack a railway junction when Truluck sighted an airdrome at Thalhein.

As Truluck reported the subsequent events:
I let down in a wide circle, dropping down into a narrow rocky gorge. We flew up this twisting gorge below the mountaintops and followed a narrow stream and railroad, flying over a small town. We then pulled up and turned 78 degrees to the left and approached the edge of the airdrome. The field was roughly square, with one paved runway running north to south, with workshops and hangars in the southeast corner. Twenty-plus airplanes were parked along the east and west boundaries on the grass, with a number dispersed in revetments along the east boundary.
My White Flight flew parallel to the field on the right-hand side and then turned left, crossing the airdrome from east to west and 90 degrees to the runway. My wingman [Lt. John A. Aranyos] and I strafed the north end of the field. Lt. [Donald V.] Peters and Lt. [Vernon E.] Kerr, [Jr.,] who turned the sharpest, [strafed] the south end.
In my first pass I opened fire on one of two Me 109s in the northeast corner of the field. I

observed a large number of hits all over the plane. My wingman fired at another 109. After passing over the 109 I opened fire on one of several [aircraft] in the northwest corner of the field [believed to be a Do 217], observing many hits. As we pulled up to the left, we saw the 109 burning.

While Truluck and his wingman were making their passes, Lieutenant Peters destroyed one Me 210 and damaged an Me 109. Lieutenant Kerr destroyed an Me 109.

Truluck related:

I and Lieutenant Aranyos made our second-pass attack from south to north on the western side of the field, coming in over the hangars down a whole line of ships. We scored a number of strikes on two ships before flying through a large fire near the center of the field. As I pulled up, I saw another column of smoke rising from the area of my most recent attack. Lieutenant Aranyos also fired at [an] Me 210 in the line and scored many hits. [A Do 217 had been destroyed and another damaged in Truluck's run.]

On their second run Lieutenant Peters destroyed an Me 109 and Lieutenant Kerr an Me 210. These pilots made a third run, with Peters damaging another Me 109 and Kerr destroying an Me 109 and damaging an Me 110.

Just northeast of the field about 10 to 12 miles away [stated Truluck] I saw another airdrome, which I later believed to be Eutingen, Germany, with from forty to fifty aircraft on it, mostly Do 217s, mostly

Ju 88s, Ju 52s, and miscellaneous single-engine planes, and a few fighters. I made one pass, strafing about eight airplanes [believed to be Do 217s] and saw a number of strikes on several of them. I pulled up and made another pass in the opposite direction but had run out of ammunition. Lieutenant Aranyos also strafed this row of planes, and as we broke off to come home, we saw two large columns of smoke coming up [from] the airdrome.

En route home Truluck and his wingman had an ordeal in stretching their fuel and maneuvering around weather. Truluck followed Aranyos in order to save his fuel, but when they entered a thick cloud formation, they went into a turn and Truluck discovered they were upside-down. He immediately righted his aircraft, then let Aranyos follow him and barely managed to get him back to England.

All total, the pilots of B Group destroyed sixteen enemy aircraft on the ground, with Captain Truluck accounting for three of them and two damaged.

The following day Col. Hubert Zemke led A Group escorting the bombers to Metz, France, where they bombed an airfield. Following the bombing, Colonel Zemke took some pilots down to strafe. Three enemy aircraft were destroyed on the ground, and several were damaged. No losses were suffered.

Colonel Zemke led the group on its first dive-bombing mission on April 29. Sixteen P-47s were

Lt. John Aranyos of the 63rd Fighter Squadron in Ol' Steel Butt. The invasion stripes are gone from the wings, but stripes are still on the lower fuselage. USAAF

loaded with clusters of 20-pound fragmentation bombs. These aircraft were escorted by another eight Thunderbolts. The objective was to have been Orleans-Bricy airfield, south of Paris, but weather prevented this attack. Zemke finally found a break in the clouds at an unidentified airfield in the vicinity of Soissons, France. Dives on the field were made at angles of from 45 to 60 degrees and pulling out at 3,000 or 4,000 feet. Results were unobserved.

The bombers were dispatched to Brunswick on May 4, but the weather was so bad that they were recalled. Scattered enemy opposition was encountered, and both A and B groups were able to destroy only three enemy fighters. Other German aircraft were sighted but were unwilling to do battle. Both groups did some strafing on the way home, and several trains were shot up and a number of locomotives were destroyed.

On May 8 Lt. Col. Francis Gabreski led A Group, consisting of thirty-six Thunderbolts, on a mission

The right side of the nose on Ol' Steel Butt told of the glory of Idaho potatoes. USAAF

with a fighter sweep ahead of the bombers attacking Berlin. It was hoped that the Thunderbolts would be able to locate the German fighters as they queued up to attack the oncoming force of Big Friends. Things did not materialize as envisioned, so apparently the German ground controllers vectored their fighters away from the Thunderbolt formation.

Lt. Frank Klibbe was leading Blue Flight of the 61st Squadron. West of Celle, Germany, he sighted two Me 109s diving toward a small hole in the solid undercast. Klibbe dived down from 20,000 feet to 1,000 feet on the tail of one of the 109s. He began to fire short bursts, and finally the 109 pilot realized he had a P-47 on his tail. At this time the enemy pilot started climbing for the clouds with Klibbe still on his tail. As they came through the cover, Klibbe hit the German again and saw strikes all over the 109, which rolled over on its back and went straight down to the ground.

When Klibbe pulled up to 1,500 feet, he met a 190 coming head-on. The P-47 pilot started a turn with the FW, and after one turn the two came at each other head-on again with Klibbe firing. The 190 immediately went into two rolls and seemed to be out of control. Lieutenant Colonel Gabreski saw the aircraft smash into the ground.

Gabreski took his squadron back up to 15,000 feet. Then a huge explosion was seen at 20,000 feet some miles away. As the Thunderbolts sped to the scene, it became obvious that the bombers were under heavy attack from a mixed force of Me 109s and FW 190s. By the time they arrived, the enemy was breaking off the contact and diving away for the deck. Gabreski managed to latch onto an Me 109 and flamed it following a high-speed chase.

Capt. Robert S. Johnson surpassed the victory record of Capt. Eddie Rickenbacker of World War I fame when he scored victories twenty-six and twenty-seven on the mission. He was flying in Gabreski's group when they sighted the bombers under heavy attack in the vicinity of Brunswick. As Johnson looked down on the bombers, he saw an Me 109 passing beneath him. Johnson rolled over and went down. He caught the 109 easily and fired at it from fairly close range. Apparently the enemy pilot thought Johnson had turned inside of him, but he was right under Johnson's nose. The 109 straightened out, and when it did, Johnson's eight .50s tore into it. As smoke poured out and the 109 rolled, its wing came off and the aircraft exploded.

As the P-47s proceeded on south, Johnson's number 3 pilot reported two FW 190s diving at three o'clock. He and his wingman apparently went down, and Johnson told them he would pick them up on the other side of the clouds. When aircraft

Lt. Frank Klibbe tells them how he got that Me 109 in typical fighter pilot fashion. Left to right, Maj. Francis Gabreski, Lt. Eugene Barnum, Klibbe, and Lt. Justus Foster. F. Klibbe

The final score for Capt. Robert S. Johnson is shown on his last aircraft, Penrod and Sam. Twenty-seven German aircraft fell to the .50 calibers of his Thunderbolts. USAAF

appeared, they were a P-47 with four FW 190s after it. Johnson told the Thunderbolt pilot to head for the clouds or turn to get away from the 190s. The pilot turned and climbed and was getting away from them and getting into a position where Johnson could help him.

Johnson reported the events that followed:

As I was going in the opposite direction, I kept making head-on passes at them, getting the last two off and getting hits on the nose of the second one. I saw only a few strikes on the FW head-on, and he rolled over with a little smoke trailing as I pulled up. I didn't watch him, as I was still trying to get the last FW off. Then the P-47, who later turned out to be my number 4 man and who had lost his leader, seemed to tire of the turn and climb so straightened out a second. At the time I saw strikes on the left side of the P-47's engine and the pilot bailed out. The FW 190 that I had hit in the engine was seen to smoke, then catch on fire and explode, by four or five [of] my fellow pilots.

The pilot of the P-47, Lt. Gordon H. Lewis, went down to join the prisoner of war rolls.

May 12 marked the initial use in aerial combat of a new fighter tactic that would be given the name Zemke fan. The tactic called for the group to fly to a designated point, from which it would disperse in three fanlike formations, which covered a 180-degree area. Although it would appear that the fanlike arc was evenly dispersed, an extra flight would be maintained in the center and could move quickly to the portion of the fan that had engaged the enemy.

Col. Hubert Zemke led A Group, consisting of twenty-four P-47s. When they reached a point some 36 miles south of Coblenz, Germany, on the Rhine River, the fan began to disperse. Upon reaching its full extension the fan stretched from Giessen, Germany, on the north to Frankfurt on the south.

Zemke's mission report is classic:

Three of us—Lt. Col. Preston Piper, Lt. Willard [D.] Johnson, and myself—had moved out to scout an area north of Frankfurt when we were bounced from above by seven Me 109s. During this engagement, my two wingmen were shot down. [Both survived as prisoners of war.] I have no idea of how many the two pilots may have damaged or even destroyed but believe there were none. [Years later Zemke learned that the pilot who downed his wingmen was Maj. Gunter Rall, commander of II/JG 11, who finished the war with 275 victories.] My escape was by outspinning and diving the enemy. As I flew westward toward home, another four Me 109s jumped me over Wiesbaden, and in the ensuing defensive battle I was again just able to elude the enemy. After outrunning these aircraft, a course of 290 degrees, magnetic, was set for England.

South of Coblenz about four enemy aircraft were seen circling at 15,000 feet, my altitude at the time being approximately 20,000 feet. My first intention at the moment was to bounce these planes from this superior altitude and pull off home. I had hardly circled before several more FW 190s and Me 109s were seen to assemble with the original four. Gradually their strength built up until an estimated thirty enemy aircraft were circling below and gradually increasing altitude as they assembled.

I continued to circle above them, calling for help to the other members of the 56th Fighter Group who were spread in the Coblenz-Frankfurt area. The purpose was that we could pull a kill on these enemy aircraft.

For more than 15 minutes I continued to circle above this concentration. As they climbed, I moved up, until my final altitude was approximately 29,000 feet. At this point I was finally throwing contrails, which were picked up by Lt. [Robert] Rankin and his wingman, Lt. Cleon C. Thomton. These two pilots moved up to within a half mile, and I told them to give me top cover while I bounced the enemy circling below.

The dive was fairly steep, and a lonesome Me 109 was picked up on the outer portion of the Lufbery below. By the time I was in firing position, he presented a 60- to 90-degree shot, and over two rings of lead were laid off before squeezing the trigger. The fire of my tracers was well ahead of him, and I allowed him to fly through the bullet pattern. At no time did I see a terrific explosion, but several hits were seen over the entire length of the fuselage.

At [the] point where I was about to ram him, the stick was pulled back abruptly and my airplane zoomed up into a climbing turn. Looking back, the Me 109 was seen to do two sloppy flick rolls, which wound up in a spin, whereupon the engine burst into flames and the pilot bailed out. Because of being so elated the fact was announced over the radio, but just soon enough for me to hear Lieutenant Rankin announce to break left, as there was an Me 109 on my tail. This plane was never seen, for Lieutenant Rankin was down on top of my position and away just as I entered into combat with four more Me 109s. However, seen far below during this combat was an airplane on fire, which was spinning down. This may have been the enemy aircraft Lieutenant Rankin shot from my tail. My further action was to break into the four Me 109s, do a half roll to the west, and outrun them. The gasoline gauge registered but 125 gallons, so after the last enemy fighters gave up, I cut everything back to the absolute minimum and moved off home by myself.

For Lieutenant Rankin it had been a very busy day before he came to Colonel Zemke's rescue. As he reported:

I was leading Whippet White Flight, and at 1155 Whippet White leader called in twenty-five–plus enemy fighters below him. I was about 20 miles away at the time. I started with my flight towards Whippet White leader. On the way to join him I ran into twenty-five–plus Me 109s climbing up in a left turn at 19,000 [feet], apparently forming up to attack the bombers.

I attacked the last two of this formation. They saw our flight coming and dropped their belly tanks. I fired a short burst at 350 yards in a diving turn to the left. The Me 109 split-essed for the deck, and I went with him. I fired another short burst, with my nose blacking out the enemy aircraft. We continued straight down, and I didn't fire again. I noticed the aircraft wings jerking violently trying to pull out. I saw he wasn't going to make it. I pulled out at 1,500 feet indicating 525mph, and the 109 crashed in flames in a small town.

I started climbing up for altitude, and when I reached 8,000 feet, I saw another Me 109 diving [at] about [a] 20-degree angle going east. I called my flight to push everything forward, and we closed without any trouble. The 109 was in a slight turn left. I closed to good range, fired a very short burst, and got a good concentration of hits on fuselage and engine. The 109's canopy flew back and just missed my wingman. The pilot bailed out, but [his] chute did not open.

. . . We started climbing up again when F/O [Steven N.] Gerick called in [an] FW 190 on the deck. He went down to attack, and I lost him and Whippet Red 4 at this time. I kept climbing up and heard Fairbank leader [Colonel Zemke] called for help. I flew for 10 minutes climbing, flying on vector 240 degrees. I joined Colonel Zemke south of Coblenz. He was alone, circling above thirty Me 109s. I called and told him I was joining him. He immediately went down to attack, and I gave him cover as thirty Me 109s pulling contrails passed directly over me and my wingman. This box of enemy aircraft kept right on course toward the bombers and didn't bother us at all. I saw Colonel Zemke destroy [an] Me 109, which blew up and went down covered in flames. As Colonel Zemke pulled up from his attack, I called him and said I was going down to attack. I got behind two Me 109s and fired on the one on the left [and] got good hits; black smoke came back, and landing gear came down. I moved over on the next one. I got many hits from dead astern, and this 109 smoked badly and his landing gear also came down. I had both these Me 109s in front [of] me going down in [a] 30-degree angle smoking and landing gear down.

I was coming around in a turn to the left [at] about 15,000 feet with many enemy aircraft still circling below. I was getting into range of two in formation and one ahead, slightly above, when for no reason all three pilots of these aircraft bailed out. I didn't fire, my wingman didn't fire, neither did Colonel Zemke. There was no other Allied fighter in the area at all. I couldn't figure this one out. . . . We make no claim on these.

I was still climbing to the left when I got on two more Me 109s. I got in a very tight circle with them and fired a short burst at each. I was unable to observe results, as deflection blacked out the enemy aircraft. I claim these damaged.

Just after this I saw [an] Me 109 come up from the box of enemy aircraft and climb up underneath Colonel Zemke. I called him to break and turned to get on the Me 109's tail. I managed to turn with him, fired a short burst, got a few hits, and this enemy aircraft started down with a very little smoke coming back. One landing gear came down at about

Lt. Robert ("Shorty") Rankin celebrates his five victories in one day on May 12, 1944. F. Klibbe

a 20-degree angle. I broke into two more Me 109s which were coming in on my wingman. As I turned, I saw the pilot bail out of the enemy aircraft that I had fired on.

We circled with the two Me 109s until my wingman had to break down to get away. I kept circling with the two Me 109s while my wingman came up and fired at one of them head-on. I saw hits, with glycol and smoke pouring out. The pilot bailed out as the 109 started down. We circled with the remaining 109. I got on his tail [and] fired a short burst, when my tracers came and I ran out of ammunition. I closed to 50 yards but could only get a good picture. . . . This was my wingman's [Lieutenant Thomton] first mission, and he did the best job of flying wing I have ever seen.

Lieutenant Rankin was officially credited with five enemy aircraft destroyed for the day.

Capt. Paul Conger was leading the 61st Squadron when he sighted a formation of forty-plus enemy aircraft. He took his flight up, and although they were attacked by four FW 190s on the way up, they pushed on to the enemy formation. Conger downed two FW 190s and then took this fight back in a line-abreast attack to break up a formation of twenty enemy aircraft.

Another pilot who heard Colonel Zemke's call for help was Lt. J. Carroll Wakefield of the 63rd Squadron. He was unable to find Zemke but did find a formation of six Thunderbolts with some twelve to fifteen Me 109s following them. Wakefield managed to maneuver onto the rear of the enemy formation and downed three of the 109s in the subsequent fight.

A Group downed fourteen enemy fighters that day and prevented several enemy formations from getting to the bombers.

B Group, led by Lt. Col. Francis Gabreski, began its sweep of the area, and once it knew that A Group

Capt. Robert Keen of the 61st Fighter Squadron got all of his six aerial victories on two missions. He also added another seven on the ground. USAAF

and that time saw the canopy come off the 190. This pilot, too, went over the side.

By now Keen had lost his wingman and was all alone. He decided too many enemy aircraft were around to be in this predicament. He was seeking cloud cover when he sighted two P-47s diving down and around a big cloud with an FW 190 right behind them. As Keen approached, the Luftwaffe pilot saw him and began to take evasive action. Keen began firing at 200 yards and closed to 100 yards. The enemy aircraft went into a barrel roll, and Keen hit it solidly, causing the aircraft to explode. Watching the aircraft go down almost cost Keen his life.

I looked behind me [reported Keen], and [an] FW 190 was on my tail about 600 yards behind me, shooting like hell. I had plenty of speed, so I started doing a climbing spiral turn. I began outclimbing and outturning him immediately. When I was about 90 degrees to him and 500 feet above, he leveled out and tried to run. I turned in as hard as I could and did a wingover on to his tail. He tried to break down and to the left. I pulled about 20 degrees' deflection at 100 yards and gave a short burst and saw a few hits in his left wing root and behind the canopy. I saw a few pieces come off, and he started burning behind the canopy and inside the fuselage. I began overrunning him. We were going down at a 45-degree angle, and my port guns had stopped firing. I rolled my trim tabs back and pulled out. I blacked out, and my oxygen mask came down around my neck. When I came out of it, I was in a shallow climb to the right and in a sharp right turn.

. . . A P-47 with a yellow tail chased [an] FW 190 past me and to my left, about 1,000 yards away. I began climbing to the left and above them for top cover. The P-47 got a 45-degree deflection shot at the enemy aircraft, mushed past to the outside of the Lufbery. I sliced inside the FW 190 and shot about ten rounds and my guns quit. I pulled up and told the P-47 to take him, as I had no ammunition left. The P-47 pulled in and took another shot at about 45 degrees, again mushed to the outside of the turn, and leveled out slightly. The FW pulled in tight and almost got on his tail. The P-47 tried to turn head-on, but the FW 190 hit him before he could complete his turn. The P-47 hung there for [a] second, then went into a slow left-hand turn. He hit and exploded. The FW 190 flew straight over the flames at about 500 feet and went into a shallow dive straight ahead. I pulled up into a cloud.

About this time the 56th began to receive the first of the P-47-D-25s, which were fitted with the bubble canopy. The increased visibility was most welcome and gave the pilots a capability of fore-warning that they had never enjoyed before.

Col. Hubert Zemke led forty-eight Thunderbolts providing penetration support for the bombers headed for Brunswick on May 19. Several abortive attempts to contact enemy fighters were made around the rear end of the bomber formations before

was heavily engaged, it began to seek the areas of combat. It was not, however, able to engage the large formations that were so prevalent in the area that day. Its limited action did result in five enemy fighters being downed for the loss of Lt. Jack E. Green, who bailed out over Frankfurt to become a prisoner of war.

On May 13 the bombers traveled deep into enemy territory and the 56th Group was a part of the penetration escort. Lt. Col. Francis Gabreski's group had been with the bombers only a short while when a sighting of "bandits" was called in, but these turned out to be P-51 Mustangs. Then thirty-plus enemy fighters were sighted that were already under attack from a group of green-nosed Thunderbolts (from the 359th Fighter Group).

Lt. Robert J. Keen was in Gabreski's flight. As the fighters turned to come in on the rear of the enemy formation, he sighted an FW 190 straggling behind the main group, so he tagged onto it. The 190 did a diving turn as Keen pulled within range and opened fire. Keen observed a few hits, so he continued to close and fire. The enemy pilot bailed out.

Keen then sighted another FW 190 about 300 yards away. He held his fire until he was well within range and then hit the 190 with a telling burst. Keen was overrunning, so he pulled up and out to the side a number of them were finally intercepted. Maj. Leslie Smith was leading the 61st Squadron when they saw fifteen FW 190s down below. He took his charges down in a head-on attack.

The Thunderbolts then outclimbed the 190s, and as the 190s split into sections of five, the men of the 56th went back down on them. Smith picked up a straggler and closed on him. Three short bursts sent him down smoking badly.

Smith immediately went back to a formation of three FW 190s and began to fire at the closest one. He got a good strike in from 30 yards, and the 190 rolled over and turned down for the deck. Smith chased it down through some clouds, and his victim was still lagging behind the other 190s when it came out. When the enemy pilot sighted the Thunderbolt still there, he pulled up very violently. Smith followed and got above him. The 190 pilot then turned west, rolled over, and bailed out.

The 56th accounted for five enemy aircraft destroyed for the day. The only problem was with Lt. Anthony S. Cavalle's aircraft, which began to smoke, and he was forced to bail out over the North Sea. Fortunately he was picked up safely by an air-sea rescue launch.

The Zemke fan got into action again on May 22. Col. Hubert Zemke led forty-eight Thunderbolts out to sweep the Munster area. The squadrons began to fan out from the Dummer Lake area. They found considerable cloud cover below, but one flight sighted a couple of trains on the deck, so they went down to investigate. As they were circling around, they spotted a well-camouflaged airdrome from which sixteen FW 190s were getting ready to take off.

Lt. Col. Francis Gabreski, leading the 61st Squadron, took three flights down to attack. The sixteen FW 190s began getting airborne. Gabreski reported:

By the time White Flight [Gabreski's] got into position for a dead-astern attack, the enemy planes picked up enough speed and altitude to give us a damn good fight. The battle started at about 3,000 feet. I took my flight ahead to attack a section of eight FW 190s flying pretty good formation, while ten to twelve FW 190s were left to the second and third flights directly behind us. I closed in on the first FW 190, opened fire at range, and saw hits all over the fuselage and wings. The plane fell off to the side and burst into flames while I pulled up for the second kill. I opened up within range, saw hits over the fuselage, and the plane broke off to the side, smoking badly. The canopy flew open and the pilot bailed out.

While still following this ship down I looked behind and saw myself wedged between two Germans coming in for the kill. I broke right for all that I was worth and made about two orbits with the enemy before I was able to outclimb the 190. It was at this moment that I saw a P-47 going down in flames and another smoking very badly. This sort of shook me, so I regained about 12,000 feet of altitude and asked the squadron to rendezvous above the airfield. Circling for about 5 minutes, I managed to get six planes together. No sooner had the planes re-formed when about twenty-plus FW 190s were sighted headed across the airdrome in very good formation.

The boys on the airfield threw up everything but the kitchen sink. The [Germans'] formation blew up, one flight going right and the other ships climbing for all they were worth. A green flare was fired from one of the ships, and the ground guns ceased firing. That was our cue. The six of us dove from 12,000 feet and picked individual targets. I picked a flight of six to my right, flying a pretty string formation. [I] closed to range [on] the first man and opened fire [and] saw hits around his fuselage and wings. The plane lost speed rapidly, trailing columns of black smoke; then it rolled over and hit the ground.

Closing from about 500 yards on the second man from the end and still holding fire, since ammunition was precious at a moment like this, I glanced to my left and saw a 190 just beneath my left wing rapidly falling behind and trying to get in position for an astern shot. I cut my throttle, drew back on the stick, and practically stalled the plane. The [German] overran me, and I fell behind him but in no position to fire. The FW 190 went into a very tight right-hand turn, with about five 190s doing the same out in front. After about three turns with six Germans in a Lufbery, I broke up in a very steep climbing turn. At this moment another FW 190 came down on me from above and got a 60-degree deflection shot at me. I kept climbing and turning till I got to 10,000 feet. Looking about, I saw a few friendly fighters about the sky, so I joined up and headed for home with four ships.

On a vector for 5 minutes, Blue 3 called in about twenty plus a short distance northeast of Bremen. The five of us made a 180 and headed in the direction of Hamburg. As I arrived over the area of our last battle, I spotted a lone FW 190 flying down on the deck. But I lost him under the overcast, so I flew over the cloud and waited at the other end, circling. [I] picked up my target again and made the bounce. [I] fell dead astern of him at 3,000 feet, just beneath the overcast, and closed to range and opened fire. My first burst was a little high, but the second connected with hits near the wing roots and fuselage. The plane appeared to snap down and when last seen was rolling off to the left, pouring out what appeared to be oil and black smoke.

The flight that had been sent down to strafe the train was led by F/O Evan McMinn. By the time it arrived on the site, the train, which consisted of only a locomotive, had passed on through the town. Regardless, McMinn gave it a burst and damaged it. It was at this time that the airdrome was discovered with the Focke Wulfs getting ready to take off. McMinn immediately went over to come down on their tails, but the ground fire was so intense that he pulled off and got on the radio to warn his fellow pilot not to try to attack the enemy fighters over the airdrome.

McMinn got off to the side of the airdrome and called for Gabreski to bring the other Thunderbolts down. McMinn got into the formation of FW 190s about the same time that Gabreski did and was most fortunate to get out of it. McMinn reported:

F/O Evan McMinn was in on a lot of action and became an ace in the 61st Fighter Squadron. USAAF

I busted into this formation of fifteen FW 190s . . . getting on one's tail, but due to my superior speed he outturned me, so I told my element leader, Lt. Praeger Neyland, to get him, and he did. I then slid onto the tail of another FW 190 that was firing at a P-47. I fired and saw smoke start pouring out. He rolled over and bailed out.

I tightened my turn and fired at another FW that was shooting at another P-47. I saw hits and saw it catch fire. It went straight into the ground.

I straightened out to look for another target and found a 190 on my tail. I broke hard left, but he hit me with a 20mm and set fire to my wing. I started to bail out but decided that I might be able to put it out. I broke away from the fight and climbed as fast as I could. I looked back and saw my wingman, Lt. James [C.] Clark, hit [an] FW 190, which started smoking. It rolled over and the pilot bailed out. . . . My wing was still smoking when I reached the Zuider Zee.

McMinn was able to make it home, although his Thunderbolt was badly damaged.

Capt. James Carter was leading Blue Flight of the 61st Squadron, and his was the last to go down to attack the formation of FW 190s. When he arrived on the scene, he noted that other 190s were pulling in on the tails of the P-47s that were attacking the formation. He immediately got on the tail of one of these and drove it off, but not before a Thunderbolt was smoking. The 190 broke off to the left, but Carter stayed with it and continued to hit it with his fire until the canopy came off and the pilot went over the side.

Carter then came under attack from an FW 190 and had to break hard left to get away. After two orbits Carter was on the tail of the 190 and pumping lead into it. The 190 split-essed and went down.

Capt. Gerald Johnson takes off in In the Mood. USAAF

Capt. James Carter taxis out in HV-J. USAAF

Carter was not able to follow owing to the low altitude of the combat. One of the P-47 pilots in the squadron had observed the combat and had seen the 190 split-ess and continue on into the ground.

The 61st Squadron had a very good day, with an even dozen FW 190s destroyed, but it lost two of its own. Lts. Cletus B. Neale and Richard M. Heineman were shot down and killed in the air battle.

The other two squadrons had to settle for ground targets for the day, but they were able to destroy half a dozen locomotives and shoot up a number of barges.

An administrative change occurred on May 25 when Maj. Don Goodfleisch took over command of the 63rd Fighter Squadron.

May 30 marked the first Droopsnoot mission for the 56th Group. A Lockheed P-38 with a plexiglass nose had been fitted with a bombsight to act as lead aircraft for formations of fighter planes doing level bombardment. Col. Hubert Zemke flew the P-38 and borrowed a bombardier, Captain Ezzel, to operate the bombsight. Twenty-four Thunderbolts, each laden with a 1,000-pound bomb, took off to strike the Criel railway bridge in France. The load was heavy for the fighters, and they were quite unstable in their formation. Upon their arrival at Criel, heavy flak began to come up, so Zemke decided to take the formation elsewhere. About 5 miles down the railroad he located another bridge at Chantilly. It was "bombs away," and the Thunderbolts knocked out three spans of the bridge.

The following day Col. Hubert Zemke led the group on a dive-bombing mission against the Luftwaffe airdrome at Gutersloh, Germany. The 62nd Fighter Squadron provided top cover for the other two squadrons of the 56th and for the 353rd Fighter Group as they dropped their bombs on the target area.

Zemke was orbiting at 21,000 feet when the 56th Group finished its bombing and the 353rd Group went down to perform its attacks. At that moment Zemke got a radio call from Lt. Col. Francis Gabreski that he saw a gaggle of aircraft coming in from the southeast. Zemke called Gabreski and informed him that Zemke's twelve aircraft were in that vicinity and not to call them the enemy. Gabreski assured him that a lot more than twelve aircraft were in the gaggle.

Zemke and his Thunderbolts continued to circle. As they flew to a point southwest of Gutersloh airdrome, he looked back over his left shoulder and saw a close formation of some thirty-plus aircraft at his level and only about 2 miles away.

The P-47s began to turn to investigate the situation, but before they could complete their move, ten enemy aircraft peeled off and began their run on one of the flights below Zemke's level. They were immediately identified as FW 190s, and an air battle had begun.

Colonel Zemke reported the battle as follows:

My lower flight broke into ten FW 190s and evaded them somehow, while I took White Flight in a steep left climb over the main enemy formation in an endeavor to pull an attack from above. In the meantime I called repeatedly to the 353rd Fighter Group down below that we were engaged directly above and to scatter.

The four of us in White Flight found that the enemy flew ahead and below us but just [too] far out of range to fire, so we opened up everything and gave chase. The main enemy formation, which now

Maj. Francis Gabreski gets settled in the cockpit. USAAF

Maj. Gerald Johnson flew this aircraft when he was commander of the 63rd Fighter Squadron. USAAF

A 61st Fighter Squadron Thunderbolt at rest. Note the
drop tank and kill marks by the cockpit. USAAF

Lt. Praeger Neyland's aircraft being made ready for a
mission. USAAF

consisted of approximately twenty FW 190s with four weavers in back, began to climb toward the northeast. They stayed in fairly close formation and moved rapidly ahead of us. At a point over Bielefeld the German flak opened up against them and partially spit them up again. We continued on, and as they formed up again, we had decreased the interval and gained about 1,000 feet on them. At Herford, while still being shot at by their own flak, they began to make a gradual right turn to come back to Gutersloh airdrome. All this time I was calling out the position of the enemy to Lieutenant Colonel Gabreski and Col. Glenn C. Duncan in the hope we could really box these bandits in.

As the enemy made their 180-degree turn to return to Gutersloh area, the four of us in Platform White Flight were able to cut off a lot of distance on the turn and position ourselves just in the rear and above them at 26,000 feet. Gabreski had, in the meantime, told me that he could give me no assistance, which I later found out was due to the fact the remainder of the group had very little gasoline left, after their dive-bombing and long climb up to altitude. For some reason or another I had been unable to contact Duncan on C-channel, so I decided to launch an attack with my own flight and at least break up the enemy formation.

Unfortunately, the enemy formation was stacked down, so my choice of attack had to be below their leader and to the rear. At any rate, a straggling weaver on the left flank was picked out, and I closed to about 300 yards to fire at him with about a 30-degree deflection shot. In short order he wove to the left a bit, thus straightening himself almost for a direct astern shot, and a concentration of my fire hit him with a hell of a jar. Immediately, this aircraft began smoking badly and fell into an uncontrolled spin toward the ground. The remaining enemy still held their formation, so I moved up on another victim, hoping they wouldn't break.

For certain, I don't know whether it was this next aircraft that I claim as probably destroyed or not, as I was almost in the midst of them by now, firing like mad. At any rate, another low member of the formation was picked up and fired at. A good lengthy burst was seen to hit this FW 190, and smoke began to appear. Just at that moment I glanced to the right and saw I was overrunning an FW 190, which would put me in a bad position, so I broke off my fire, pulled up slightly to the right, and concentrated on the FW 190 I had begun to overshoot.

This bandit was given a real burst that sent him smoking downward with debris flying, and I concentrated on an FW 190 which was several hundred feet ahead of me and above. He was turning to present a 30- to 45-degree angle to my direction, so I pulled up, laid off about what I thought was a

Lt. Samuel O. Stamps taxis out for takeoff in Tinkle.
USAAF

proper lead, and opened up. He immediately began to jinx, and I sprayed ammunition ahead of and in the rear of him as I closed. My ammunition gave out about this time, so I rolled to the right and in back of him.

Because I was unable to see him again, I claim this FW 190 as only probably damaged, for I am not too certain of my claim. . . . Soon the remainder of my flight was with me, and we looked down on Gutersloh airdrome before proceeding home. It is interesting to note that this combat, which I believe was over Detmold, Germany, consisted of but one pass at terrific speed by four aircraft. It was enough to cause twenty enemy planes to split and run as a flock of chickens hit by a car. All my ammunition was shot in one pass of less than 2 minutes, which is inconsistent with the life of gun barrels, but everyone in two fighter groups returned home from a dangerous low mission.

In addition to the two aircraft destroyed by Colonel Zemke, the balance of the flight was credited with another three.

Capt. Walker ("Bud") Mahurin's aircraft. USAAF

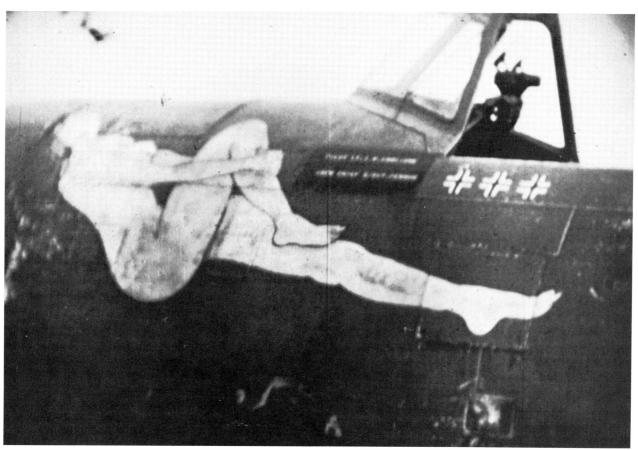

Capt. Gerald Johnson's In the Mood. USAAF

112

Chapter 8

D-day and Ground Support

In late May and early June of 1944 all the men of the 56th Fighter Group were full of speculation and hope that the Allied invasion of the Continent would soon be forthcoming. Allied air forces roamed supreme over the Channel, as most of the Luftwaffe fighters had departed their bases on the coast. Tactical air missions had been the order of the day, with railroads, highways, and bridges prime targets. The first five days of June proved to be quite uneventful, but following a mission on the fifth, Col. Hubert Zemke was called to a meeting of group commanders that afternoon. Later in the day orders came down to paint the black and white invasion stripes on the aircraft.

At 2000 hours Zemke called the intelligence and operations officers into the briefing room, locked the door, and passed on to them the details of D-day. The first pilots learned the details at a very early morning briefing, and the first mission was airborne at 0336 hours. The Thunderbolts roared down the runway, and the air was filled with the red and green navigation lights of the aircraft. These

Two 61st Squadron aircraft taxi out in their new D-day invasion stripes. The 56th flew from before dawn until after dark in support of the ground troops. P. Conger

P-47s patrolled the Strait of Dover to see that no enemy aircraft broke through to get at the massive convoys that lined the English Channel.

By midmorning the Thunderbolts of the 56th got busy with tactical air strikes. The third and fourth missions of the day were skip- and dive-bombing strikes, with limited damage inflicted. No enemy aircraft were encountered.

The fifth mission of the day was flown by the 62nd Squadron with Capt. Fred Christensen leading. The Thunderbolts skip-bombed in the Rambouillet, France, area, and a number of locomotives and freight cars were destroyed. Lt. William W. McElhare encountered and shot down an FW 190, one of the few to be met during the day.

The seventh and final mission of the day was flown by P-47s of the 61st and 62nd Squadrons. They were assigned to patrol an area bounded by Rouen, Evreux, and Bernay, all in France. Fanville airdrome was attacked, but only staff cars, trucks, and lorries were present. Col. Hubert Zemke encountered and downed an FW 190, and Capt. Mike Gladych another. These were knocked out of a flight of four that attempted to flee when met. The 56th

suffered its only pilot loss of the day on the final mission, when F/O Evan McMinn was shot down and killed while strafing a truck convoy.

June 7 was even busier than the sixth. The group flew eight missions during the day and was quite successful. The first mission was the most tragic. Fifteen P-47s set out to drop fragmentation bombs south of Bernay, but three pilots were lost on the mission. Lts. Alfred Evans, Jr., and Donald Furlong were both killed in action, and Lt. Eugene E. Bennett was downed but managed to evade capture and return to England in September.

The third mission of the day was carried out by the 63rd Squadron with Capt. Russel B. Westfall leading. Its target was at Gournay, France, where the Thunderbolts dropped their bombs on the marshaling yards inside the town. Three locomotives were destroyed, and a number of other locomotives and freight cars were damaged. The rails were left in a tangled mess. Lt. Harry F. Warner's P-47 exploded in the vicinity as a result of the concussion of his bombs, which exploded as soon as they hit the target.

Lt. Dayton Sheridan's aircraft in D-day markings. The stripes were rapidly applied without the exacting dimensions of the squadron painters. USAAF

Lt. Joseph R. Curtis was just off the target when he noticed a lone aircraft out at three o'clock and 500 feet. He hit his water injection and sped over to close the range on an FW 190 that was carrying two external fuel tanks. As Curtis maneuvered with the enemy aircraft, the 190 pilot reversed his turn, giving the P-47 pilot a great deflection shot. Hits were scored, and the right wing of the 190 hit some trees, which sent the aircraft cartwheeling across the ground.

Lt. Col. Francis Gabreski led the fourth mission of the day, which was a dive-bombing run to Chateaudun, France, where a railroad crossing was bombed with good effect. On the way home the P-47s circled the airfield at Dreux hoping that they would find a target. Two flights let down through the overcast and headed off in pursuit of two FW 190s. At this moment Gabreski sighted about twenty-plus enemy fighters out at nine o'clock flying at about 2,000 feet.

Gabreski called the gaggle in and attacked two Me 109s. One broke, but the other went into a left-hand turn, and Gabreski sprayed it with a good burst. The 109 seemed to lose power, and Gabreski overran it. As Gabreski looked back, he saw the other pilot bail out.

As Gabreski regained his altitude, he sighted four FW 190s out to the right and about 1,000 feet below. Gabreski shoved the throttle forward and went down. He caught one of the aircraft just as it dived into haze, and hit it with a solid burst. An explosion took place, and fire emerged from the fuselage. The FW 190 flew on into the ground. This marked Gabreski's twenty-fourth aerial victory.

The balance of Gabreski's flight also did quite well. Capt. Mike Gladych got one, F/O Steven Gerick downed two, and Lt. Joel I. Popplewell destroyed one.

The fifth mission of the day was carried out by sixteen Thunderbolts of the 62nd Fighter Squadron, which dive-bombed marshaling yards at Poix, France. Four sets of tracks and over twenty freight cars were destroyed. On the way out Lt. George E. Bostwick and his flight were bounced by three FW 190s. The P-47s broke into the 190s and then went into a big cumulus cloud.

When Bostwick came out of the cloud, he found himself directly astern of an Me 109. As he opened fire, smoke was seen to emit, and then the Me pilot pulled up as if to go into a loop. Bostwick followed the enemy pilot, firing intermittently, until his P-47 stalled out. When he recovered, he saw his target coming out of a cloud, inverted and in flames.

Lts. Mark L. Moseley and Jack W. Pierce caught a Ju 88 bomber taking off from an airdrome at St. Andre de L'Eure, France. They followed it until it was about 5 miles southeast of the field. They then took turns making passes until they sent the bomber down in flames.

Lt. Wendel A. McClure was lost on the mission, but he managed to evade capture and returned to England in September.

Col. Hubert Zemke led the 61st Squadron for the group's seventh mission of the day. The Thunderbolts dive-bombed Gournay marshaling yards with good results. Zemke took a half dozen P-47s down to investigate what he thought was a truck convoy, but the objects turned out to be piles of stone.

As the P-47s climbed back up, they were warned of enemy aircraft in the area by Lt. Robert Rankin, who was flying top cover. At that time the Thunderbolts were jumped by some fifteen FW 190s and Me 109s. The P-47s broke into the attack,

Capt. George Bostwick became a top scorer of the 63rd Fighter Squadron late in the war. USAAF

115

and Zemke fired at two FW 190s without effect. He immediately had to break into an Me 109 that was firing at him. This aircraft fired and kept going.

Zemke continued to go after four FW 190s that were slowly climbing toward Paris. South of the city they did a right turn to head west, which put Zemke farther behind. Somewhere near Chartres, however, the 190s did a 180 and headed east. This put Zemke almost directly over the enemy aircraft. As he drew to a point about 2,000 yards behind the four, the leader did a 45-degree turn to the southeast and all began to cross over. Zemke picked out the last FW 190 and opened fire using about 20 degrees' deflection. The 190 absorbed a full blast from the eight .50s and went down in flames.

The remaining three 190s completed their turn and went into a three-company front. Zemke picked out the element leader and closed to about 300 yards directly astern. Zemke recalled:

> He rocked his wings, and I would rock my wings in return. He probably thought I was his wingman, who I had just shot down in the crossover turn, and was saying over the [radio telephone,] "Hans, you bastard, move up in line abreast and stop flying in back of me." At any rate, I fired and fired at this pilot to finally tag him with a decent concentration, and he nosed over to go straight down.
>
> This left two FW 190s still flying line abreast and unconcerned, so I slid over in back of the flight leader and opened fire. My tracers showed just as I hit him, and the jinx was up, for he immediately began kicking rudder to roll over on his back, and I swung over on the last man to shoot at him as he went down. No hits were seen, but I claim a damaged against the flight leader. Both were seen running like mad in a steep dive, so I climbed to 29,000 feet and came screaming home.

The 63rd Squadron flew the eighth and last mission of the day and destroyed more railroad tracks and freight cars. Lt. Eugene Timothy went down and strafed ten cars, which exploded with such force that the concussion could be felt at 10,000 feet. Lts. Marvin H. Becker and Sam B. Dale, Jr., teamed up to down an FW 190 on the way home.

Two missions were flown on June 8. The first was executed by the 62nd Squadron, which dive-bombed Dreux. It left an ammunition dump in flames and then encountered enemy aircraft on the

The all-silver Thunderbolt flown by Capt. James Carter of the 61st Fighter Squadron. USAAF

Lt. Billy G. Edens was a constant scorer with the 62nd Fighter Squadron until he was downed on September 10, 1944. USAAF

way home. Lt. Billy G. Edens saw two fighters taking off from the airdrome at St. Andre de L'Eure. His flight leader, Lt. Mark Moseley, took the flight down and opened fire on an FW 190. As Moseley closed to pointblank range, the enemy pilot bailed out and the aircraft exploded. Moseley then pulled up on the leader and hit him with heavy strikes on the fuselage, and the aircraft went down to crash and explode.

While this was going on, Edens observed other enemy fighters taking off from the airdrome. A 109 was after Moseley as he concentrated on his victim, and Edens closed in on the stern of the 109. He opened fire from 500 yards, then closed to 100 yards, and the 109 went down in flames.

A second 109 went after Moseley, so Edens lined up on this one and opened fire at 100 yards. As Edens closed to pointblank range, the 109 broke sharply to the left and exploded.

A third FW 190 came in front of Edens, climbing about 300 or 400 yards away. Edens opened fire and did not see initial strikes. The enemy aircraft seemed to hang in the air and then fell off on its left wing and crashed.

Lts. George H. Van Noy, Jr., and George H. Butler both downed Me 109s to give the flight a total of seven victories for the encounter.

For the balance of the month skip-bombing and dive-bombing would be the order of the day. Weather grounded the fighters on June 9, but they were airborne again on the tenth to fly four missions. These were all skip-bombing and dive-bombing missions against rail targets, and most were quite successful. A loss was suffered on the third mission of the day when F/O Joseph Vitale was shot down by flak. He bailed out successfully and also evaded successfully, returning to England in September.

A group mission to sweep the Paris area on June 12 stirred up a bevy of German fighters. Lt. Col. Francis Gabreski and the 56th had been patrolling the Paris area for about half an hour when the 353rd Fighter Group reported that it was engaged west of the city. The 56th Group immediately headed for the fight, but when it arrived, nothing of consequence was in sight. The 56th continued on between Chartres and Beauvais when someone called in a few planes flying north on the deck. Gabreski couldn't spot them but was told to make a 180 left and they would be directly below him. He did so, and lo and behold, a dozen Me 109s were ahead in a beautiful formation down at 3,000 feet.

Gabreski took his charges down from 14,000 feet and closed on a 109. As soon as he came in range, he opened fire and saw strikes all over the aircraft. Flames billowed out, and the Thunderbolt pilot barely missed colliding with the enemy craft.

As he regained his altitude, Gabreski spotted four more Me 109s at quite a distance and below him. He gave his aircraft full throttle and managed to intercept one of the 109s down at 6,000 feet. His target went into a steep right-hand turn, but Gabreski hit it in the fuselage and cockpit. Once more the aircraft fell off burning and Gabreski barely managed to keep from hitting it.

High scorer for the day was F/O Steven Gerick with four. Gerick was the pilot who had positioned Gabreski over the enemy formation. As he reported:

I also did a 180 and placed myself in line of a 109's tail at about 25 to 30 degrees' deflection and 150 yards behind. I chopped my throttle completely to avoid overshooting and gave the enemy aircraft a short burst, which blew it up.

I turned hard left, still with the throttle closed. I positioned myself on another 109's tail within 100 yards or so. Again I fired a short burst from some 20 degrees' deflection, and after firing, the 109 broke out in flames and headed for the ground, where he hit and exploded.

Still in the center of the enemy formation dodging 109s and firing at some, I decided that I better get out. When I was about to break off the dogfight, a 109 forced me to take evasive action, as he was well in range and firing for all he was worth. I broke, and

The Thunderbolts of the 56th line up for takeoff. By this time many different models and paint schemes are evident. USAAF

just as I did, a 109 came in my line of sight, when I fired at him in a slight diving turn, which set the enemy aircraft on fire.

I did not have any time to see what happened to him, as I was all alone in the enemy formation. I continued my evasive action and caught sight of two 109s flying alone on the deck. I closed on the tail-end Charlie, firing at him in very short bursts, when apparently my attack drove him into crashing into the ground.

When I finished him, I looked around for any aircraft that might be on my tail and noticed a 109 crashed in a farmer's field, which I believe was my third, the one I set on fire. I continued my attack on the remaining 109 in a right-hand turn but did not fire due to the fact I could not draw any deflection. We began a rat race on the deck when another 109 joined the fight. We three continued turning, as none of us could get on the other's tail. I tried water injection, which helped me in getting on one of the 109s' tail, but the other would slide out and make me break my attack. After some 5 minutes of this turning and sliding-out maneuver I could get some head-on shots, which I believe did some damage, and when he came around again, I noticed one 109 streaming glycol. We made about three head-on attacks on each other. The enemy aircraft could not

hit me, but it did not stop them from firing on me. [We were] still turning when another 109 joined the fight, making it three to one, which I thought rather unfair. At this time I yelled for help, giving my position in relation to the airdrome where we first noticed the 109s. To make things even worse another 109 came in.

By some stroke of luck two red-nosed Thunderbolts came diving down and the 109s broke off their attack on me. I broke up to a right climbing turn [at full power].

Another dive-bombing mission went out on June 13 in the Saumur, France, area. Once more bridges and marshaling yards were the targets. One casualty occurred. F/O Z. Janicki, one of the Polish pilots attached to the 56th, did not return.

On June 16 the group flew area patrol around Dreux. Four Me 109s were encountered, one of which was shot down by F/O Steven Gerick. Lt. Timothy Sullivan of the 61st Squadron was last seen over the beachhead. He was not heard from again.

June 21 saw two groups set out on missions. One was an area patrol led by Lt. Col. Francis

Lt. Col. Francis S. Gabreski receives the Distinguished Service Cross while Capt. Fred Christensen is awarded the Silver Star. Note the Polish wings worn by Gabreski above his USAAF wings. USAAF

Capt. Fred Christensen in one of the earlier Rozzie Geth Thunderbolts that he flew so successfully. USAAF

Gabreski. The Thunderbolts strafed four trains. Lt. Harold Matthews was lost when he did not pull up after making a strafing run on one of the trains.

On June 22 a patrol mission was flown in the Compiegne, Abbeville, and Beauvais region of France. Some targets were bombed, and an airdrome was strafed. Lt. Charles E. Tucker was killed in action on the mission.

Lt. Col. Francis Gabreski led the group on June 27 when the Thunderbolts were dispatched to dive-bomb the airdrome at Connantre, France. Twenty-pound fragmentation bombs were used, and the field was well covered. Intense light flak was encountered at the airdrome, but it proved to be inaccurate and no losses were suffered.

Following the dive-bombing, the P-47s came under attack from about ten Me 109s. Fortunately, no one was hit and the enemy aircraft scattered.

Gabreski's squadron was now scattered. After searching the skies for more of the enemy he received a call for his number 4 man that his fuel was getting low. Gabreski decided to make one more pass over La Perth airfield. As he dropped down low, he noted two Me 109s rolling along that had just landed. He then began to scan the sky for more aircraft coming in and sighted one at 4,000 feet. Gabreski went down after it, but owing to cloud and airfield camouflage, he lost his target.

As Gabreski pulled up, he sighted four more Me 109s ahead and above. He climbed up behind the first and gave it a short burst. He then picked another target and closed rapidly, firing all the way. The 109 began to billow flames, which were followed by a violent explosion in the fuselage.

Gabreski got a call from his wingman, F/Lt. Withold A. Lanowski, who was after another Me 109. Gabreski followed Lanowski, and they chased

The armorers of Capt. Fred Christensen's aircraft are loading up the belts of ammunition as Christensen looks on. USAAF

the enemy at full throttle right down on the deck. Lanowski opened fire at 300 yards and observed hits on the craft, which then crashed into the ground.

Capt. Fred Christensen was leading the 62nd Squadron, which provided top cover for the dive-bombers. A few Me 109s were sighted in and out of the overcast, but these were chased with no encounters of consequence. As the Thunderbolts headed for home, they were bounced by four Me 109s between Cambrai and Lens, France.

Christensen's number 4 man caught the brunt of the attack and had three 109s on his tail. The fourth Me 109 went after the number 3 Thunderbolt. Christensen attacked and hit one of the 109s with a good concentration of fire. An explosion took place behind the cockpit, and the aircraft went down in flames. With this two of the 109s split-essed and headed for the deck.

Christensen and his number 3 man then approached the remaining 109, which was in a tight Lufbery with the number 4 P-47. When the other two Thunderbolts arrived, the Luftwaffe pilot broke into a split-ess and started a dogfight that ranged from 7,000 feet to the deck. This pilot appeared to be very experienced, and the P-47s were never able to get a shot at him. He disappeared in ground haze after he split-essed from 1,500 feet.

Altogether it had been a profitable day for the men of the 56th. They had a successful bombing mission and destroyed eight enemy aircraft in the air without loss.

The rest of the month was taken up in continued dive-bombing and strafing. On June 30 bridges and marshaling yards were hit and several trains were shot up. An airfield north of Auxerre, France, was strafed. Lt. Marvin Becker shot down an all-silver Ju 88 south of Noyen, France. Lt. Charles Tucker caught and shot down a V-1 "buzz-bomb." The ramjet-powered missiles were the scourge of southern England at the time. Tucker was not a member of the 56th, but belonged to the air-sea rescue squadron that was also based at Boxted, England.

The 56th Group celebrated Independence Day on July 4 by flying two missions. The first mission was uneventful and entailed providing close escort to a bomber force striking Beaumont-sur-Oise airdrome in France. The second mission of the day was quite different. Forty-eight Thunderbolts, each laden with two 250-pound general-purpose bombs, set out to dive-bomb Conches airdrome in France. Cloud conditions over the base delayed the strike, and when the target was found to be overcast, the P-47s went hunting for other targets. A small hole in the clouds was found, and two flights bombed a marshaling yard. The 62nd Squadron was called to proceed north of Evreux marshaling yard for bombing.

On the way, Capt. Mark Moseley, who was leading Blue Flight of the 62nd, sighted aircraft on

Thunderbolts from the 63rd Fighter Squadron get airborne for a mission. Note the new camouflage schemes and the drop tanks under each wing. P. Conger

an airfield below him. Moseley then spotted an FW 190 stooging around on the deck. Moseley jettisoned his bombs and went down to attack. As he and his flight arrived under the cloud layer, they spotted a gaggle of thirty to thirty-five Me 109s flying north. At this point Moseley called the rest of the squadron down. As he did so, he sighted seven more Me 109s at 2,000 feet above, covering the gaggle, so he climbed up toward them.

By this time White and Red Flights had entered the picture, and fights broke out all over the place. Moseley got into a Lufbery with one of the 109s. After several circles Moseley tried with a short burst but missed. Then the 109 pilot pulled his nose through and hit Lt. Dayton C. Sheridan. Moseley was then able to get in a good 60-degree deflection shot and got heavy strikes on the 109. The enemy pilot bailed out.

Lt. Wiley H. Merrill, Jr., was a member of Blue Flight. When it attacked the gaggle of Me 109s, he immediately pressed his attack on two of them from astern. He moved in to very close range on one of them and got heavy strikes all over it, and the enemy aircraft rolled over and flew into the ground.

A scorer on the July 4 mission was Lt. Dayton Sheridan (left). USAAF

Lt. Dayton Sheridan's aircraft carried the unusual name Nigger Haid. S. Sox

Merrill went after another 109 but was cut out by another Thunderbolt. He then sighted a 63rd Squadron fighter with an Me 109 on its tail and proceeded to shoot the 109 off. The enemy aircraft flicked over, went straight down, and crashed.

As Merrill pulled up with three other Thunderbolts, someone called in seven bandits coming in at seven o'clock. At the same time Merrill sighted twenty-plus enemy aircraft coming in from five o'clock above. He broke into them and got into a Lufbery with their tail-end Charlie. During the ten orbits that they made together, the 109 pilot got some good strikes on Merrill. Some of the 20mm shells exploded in the cockpit, piercing Merrill's feet and some instruments. Merrill finally pulled in tight enough to get good deflection and scored heavily on the fuselage and wings of the 109. The enemy pilot flicked away quickly, but Merrill could not follow him.

Merrill and his shot-up Thunderbolt made it back to an emergency field in England, where he crash-landed.

Lt. George Bostwick came down on the Me 109 gaggle with White Flight. He immediately picked a target on the outside of the formation. The 109 tried to turn into him as he closed astern, giving Bostwick a good deflection shot. The fire from Bostwick's guns clobbered the Me, which rolled over, crashed, and exploded.

Bostwick climbed back up and then went down after two Me 109s on the deck. He lined up on the one on the right, but three other Thunderbolts came flashing down and prevented that attack. Bostwick then went after the 109 that broke left. When the German pilot discovered he had a P-47 on his tail, he tried to break right, but Bostwick caught him in the turn and blasted away. Enemy aircraft number 2 went down to crash.

As Bostwick pulled off to the right, he found himself in a perfect position to attack his third target. He opened fire from dead astern and held it until he was only 50 yards away. As Bostwick passed over the enemy aircraft, the pilot bailed out but hit the tail plane.

The 63rd Squadron, led by Col. Hubert Zemke, had dive-bombed the marshaling yard and was on its way home when enemy aircraft were reported over Evreux airdrome. The Thunderbolts headed in that direction, and on arrival one target was destroyed by F/O Robert W. Magel. Lts. Walter Frederick and Joseph Curtis picked up a dogfight that they found on the deck. Curtis got on the tail of a 109, and the enemy pilot bailed out before Curtis could open fire. Curtis then picked up another Me 109 and got a

few bursts into it. As it began to spin, Frederick came in and finished it off.

Frederick then got after an FW 190 and chased it all over the deck. He closed and fired bursts and saw strikes, but the aircraft would just not go down. Frederick stated:

> We both hit trees on the deck, and once I saw his prop dig up dirt from a field. As my tracers appeared, I knew my ammo was low but kept on firing, the last of my ammo getting in his right wing. I damaged this 190 severely, but he still wouldn't go down.

Seventeen German fighters did, however, go down to the guns of the 56th that day. One casualty occurred: Some FW 190s came up to pursue one flight that was on its way home with all of its ammunition expended. This flight was bounced, and at this point Lt. Sam B. Dale, Jr., was last seen.

The following day Lt. Col. Francis Gabreski led the group over France, where it was to pick up and escort the bombers that were on the final leg of their journey home following a shuttle mission to Russia. The bombers were late arriving, and when they did appear, they were under heavy escort. Some of the Thunderbolts of the 56th went out looking for targets of opportunity.

Capt. Fred Christensen was leading the 62nd Squadron and was north of Evreux when he sighted a lone FW 190 down below. He called his charges on the radio and told them to cover him while he attacked. As he broke down, he was sighted by the enemy aircraft and it fled into the clouds. As Christensen pulled out, he noticed fifteen-plus FW 190s circling over Evreux airdrome.

Christensen broke through the overcast and went after two FW 190s. As he closed, he was in turn attacked by two FW 190s. Lt. Jack Pierce shot one off Christensen's tail. Lt. Robert C. Cherry chased the other 190 all the way to Paris, using water injection, and never could catch it.

The chase for Christensen's targets went on for about 5 minutes before Christensen finally hit one of them with a long burst from maximum range. The aircraft were right down on the deck, and after the 190 was hit, it dropped slightly and hit its left wing on a tall chimney. The 190 crashed in the town, and debris and flames covered a large area.

Gabreski took his P-47s down to chase the 190s after Christensen called them in. He saw a Thunderbolt pursuing an Me 109, but since Gabreski had altitude and range, he dived down after the 109. Just as he was closing, however, he saw the other Thunderbolt close and get hits all over the 109, which went into a cloud formation. Gabreski orbited and waited for the 109 to emerge, but as it did, the pilot bailed out and the aircraft continued down

LM-A of the 62nd Fighter Squadron coming in for a landing. The bubble canopies that came along in May of 1944 made a world of difference in pilot visibility. USAAF

Lt. Col. Francis Gabreski holds a squadron briefing pointing out the route for the day's combat mission. This photo was made a few days before Gabreski went down strafing. USAAF

toward the ground. Gabreski later learned that F/O Withold Lanowski had downed this enemy aircraft.

Gabreski climbed back to altitude and sighted three more Me 109s. As he attacked, two of them dived and one went into a climbing turn to the left. Gabreski reported:

After about three turns at 3,000 feet I got in a few bursts without results. My firing must have shook the [German], as he dove to the deck in a straight line. I closed in very rapidly. Still a bit out of my range the [German] made a left-hand turn. I gave him about two rings of deflection, which put him out of my sight. I pressed the trigger and let the pilot fly into sight. The Me 109 was smoking very badly. The [German] leveled off, and I closed in for the kill, getting hits all over the fuselage. I broke off my attack after overrunning. Before completing a 180-degree turn I saw the pilot's chute open at about 200 feet off the ground.

This was Gabreski's twenty-eighth aerial victory—a record that would stand as the top aerial score in the European theater of operations.

Lt. Robert J. Keen was the top scorer of the day. He took his wingman into a bevy of twelve Me 109s and knocked one of them down immediately. He chased his second victim in and out of the clouds until he finally sent him crashing to earth. After that he was involved with numerous Me 109s until he finally caught two flying alone just above the clouds. When the two broke in opposite directions, he went after one and hung on until he shot it to pieces. The enemy aircraft went down in flames.

All total, the group was credited with twelve enemy aircraft destroyed for the day. The lone loss was Lt. Timothy Sullivan, who was shot down by a flight of FW 190s as he and his wingman went down after some Me 109s west of Evreux.

Col. Hubert Zemke led the group on July 6 when it took off to bomb the airfield at Evreux. Each Thunderbolt was laden with two 250-pound bombs. All was going well when south of Bernay the group was bounced by some forty Me 109s and FW 190s. The attackers began diving down in twos and threes, leaving the balance of the enemy fighters up as top cover. Colonel Zemke had the P-47s salvo their bombs and shoved his throttle forward and went after the attackers head-on.

The final Rozzie Geth *flown by Capt. Fred Christensen showing all the victory markings, including the ones for the six Ju 52s that he downed on July 7, 1944. USAAF*

A flight of Me 109s had just passed below Zemke's flight when one of them got on his tail. He called for help, and Lt. George Bostwick went into water injection and was soon on the tail of the 109. As Bostwick opened fire, the enemy aircraft went into a roll and then split-essed. Bostwick stayed right with it and fired short bursts as they dived straight down. Both aircraft went into compressibility, and finally Bostwick began to come out of his dive at about 7,000 feet. It looked as though the 109 would, too, but it never quite made it. It smacked into the ground at a 45-degree angle.

As the enemy aircraft came down on the Thunderbolts, Capt. Mark Moseley took his flight up in a climb toward the aircraft that were flying top cover at 20,000 feet. He didn't level out until he reached 26,000 feet. That put him in the position of the attacker. He then went back down, attacking two Me 109s and staying with one target after the enemy split. Moseley continued to fire and get hits on the

109 until he left it at 10,000 feet, spinning and in flames.

When the 63rd Squadron came under attack, it became aware of the heavy black exhaust streamers that the 109s were leaving as they roared down to the attack. Suddenly, one of the Me 109s exploded. It was deemed that this was probably due to the excessive manifold pressure that it was pulling in its steep dive.

The 63rd Squadron entered an unusual claim for an Me 109 damaged in the ensuing combat. Lt. Joseph Curtis found himself with two Me 109s on his tail and six more giving them top cover. Curtis made a couple of orbits with the two 109s before he realized that he was still carrying his external fuel tank. Once this was released, he was able to tighten his turns considerably. The freak accident came when his tank was seen to hit the wing of one of the 109s, damaging the wing considerably. Curtis last saw this aircraft in a tight spiral to the left. He continued to turn with the remaining 109 without

A quartet of 20-plus victory aces: left to right, Col. Hubert Zemke, Lt. Col. Dave Schilling, Lt. Col. Francis Gabreski, and Capt. Fred Christensen. USAAF

The Silver Lady was Capt. Leslie Smith's aircraft but was also flown on several successful missions by Polish pilot F/Lt. Withold Lanowski. USAAF

Maj. Mike Gladych flew a Thunderbolt named Pengie III. Here are Gladych and his ground crew. USAAF

either getting any shots in. Suddenly, the 109 broke down and away and it was all over. Fortunately, the six enemy craft that had been overhead were gone, too.

The Thunderbolts were credited with five enemy fighters destroyed but lost Lt. Samuel J. Lowman when they were jumped by the enemy fighters.

Lt. Col. Francis Gabreski led the Thunderbolts escorting the bombers deep into Germany the next day. A number of enemy aircraft were seen, but the 56th did not have the opportunity to engage. Escort had been broken and the squadrons headed home when Capt. Fred Christensen, leading the 62nd Squadron, noted quite a bit of activity taking place over Gardelegen Airdrome, Germany. He let down from 17,000 feet and sighted a dozen Ju 52 trimotored transports flying toward the airfield.

Christensen entered the traffic pattern from above, went past the last Ju 52, and opened up on the next one. He hit it in the wing and left engine. As he overran it, the aircraft burned and exploded in midair.

He then lined up on a second transport and hit it from very close range. It went down in flames. He caught the third Ju 52 in a turn to the left and hit it with a deflection shot. The right wing caught fire. The pilot tried to land it short of the airdrome but didn't make it.

All the while Christensen had forgotten to release his auxiliary tanks during the combat. Suddenly his engine quit. Frantically, he switched tanks and dropped the auxiliaries. He then found another Ju 52, which he began to fire on. This pilot tried to shove his nose down to evade, but he didn't have enough altitude to pull out. The aircraft crashed into the ground.

Christensen closed to pointblank range before he opened fire on his fifth victim. As he sprayed the wings, the fuel tanks burst into flames. The aircraft peeled off to the right and went into the ground.

The P-47 pilot then pursued his sixth victim right over the airfield. Flak was coming up hot and heavy, but Christensen continued to press his attack until this transport, too, burst into flames and crashed.

Lt. Billy G. Edens shot down his first two Ju 52s in much the same manner as did Christensen. He, however, came upon his third target at only about 50 feet in the air. He closed too rapidly, and as he pulled up, the tail of his Thunderbolt hit the tail of the Ju 52, causing it to crash, hitting buildings and burning.

Capt. Michael J. Jackson also accounted for one of the Ju 52s, giving the 62nd Squadron credit for ten out of the formation of twelve aircraft.

Encounters with enemy aircraft were limited for the balance of the month, as the group returned primarily to escort missions. As with all combat operations, however, casualties occurred. Lt. James Palmer was lost on the escort to Munich on July 13, and Lt. Robert Jenkins was lost on a dive-bombing mission to La Chapelle, France, on the fifteenth.

Maj. Don Goodfleisch finished up his combat tour. On July 17, as he prepared to return to the United States, he was replaced as commander of the 63rd Fighter Squadron by Maj. Joseph L. Egan, who had returned to the 56th for a second tour of combat. Regretfully, when Egan took the squadron on an escort mission to Augsburg two days later, he was lost. The P-47s went down to strafe an enemy airfield, and Egan's aircraft took a 20mm hit near the cockpit. His Thunderbolt did a slow roll and crashed into the ground.

Capt. Mike Jackson rapidly became one of the leaders and scorers of the 62nd Fighter Squadron after he joined the unit in the summer of 1944. USAAF

Lt. Col. Dave Schilling led the group on July 20 when the Wolfpack furnished penetration support for the bombers that went after targets in the

Lt. Col. Francis Gabreski's final aircraft shown shortly before takeoff. Gabreski got too low strafing on July 20, 1944, and fouled his propeller on the ground. End result: prisoner of war camp. USAAF

All in a Day's Work

Lt. George Bostwick joined the 62nd Fighter Squadron of the 56th Fighter Group in the spring of 1944 and became one of its leading aces before the end of the war. As with all combat men he had an unusual experience, but he would never have survived his had he not been flying the rugged P-47.

It started on the morning of July 4, 1944. The group lined up for takeoff, and all was going according to plan until Bostwick's leader, Maj. Lucien Dade, had engine trouble and pulled off the runway. Dade's wingman was a novice and didn't seem to know what to do but was finally waved off to the side.

Bostwick's Thunderbolt was loaded down with fuel, including drop tanks, and two 1,000-pound bombs. By the time the obstacles were overcome, he was already 1,000 feet down the runway. He poured on the coal, but when he reached the end of the runway, he didn't have good flying speed. Bostwick decided to bounce the aircraft on a highway at the end of the runway, and then he was off across a wheat field. Still rumbling along on the ground he plowed through a series of hedgerows. Somewhere along the way he clipped his left wing on a tree and the 1,000-pound bomb on the right wing came loose and was bouncing merrily along under the wing.

By this time Bostwick was airborne, and his first thought was immediately to abort the mission. But then his engine seemed to be running O.K. and the fuel from his drop tanks was transferring properly, so he set off to catch the squadron, which was en route to Conches, France.

When the group arrived at Conches, it was directed to a large number of enemy aircraft, which it bounced from above. The P-47s had a field day, and Bostwick shot down three Me 109s. He felt he should have gotten four if he had not wasted some of his ammunition. On the way home Bostwick and his wingman were alone and Bostwick began to have trouble with his propeller. The farther they went, the more vibration he had.

Bostwick arrived home with an airplane vibrating so badly that he could not read some of the instruments. As he got ready to land, he had his wingman check his landing gear and discovered that his right wheel had been crushed in his accident before becoming airborne. Bostwick came in and made a two-wheel—tail wheel and left main gear—landing. It was found that his wing was bent and his prop blades were bent from going through the hedgerows, but still he had flown the mission.

Russelsheim, Germany, area. The group encountered no enemy aircraft in the air, but the 61st Squadron noted a number of aircraft on an airfield in the area.

Lt. Col. Francis Gabreski, leading the squadron, sent one flight down to strafe. Lt. Praeger Neyland, leading the flight, made his pass and reported good shooting below and little or no flak on the field. At that, the entire squadron took turns making their runs on what turned out to be primarily He 111 bombers. Gabreski made two runs, but apparently he got his nose a bit low and struck a knoll on the field. The impact was sufficient to bend his propeller blades and make further flight impossible. He bellied his Thunderbolt in, scrambled from the cockpit, and ran for the woods. Gabreski remained loose for a few days but was turned in by a farmer who called the police, who came and took him prisoner.

On July 22 Maj. Gordon E. Baker replaced Lt. Col. Francis Gabreski as commander of the 61st Squadron and Maj. Harold Comstock, who had just returned to the group for his second combat tour, took over the 63rd Fighter Squadron.

Chapter 9

A Slower Pace

August 1944 saw a drastic change in operations for the 56th Fighter Group. Since D-day it had flown a number of tactical missions, but by and large it had gone back to bomber escort duties. August brought about a reversal in its type of missions. It flew twenty-eight tactical missions, most of which involved dive-bombing and strafing. Only a half dozen escort missions were conducted during the month.

As Allied troops sought to break out in France and thrust to the north and east, it was essential that the rail systems, principally in France, should be

A close-up shot of Lt. Roach Stewart's 63rd Fighter Squadron aircraft. The tail of his wingman is visible just above the national insignia. USAAF

Capt. Donovan Smith's Old Cock III. USAAF

Lt. Sam Aggers taxis out in Sad Sam. USAAF

put out of order and kept that way to prevent German supplies and troops from arriving on the invasion front. Many of the 56th Group's missions were flown in conjunction with its partner in bombing: the 353rd Group.

On August 4 a dive-bombing mission was flown against marshaling yards at Saarebourg, France. Quite a bit of glide-bombing was done, and the effects were significant. One direct hit was scored on a roundhouse with a dozen locomotives inside. Other glide-bombing hits were made on a cement factory. Over 100 freight cars were damaged. Lt. Richard B. Anderson caught a lone FW 190 in the area and shot it down. Lt. Roach Stewart's Thunderbolt was seen to begin smoking, and then it burst into flames. No parachute was observed.

Lt. Col. Dave Schilling led A Group on an escort mission the following day. The Wolfpack went nearly to Bremen with the bombers and met no enemy opposition. On the way out three Me 109s were encountered and one of them was downed by Lt. Arthur C. Maul.

B Group, under the command of Maj. Sam B. Dale, Jr., escorted bombers to Kiel. On the way out they sighted two four-engined flying boats on Selenter Lake east of Kiel. Maj. Gordon Baker took his flight from the 61st Squadron down, and on his strafing pass he set one of the flying boats on fire. The other members of the flight completed the destruction of the other flying boat.

A late-afternoon mission was led by Col. Hubert Zemke against the airfield at Plantlunne, France. Each Thunderbolt carried a 250-pound bomb, and twenty-three of them bombed the airfield. Six He 111 bombers were destroyed by the 56th Group. This mission was flown in conjunction with the 353rd Fighter Group, and it, too, was successful

Lt. Col. Lucien ("Pete") Dade took over the 56th Fighter Group when Lt. Col. Dave Schilling left in January 1945. USAAF

Lt. Col. David Schilling, commander of the 56th Fighter Group following Zemke. USAAF

Two 56th Group Thunderbolts lined up and ready for takeoff. USAAF

in that it destroyed twenty enemy aircraft on the ground.

Tragedy struck on a dive-bombing mission against the marshaling yards at Albert, France, on August 7. F/O Robert W. Magel was shot down by flak and became a prisoner of war. A midair collision occurred between the P-47s flown by Lts.

The nose of Capt. Eugene O'Neill's aircraft sported the comic strip character L'il Abner. USAAF

Hun Hunter *was one of the P-47s flown by Capt. Donovan Smith. USAAF*

Arthur Maul and Warren S. Patterson as they pulled up from dive-bombing. Maul was heard to say that he was bailing out, but no parachute was ever seen. Patterson made it back to base.

A successful dive-bombing mission was flown against the Muizon, France, marshaling yards on August 10. Thirty-eight railroad and ammunition cars were destroyed.

August 12 was a momentous day in the history of the 56th Fighter Group. Col. Hubert Zemke turned over the command of the group to Lt. Col. David Schilling. Zemke departed to take over the command of the 479th Fighter Group, which at that time was a P-38 unit.

The most destructive mission of the day was a dive-bombing foray to the Fournies-Mauberge, France, marshaling yards. The P-47s carried 250- and 500-pound bombs and used them effectively. Fourteen locomotives were destroyed, and at least ninety rail cars were destroyed and many more damaged. Lt. William H. Barnes was hit and seen to belly in. He would become a successful evader.

Capt. Roy T. Fling sighted an all-silver Me 109 and downed it near Mauberge. Maj. Mike Gladych was in the vicinity of Cambrai when he saw two Ju 88s flying down on the deck. He went after them, and when they split, he hung onto the leader. Gladych's visibility was limited owing to oil on the windshield, but he opened fire anyway. He was low enough that he saw his fire raking the ground, so he moved the pip up and scored good hits on the twin-engined craft. To his surprise the Ju 88 bellied in and hit a tree before it came to a complete stop.

Another administrative change came about on August 13 when Maj. Lucien Dade was appointed deputy commander of the group and Maj. Michael Quirk took command of the 62nd Fighter Squadron.

The group flew a successful dive-bombing mission against the marshaling yards at Braine—le Comte, France, on August 15 but lost Lt. Robert A. Campbell to flak. The next few days were all taken up with dive-bombing missions against rail targets, with spectacular results. Fourteen locomotives were destroyed on the seventeenth, and thirty-one box cars were destroyed while utilizing spike bombs for the first time on the eigthteenth. An outstanding mission took place on the twenty-seventh when the Kaiserslautern area of Germany was attacked. Fifteen locomotives and forty freight cars were destroyed. Lt. Jack Price was lost on this mission when he did not pull out from a strafing run.

Lt. Col. Dave Schilling led the group on a strafing and dive-bombing mission targeted for the Saarbrucken, Germany, and Nancy, France, area on August 28. So much cloud activity was encountered, however, that they were forced to go 20 or 30 miles north of Trier, Germany. As the Thunderbolts arrived in the target area, several He 111s began to show up. The first was destroyed by Lt. Walter R. Groce of the 63rd Fighter Squadron.

At that point Lieutenant Colonel Schilling's wingman sighted another He 111 down below, so Schilling went down after it. He quickly got on the tail of the aircraft and opened fire. The first burst missed, but the second scored hits all over the aircraft. The He went into a hard right turn and took another dose of lead, and the right engine began to smoke and burn. Schilling gave it a final burst and pulled up and over the bomber, which was then burning from both engines. It crashed into the side of a mountain.

Four He 111s were destroyed, as well as a Ju 88, which was shot down by Capt. Mike Jackson. To finalize the day Lt. Walter L. Flagg shot down a stray Me 109 on the way home.

The bombing and strafing had gone well, too. Two locomotives and a number of freight cars were destroyed or damaged. Eleven trains were strafed, several of which were troop trains. No Thunderbolts were lost on the mission.

Only ten enemy aircraft were destroyed in the air and another nine on the ground for the month of August. The impressive figures came in the destruction of transportation targets. The 56th Fighter Group destroyed ninety-eight locomotives and damaged another 177. The total freight car destruction was 154, and hundreds more were damaged. Multiple rail cuts were made, and roundhouses and associated railroad installations and equipment were destroyed. With complete air supremacy for the Allied air forces no railroads or highways were safe for German troop and equipment movement. The Germans had only one option remaining: Retreat at your own risk.

September was another month in which tactical missions predominated. Although the amount of destruction inflicted on the enemy reached record heights, it was the most costly that the group would endure. Dive-bombing and strafing were the primary missions, and the pilots of the 56th proved themselves to be most proficient.

Two missions were flown on September 1, with the first a dive-bombing mission directed at targets in Eindhoven, Holland. The second was a strafing sweep in the St. Trond and Namur, Belgium, area. The Wolfpack caught a train loaded with V-1 rockets and blew it sky high. A truck convoy was strafed on the highway east of Liege, and over fifty trucks were destroyed.

The group went back to Belgium the following day. It shot up more motor convoys and did some flak-busting work by destroying five enemy gun installations.

The big day came on September 5 when two strafing sweeps were made. The first mission was led by Maj. Lucien Dade and was primarily directed

The well-known red-reared Donald Duck that graced the nose of Capt. Mike Quirk's aircraft. USAAF

at airfields. First to be hit was Merzhausen, Germany, airdrome, where seventeen enemy aircraft were claimed to be destroyed. The group then proceeded to Limburg, Germany, airdrome, where another six enemy aircraft were destroyed on the ground. Top scorers for the day were Capt. Mike Jackson with 4.5 and Capt. Herman E. King with 3.5 enemy aircraft destroyed at the airdromes.

The 63rd Squadron was strafing targets on the autobahn 10 miles northeast of Coblenz when it was attacked by Me 109s. Lt. Cameron M. Hart reported:

We had just gone down to strafe in the target area and had only made two attacks when we were bounced at 300 feet by six or seven Me 109s. I saw them coming and called the leader to break.

When I broke, I met an Me 109 coming at me head-on from above. I pulled up into him and made an attack, observing hits on wings. He was still firing over my head when he passed over me. I kicked it around and saw him going down to the deck. I lost sight of him on account of another enemy aircraft passing in front of me.

I was all alone after the first engagement and in a tight climbing turn with another Me 109. I was using water injection and still couldn't get quite enough lead. I saw strikes on his tail, with range about 300 yards, 20 to 30 degrees' deflection. I kept trying to increase my lead and was really clobbering him when he reversed his turn. I closed on him again, firing from astern, and observed parts fly off, as well as the canopy. The enemy aircraft was on fire and smoking badly, going into the ground and exploding.

Hart went after another Me 109, chasing it up to about 12,000 feet. He finally caught it, and once he

Lt. Ralph Johnson's Kentucky Pud II. USAAF

The cowling of Pistol Packin Mama *from the aircraft of Lt. Praeger Neyland. USAAF*

was on its tail discovered he had no ammunition left. The 109 broke and went down in a steep dive with Hart right behind. The P-47 pilot finally pulled out at about 2,000 feet, with the 109 still screaming downward. The 109 was not seen again.

The 63rd Squadron was credited with six Me 109s destroyed in the air during the battle that took place. Two pilots were lost on the mission. Lt. William Heaton received a direct flak hit while his flight was attacking a train, and Lt. Chester Frye was last seen in flak in the Aachen area. Frye survived as a prisoner of war. Lts. James M. Jure and William D. Clark, Jr., were both shot up by flak but bellied their aircraft in safely in friendly territory.

The second mission of the day was led by Lt. Col. Dave Schilling, who reported:

I was leading the 63rd Squadron, and when we reached Gelnhausen, Germany, airdrome, I told my Red and Blue Flights to orbit the field while I took my flight across the field to draw out any flak that might be around. On our first pass we came across the field from east to west along the south side of the airdrome. My number 2 man and I were the only ones to fire on this pass, silencing flak positions on the east side of the field on the way in. I also fired at two FW 190s located near the southeast corner of the field and raked my fire through a blister hangar near the center of the south side of the field, as I strafed the whole south side. Lt. [Charles M.] Rotzler, my wingman, also strafed the entire length of the field, damaging some FW 190s which were lined up just in front of the hangar on the west side of the airdrome. The flight then dropped to the deck and pulled up about 2 miles from the field.

The flight's second pass was made in the same direction over the southern hangar line. Lieutenant Rotzler destroyed an FW 190 camouflaged under a tree, and Lieutenant [Edward M.] Albright[, Jr.,] blew up a Ju 52 in flames in the southeast corner.

The third and fourth passes were made the same as the second. This time I destroyed an FW 190 east of the large hangar near the southwest side. Lieutenant Rotzler destroyed an FW 190, and Lt. [Robert J.] Daniel destroyed an FW 190 in the same area.

I then called in that the flights should change their direction of attack due to the smoke and the availability of the target, and to come in from the south to the north on the west side of the field. Three passes were made in this direction by my flight.

On my sixth pass I saw two planes in the hangar near the southwest corner of the south side of the field and concentrated on them. Lieutenant Albright spotted another one in the hangar and destroyed it. The hangar burst into flames from my attack and burned to the ground, destroying everything in it. Lieutenant Rotzler destroyed an FW 190 in the southwest corner on his fifth pass. On his sixth pass he suspected flak firing from the hangar on the west side of the field. Raking his fire down the entire length of the building, he scored many hits on the planes inside. On his seventh pass Lieutenant Rotzler destroyed what he believed to be [an] Me 109 on the north side of the field.

On arrival it was estimated that fifty-plus enemy aircraft were at Gelnhausen airdrome, mostly single-engined fighters. When the Thunderbolts of the 65th departed, they claimed that forty-six of these aircraft had been destroyed. As the P-47s winged for home, flames were coming up from all over the airfield and it lay under heavy clouds of smoke. Heading up the scoring for the strafers were Capt. Robert J. Keen with six FW 190s destroyed, Lieutenant Rotzler with five, and Lieutenant Colonel Schilling with five.

On the way out Schilling called in an FW 190 flying down the Rhine River. He asked someone to make an attack, as he was out of ammunition. Lt. Eugene A. Timony spotted the aircraft about 4,000 feet below him and moved in on it. Apparently the Luftwaffe pilot never saw what hit him. Timony closed to about 400 yards and opened fire, moving in to 100 yards. Timony broke off firing, pulled up alongside the 190, and watched the pilot release his canopy, climb out, and slide off the left wing.

For all the destruction that was wrought on the enemy, the Wolfpack suffered only one loss. Lt. Earl Hertel, who was last seen in the Cologne area, turned up on the prisoner of war rolls.

The Wolfpack was out strafing again the following day. On a sweep from Aachen to Liege a stream

Capt. Cameron Hart became an outstanding leader and ace in the 63rd Fighter Squadron. USAAF

of trucks, tanks, armored cars, and horse-drawn vehicles was encountered and shot up. At least thirty trucks were destroyed. A number of German military personnel were caught in the open and worked over. As the fuel shortage became more acute in Germany, more horse-drawn vehicles would be on the road for the balance of the war.

Maj. Gordon Baker led a dive-bombing mission on September 8. Trucks and cars were found parked along the road southwest of Bonn and bombed and strafed, destroying all. Fifteen-plus He 111s and FW 190s were found at the airdrome at Euskirchen, Germany, and strafed. Seven of them were destroyed. Lt. George Bostwick was credited with three of them.

Dive-bombing targets in the Dutch Islands provided the action on September 9. Esschen marshaling yards were bombed, and several truck convoys were strafed. Lt. Everett A. Henderson was killed when he failed to pull out while strafing. Lt.

Lt. Sam Agger's trademark Sad Sam. USAAF

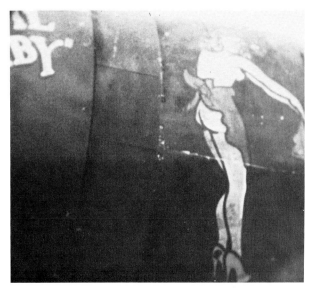

Devil Baby *was flown by Lt. Hillyar Godfrey. USAAF*

This risque artwork adorned one of the aircraft flown by Lt. Charles Clamp. USAAF

Princess Pat *was the Thunderbolt flown by Lt. Charles Reed. USAAF*

The Doublebolt, a P-47 that had been modified and fitted with a second seat behind the pilot's. USAAF

Another photo of Doublebolt. The aircraft was usually used as a "hack" or VIP aircraft. USAAF

Roy T. Fling did not return from this mission and was found to have been killed.

Capt. Michael Quirk led the group on September 10 when it returned to escort duties. Escort was broken in the Wurzburg, Germany, area without any encounters with the Luftwaffe. When the Thunderbolts went down to strafe Wertheim, Germany, airdrome on the way home, however, it was a different story. Thirty-plus enemy aircraft were

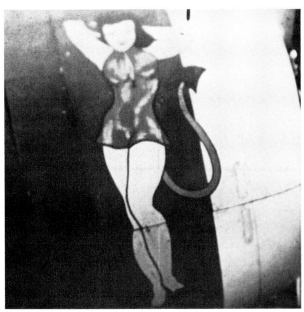

This artwork was on the right side of Lt. Tony Carcione's aircraft. USAAF

sighted, so the P-47s went after them. Two He 111s were destroyed but at significant loss to the 56th.

Captain Quirk, group leader, was hit by light intense flak and bailed out in the woods just north of the airdrome. Lt. Billy Edens, another of the group's up-and-coming aces, was shot down strafing a flak train near the airdrome and was forced to belly in at Trier. Both pilots were taken prisoner.

With the loss of Capt. Michael Quirk an administrative change had to be made and Maj. Leslie Smith was appointed the new commander of the 62nd Fighter Squadron.

Escort was provided the bombers on September 12. The mission was led by Lt. Col. Dave Schilling. Twenty-plus Me 109s were encountered in the vicinity of Brandenburg, Germany. These were engaged, and three of them were shot down by pilots from the 61st Squadron. One flight from the 62nd Squadron was bounced by a half dozen Me 109s, and one 109 was downed. No losses on the mission were incurred for the 56th.

Capt. Harold Comstock led the group on a dive-bombing mission to Ahlorn, Germany, airdrome on September 16. The Thunderbolts carried 260-pound fragmentation bombs and got good hits on the airdrome. Three enemy aircraft were destroyed by the bombing, and another three were destroyed by strafing runs following the bombing.

September 17 marked the initiation of Operation Market Garden in Holland. The British 1st Airborne Division plus the U.S. 82nd and 101st

El Diablo *was flown by Lt. Anthony Cavallo. USAAF*

Capt. Felix ("Willie") Williamson flew this aircraft. USAAF

Airborne Divisions were dropped in Holland to take vital bridges that would enable Allied forces to push all the way to Arnhem, Holland, which would provide a jumping-off point for an offensive directly into Germany. The mission of the 56th Fighter Group was to take out enemy flak positions in order to prevent the transports and gliders participating in the attack from being downed in great numbers. The Thunderbolts also went after enemy ground targets to further support the airborne troops once they were on the ground.

The group knocked out at least twenty flak positions on the ground in addition to shooting up some railroad rolling stock. One 56th pilot was lost; Lt. Edward M. Albright was shot down and did not survive the mission.

September 18 brought about a mission that was almost suicidal for the 56th Group. Although he had not been slated to lead the mission, Maj. Harold Comstock was awakened at 0400 and told that he would do so. When we went to operations to read the mission order, he was all but appalled. The Thunderbolts were to fly a flak-busting mission in the Turnhout area of Holland in support of B-24s that would be dropping supplies to Allied airborne troops from an altitude of 250 feet. The Wolfpack was to go in at low altitude to silence the flak batteries before the bombers arrived. The Thunderbolts were not to fire until they were fired upon, lest they shoot up an Allied installation! The mission would be flown AT ALL COSTS.

Thirty-nine P-47s took off and set course for Holland. The weather was so bad that it was impossible to hold the group formation. The cloud cover combined with the low altitude at which the mission was flown prevented the Thunderbolts from making the rendezvous with the Liberators as planned. Southwest of Groesbeck, Holland, some of the bombers were finally joined and the fighters set out after the flak targets as best they could. The Germans made it all but impossible to hit their flak installations, as they would track the fighters down on the deck and wait until they were alongside to open up. Then all hell would break loose. Ground fire was horrendous; Thunderbolts were hit all over the target area, and many were shot down.

Lt. Frank Klibbe's Little Chief. *USAAF*

The pilot of the colorful Naughty Marietta *is unknown.* USAAF

A rough and ready El Shalf-toe. The pilot is unknown. USAAF

Regardless of the overwhelming obstacles, the men of the 56th did their job. Fourteen flak positions were destroyed, as were some other assorted ground targets. Sixteen P-47s failed to return to base, however. For the twenty-three that did return, a dozen suffered extensive battle damage. Fortunately, most of the pilots who were downed either crash-landed or bailed out over friendly territory. Lt. David Kling crash-landed west of Turnhout; Lt. Charles Rotzler belly-landed near Brussels; Capt. William F. Wilkerson bailed out south of Aachen; Lt. George Van Noy, Jr., belly-landed east of Charleroi; Lt. Philip F. Fleming crash-landed on the French coast near St.-Quentin; Lt. Herschel C. Womack landed wheels-down at an RAF base in Belgium; Lt. William G. Bartle bailed out south of Tilburg, Holland; Capt. Paul Conger landed at a Royal Canadian Air Force base near Brussels; Lt. William

M. Hartshorn broke his ankle when he bailed out near Schjudel, Holland; Lt. James Hodges, Jr., broke a leg when he crash-landed in Belgium; and Lt. Thomas Guerrero was recovered in Belgium. Five pilots did not come back. Lts. Robert G. Kelley and William W. McElhare became prisoners of war. Capt. Gordon S. Stevens, Lt. Elwood R. Raymond, and Lt. Trevor A. Edwards were killed in action.

Although the 56th Fighter Group received a Distinguished Unit Citation and other accolades for the mission, the question still remains: Was the mission worth it for the damage that was inflicted on the enemy, and contrary to the explicit order of AT ALL COSTS should the mission have been aborted as suggested by higher authority?

On September 21 the group went back to Holland to escort the 1st Allied Airborne Army dropping more paratroops and supplies in the

Capt. Donovan Smith's last Ole' Cock. This aircraft was in an unusual two-tone camouflage paint scheme. Note the rocket tubes fitted under the wings. USAAF

Arnhem area. Lt. Col. Dave Schilling led. As he crossed the small town of Lochem, Holland, he sighted one FW 190 and one Me 109 directly in front of him heading west. He immediately went after the 190 and opened fire from 500 yards. Strikes were observed all over the aircraft, and the enemy did a half roll and went in from about 900 feet.

Schilling then sighted a P-47 with an FW 190 on its tail about 2 miles away. Schilling climbed to about 1,000 feet. As he approached the enemy aircraft, it went into a slight left-hand turn. Schilling opened fire from about 700 yards but held the trigger for about 5 seconds and got a heavy concentration of hits. The enemy pilot rolled over and bailed out as the plane went down in flames.

Schilling's third victim was sighted as it headed east. Schilling turned right to get on its tail, and as he did so, the FW 190 went into an orbit with him. Schilling closed to 400 yards and got off a long burst with 45 degrees' deflection. Hits were scored, and the enemy aircraft spun in and crashed.

Maj. Mike Gladych encountered several FW 190s in the area and shot down two of them, one off the tail of his wingman.

Numerous fights broke out beneath the overcast as the enemy fighters went after the transports and gliders in the area. Before the day was out the P-47 pilots of the 56th claimed fifteen enemy aircraft destroyed. Two pilots were killed in the action: Lts. Oscar Cagle and Harold Spicer were last seen in combat with the FW 190s.

Another administrative change took place on September 26 when Maj. Gordon Baker was moved up to group headquarters and Capt. Donovan Smith took over the 61st Squadron.

The following day the group escorted the bombers on a mission to Kassel. No enemy opposition was encountered, and the Thunderbolts did

Another photo of Capt. Donovan Smith's aircraft, this time in complete profile and fitted with drop tanks. USAAF

some free-lance strafing on the way home. Lt. Walter H. Pitts was lost on the mission when he failed to pull out while investigating a convoy at low level.

The role of a tactical fighter unit during September turned out to be an expensive one. True, the group had fulfilled its mission in support of ground troops and airborne operations, but it had never suffered the losses in aircraft and men that became its lot during the month many had speculated would end the war in Europe. During that thirty-day period, the group lost eleven pilots killed in action, another six taken prisoner of war, and one killed in an accident.

October 1944 was the leanest month ever known by the 56th Fighter Group—and, for that matter, all the fighter units of the 8th Air Force. The 56th went back to the bomber escort mission, but this brought about almost no action. The Luftwaffe refused to come up as it licked its wounds and

attempted to reorganize for the defense of the Reich. The bombers of the 8th Air Force continued their offensive against German industrial targets and particularly against oil targets. With the loss of the Romanian oil fields to the Russians in August of 1944 the Third Reich was sorely strapped for petroleum and it began to depend heavily on the synthetic oil refineries for its needs. It was against these refineries that the strategic air offensive would concentrate.

On October 5 the bombers of the 8th Air Force went out in force to strike against industrial and oil targets. The Wolfpack made rendezvous with them in the Dummer Lake area and swept out ahead of them on their way to Paderborn, Germany. Southwest of Lippstadt, Germany, two Me 109s were seen circling an airdrome. The Thunderbolts engaged but only managed to damage one of them.

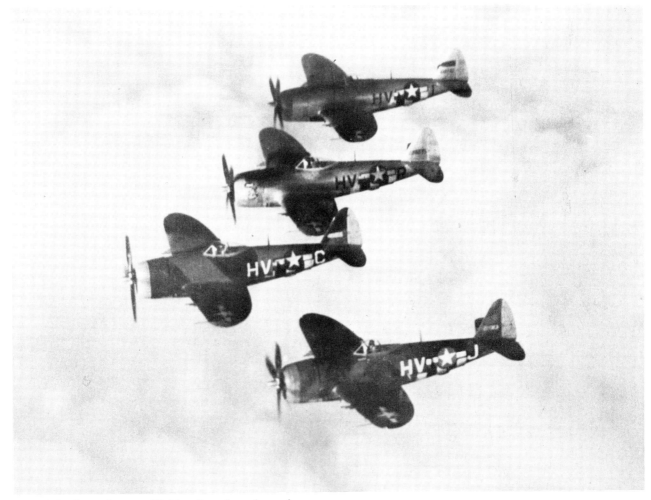

One flight from the 61st Fighter Squadron formed up nicely. Two are in camouflage paint scheme, and two are not. USAAF

While the bombers were pounding away at Paderborn, the 56th sighted aircraft on an airfield south of Geseke, Germany. Lt. Col. Dave Schilling led an attack against four light flak positions, and once they were silenced, the field was worked over. Fourteen enemy aircraft were destroyed on the ground, and Schilling was top scorer with three Me 210s.

Lt. Julius DeMayo was lost on an escort mission to Coblenz on October 11. The following day the Thunderbolts were vectored to the Dummer Lake area, where bandits were reported. A dozen FW 190s were sighted flying in American-style formation, but when engaged they immediately dispersed. One FW 190 was shot down by Lt. James E. Lister of the 63rd Squadron.

Except for two dive-bombing missions on which the P-47s carried parafrags the balance of the month saw nothing but boring, unopposed escort missions. The first dive-bombing mission was on October 15 and took place in the Gutersloh area. The second was in the Nienburg area, where the Thunderbolts not only bombed, but did considerable ground strafing. Unfortunately, two pilots were killed on this mission: Lts. William J. Osborne and George R. Choate.

The scoreboard for the month gave the 56th only one enemy aircraft destroyed in the air and fifteen on the ground, for the loss of three pilots.

Thunderbolt Toughness

Lt. Charles T. McBath of the 63rd Fighter Squadron was doing some strafing when his aircraft was hit and damaged, creating what he thought was a bailout situation—but thanks to the Republic Iron Works he made it home. As McBath related the events of the day:

We were strafing rail and road transportation north of Schweinfurt, Germany, when at a split in the railroad tracks Capt. [Walter] Flagg and I [were] sent down to strafe some fifteen or more box cars standing on a siding.

While strafing the cars lengthwise, the whole train suddenly exploded in front of me, with flames shooting way up and smoke belching from the explosion. As I was so close I had no other alternative but to fly right through the base of the explosion, which immediately engulfed me in complete darkness, punctuated by large spurts of flame, completely covering my plane. Then I felt as if I had flown into the train, because the plane reacted similarly to one that is being bellied in, and the inside of the cockpit seemed to be on fire. Coming out of the smoke, a quick backward glance revealed a dense cumulus cloud reaching some 5,000 feet with flames up to 1,000 feet.

I also noticed that my airplane was severely damaged, so I readied myself to bail out. The right side of the engine was spouting oil in a heavy stream, and the engine itself was smoking badly. One foot was blown off the left stabilizer, and it partly jammed the elevator actions. Both wings had numerous holes in them, my right wing being partially on fire, and the right side of the canopy [was] completely blown off. To add to my troubles the prop was set at 1800rpm and I was unable to change its pitch.

Being over enemy territory, I gave a second thought to bailing out and then decided to see if I could keep going and maybe make it safely to a point behind our lines. I started due west, attempting to avoid an intense barrage of flak at 3,000 feet. Shortly afterwards my flight leader, Capt. Walter Flagg, called me on the [radio] and guided me safely around a heavy barrage of rocket flak through which I would otherwise have flown had he not been there. Again I contemplated bailing out. Smoke and oil from the engine filled the cockpit, and the plane was liable to explode at any second.

I called in, asking how long it would take to get to friendly territory, and was told that it would be about 20 minutes. With this in mind I stayed with the ship, but after 30 minutes I was still fairly deep in Germany. The smoke was heavier, and, by now, the oil had covered the entire fuselage. The cockpit was so badly flooded with oil that I couldn't see the instruments. My hands and feet kept sliding off the controls. The elevators were jammed to about 5 or 10 degrees' play, and I could sense the stick jam when I tried to climb.

Throughout the entire flight back Captain Flagg stayed with me, offering me protection from any possible enemy attack, giving me courage, advice, and confidence without which I am sure I could never have gone that far. About 35 miles from the front lines, Captain Flagg talked me in to a field where I made a blind and wheels-up landing. Landing, my plane ran off the runway and I jumped clear while a fire crew sprang up immediately to put out the small fires in my smoking engine. To this day I will never know or understand how my aircraft flew from the scene of the explosion, but thanks to a P-47 and, even more so, to Captain Flagg's intrepid nature, guidance, and judgment, I was able to get back to friendly territory.

Chapter 10

Winter Actions

An escort mission to Gelsenkirchen, Germany, on November 1, 1944, marked the group's first encounter with one of the German jets. About 25 miles south of Enscheda, Holland, Maj. Harold Comstock sighted a brownish contrail coming in from the east at about 38,000 feet. The craft then went into a 25-degree dive toward the rear of the American bomber formation.

Lt. Walter R. Groce reported what then transpired:

The jet then made a diving turn to the left, and I pushed everything forward and started my dive on it. I saw that this was useless, so I cut back my throttle and decreased my dive, which enabled me to hold altitude. The Me 262 then made a 180 to the right, and I also made a diving 180. I saw the jet just below me and to the right, and going like hell bent for election. At this time there were also some other P-47s and P-51s after him, but they did not appear to be within range. [These came from not only the 56th, but also the 20th and 352nd Fighter Groups in a wild chase.] Attempting to close on him, I ended up behind him in a horde of 47s and 51s. Then I called over the [radio]: "Spread it out. We'll get him if he turns." I started slightly northeast as the jet made a climbing turn to the left, which led me to believe that he would almost have to be heading towards me. I turned into him a little more, but as he was slightly above me, I closed in and pulled up.

As I came within range, I immediately began to fire. I must have been going up in at least a 70-degree angle, and in order to pull enough deflection I had to pull my nose through him. When he came into view over me, I saw some of my bullets strike the underside of his starboard engine, which put it out of operation and on fire. The jet then went into a flat spin, the pilot bailing out, with his chute opening almost immediately thereafter.

I was on my back so rolled out and went down to take some pictures of the spinning jet, as well as to give him a few more bursts of fire.

In the general melee several pilots had fired at the Me 262. After careful evaluation the victory was split between Lieutenant Groce and Lt. William Gerbe of the 352nd Fighter Group. As was later learned the pilot of the Me 262 was Obfw. Willi Banzhaff of Kommando Nowotny, who had just shot down Lt. Dennis Alison of the 20th Fighter Group when he was intercepted by pilots of the 56th Group.

The 56th encountered 262s again on November 2, and although one Thunderbolt was damaged, no decisions resulted. The next sharp action for the Wolfpack came on the fifth when it swept ahead of the bombers destined for Karlsruhe, Germany. Trains and rolling stock were strafed en route, and several locomotives and freight cars were destroyed. Two pilots were killed during the attacks, however: Lts. Robert E. Healy and Albert L. Henry.

November 9 saw the group dive-bombing marshaling yards in the vicinity of Aschaffenburg, Germany. This mission was successful in that sixteen locomotives were destroyed and a number of trucks that were on flatcars on one of the trains were destroyed or damaged.

Maj. Harold Comstock led the group on November 18 when it went on a strafing mission directed at an underground oil storage depot at Langenselbold, northeast of Hanau, Germany. Ground haze caused Major Comstock to go by the target without seeing it, but Capt. James R. Carter of the 61st Squadron spotted it. Carter asked permission to strafe the well-camouflaged target, and upon receiving the go-ahead went down after it.

Carter reported:

We approached on the deck from the south about 5 miles out and were to turn right at the flak tower southwest of the oil dump and strafe going 90 degrees to the railway, heading about northeast. I missed the target this time . . . I re-formed and climbed to 8,000 feet. We dive-strafed this time with good results, getting five or six explosions with resulting fires from storage tanks of a medium size.

On recovering from my dive I spotted [an] Me 109 and completed almost a 360-degree turn before I got behind him. He was at 1,000 feet flying parallel to the railway track from Hanau to Gelnhausen and on the south side of the tracks heading east. I fired from about 300 yards with small deflection and got a few meager hits. My K-14 gun sight didn't seem to be working, so [I] switched to fixed and fired quite a long burst, which blew pieces and the canopy off. The enemy aircraft crashed and burned. . . .

Just south of the target at 8,000 feet I started a right turn to the north to cross over when I saw, and heard it reported, sixteen or more FW 190s coming in on us from out of the northeast at about five o'clock to us. They were flying a formation very similar to ours and had evidently come down from not more than 2,000 feet above us—at first sight I thought it might be Platform [62nd Squadron]. We broke into them, and the fight started. Three or four took turns firing at us from about 90 degrees on down, and finally one hung on me. At different times I'd take snap shots at other 190s as they crossed in front of me. P-47s and 190s were all over, but this one joker stuck tight to me, firing for the most part out of range. I could outturn him until he'd stall, but on recovery he could accelerate faster, and again he'd be on me. About the fifth such turn I felt my plane on the verge of snapping, and he only had about 70 degrees' deflection, which seemed too little to me, so I rolled it over and hit the deck with water injection.

As long as I'd fly straight, I would gain slowly and increased my lead to about 1,000 yards. I hung to the ground with full power praying he'd run out of ammo or get tired. Just when I thought he'd do neither, he pulled up. That old 47 sure put out for 20 or 30 minutes.

Capt. Mike Jackson was leading 62nd ("Platform") Squadron flying top cover while the 61st under Captain Carter went down to strafe. When Jackson got the call from the 61st that the FW 190s had shown up, he led his squadron down to do battle. Jackson saw two P-47s chasing an FW 190 that was trying to outclimb them and outturn them. He cut in between the P-47s and the FW, as he was climbing faster and outturning the German pilot. Jackson opened fire and immediately saw strikes. At

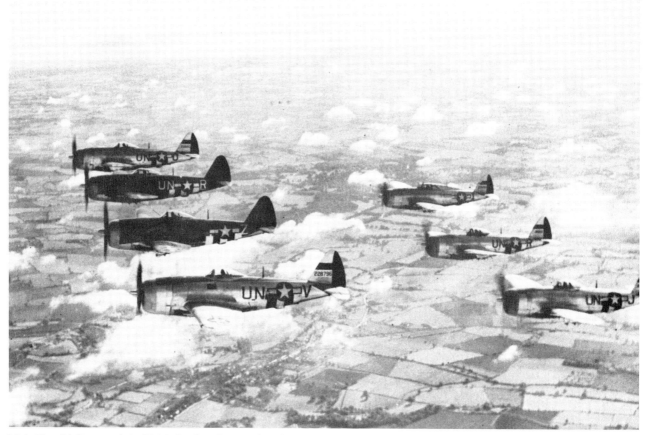

Maj. Harold Comstock in UN-V leading his 63rd Fighter Squadron over the green fields of England. USAAF

this point the Thunderbolt began to stall, so he leveled off. The FW 190 pilot jettisoned his canopy and bailed out.

After Major Comstock had missed the target, he took the 63rd Squadron on a strafing mission against a train in the area. He took his flight down, and he destroyed the locomotive while the rest of the flight took care of the freight cars.

After breaking off he saw light flak coming up from a wooded area. He flew over to investigate and discovered a small airfield with the aircraft dispersed in the woods. The 63rd Squadron proceeded to strafe these aircraft and destroyed five of them.

Lt. Ramon R. Davis, who was strafing the airfield, heard one of the other squadrons call over the radio telephone that enemy aircraft were in the area. At first he couldn't find them, but then he sighted an FW 190 flying right down on the deck. Davis caught the 190 and opened fire from about 400 yards. When the 190 was hit, it pulled up in a steep climb. Davis then cut the 190 off, fired again, and saw the pilot jettison his canopy and bail out.

The Wolfpack destroyed eleven enemy aircraft in the air in the combats that took place in the area. It suffered two losses, as Lt. Jack DeMars was killed and Lt. Gordon J. Blake went down to become a prisoner of war.

Maj. Harold Comstock led the group out once more on November 27, on what was to have been another strafing mission. When they arrived in the Dummer Lake area, Nuthouse Microwave Early Warning (MEW)—a radar station on the Continent that vectored U.S. fighters to enemy aircraft in the area—vectored them to the south where a large number of enemy aircraft were sighted. The P-47s chased the opposition in haze for some time but lost them except for three Me 109s that were caught and destroyed by members of the 63rd Squadron. Lt. Russell Frederickson and his wingman went down after two of them. Frederickson stated:

We turned with them in a circle about six times before I could get in position to shoot. Closing to about 400 yards astern of the rear enemy aircraft, I opened fire and scored many strikes on his fuselage and wing roots. Smoke started pouring from under

Teddy, the P-47-M flown by Maj. Mike Jackson of the 62nd Fighter Squadron, with northern European camouflage paint scheme. M. Jackson

the fuselage, and then a big burst of flames [came] out as pieces began to fall off the plane. . . . I then went after the leader of the two.

I again closed to [within] about 400 yards [of the leader] and opened fire. Strikes were seen. . . . Pieces were also seen coming off the aircraft as it continued downwards to explode as it hit the ground. Neither pilot was seen to bail out.

Lt. Leo J. Czarnota was lost on the mission when his engine cut out south of Dummer Lake. He was forced to bail out and became a prisoner of war.

The last day of the month the group flew another escort mission and then did some strafing in the Neuenkirchen, Germany, area. Four locomotives were destroyed, and a number of freight cars were shot up. Lt. Alben G. Calmes did not return from the mission and was later reported as killed in action.

Maj. Paul Conger of the 63rd Squadron led the Wolfpack on a fighter sweep ahead of the bombers on December 2. For the first time in over a month the Luftwaffe came up in force. Conger's description of the air action that day gives a good example of

the coordination between Nuthouse and the Thunderbolts:

Our mission was a fighter sweep ahead of the bombers, and we flew to the vicinity of Coblenz between two cloud layers at approximately 20,000 feet before making a sweeping turn to the north, being in constant touch with MEW control— Nuthouse.

After 10 minutes of flying due north, Nuthouse reported bogeys 30 to 40 miles still due north of us. I continued the vector at 20,000 feet with a solid thin overcast 1,000 feet below us. The next report from Nuthouse was, "Bogeys are now south of you." I immediately made a 180-degree turn, but as yet we had seen nothing.

Assuming that what Nuthouse was reporting must be below the overcast, I went down through in a shallow dive. As we broke out, I observed twenty or more single-engine bogeys, flying about 2 or 3 miles ahead of us in a hostile-type formation: tight line abreast, operating in sections of eight, each section close to line abreast but stacked down.

As we close[d] in, we stayed quite well hidden in the overcast for nearly 5 minutes before we could identify them. Finally the gaggle became obviously Me 109s, carrying belly tanks. They still had not

Lt. Townsend Parson's Barbara Bee *of the 62nd Fighter Squadron. This one is laden with 108-gallon drop tanks.*
P. Conger

seen us, so I called the group to drop belly tanks. The fun was on.

I closed to the middle of the formation, as my squadron was nearing an offensive line-abreast formation, too. I closed to 200 yards and throttled back, indicating only 210mph. Not having to span the Me 109 with the K-14 sight at all, I gave a 2-second burst at what I assumed to be the lead ship. I immediately observed hits on the canopy and fuselage, and the 109 was definitely out of control as it went off to the left. A second later the pilot bailed out. His plane, still intact, spun downward.

The Jerry formation was still doing very little evasive action, so I skidded to the right and picked out another Me 109. I gave it a quick spurt at about 200 yards, observing plenty of hits in the canopy and coolant. Pieces were seen to fly off, and the right side of the engine was on fire as the 109 went into a tight turn to the right. Then two more small explosions occurred, [and] the enemy aircraft went into an uncontrollable, inverted flat spin.

Unfortunately, as I was turning for further engagements, two Me 109s bounced me at 18,000 feet. I tried to turn right and climb, but after two turns with them they were outclimbing and outturning me. I finally went straight down and was able to outdive them as I hit the bottom cloud layer at 5,000 feet.

The pilots of the 63rd Squadron were credited with nine of the eleven Me 109s destroyed for the day. Most of the 109s went down in uncontrollable spins after being hit by astern attacks from the Thunderbolts. Lt. Richard B. Anderson stated that his victim shed one of its wings while in a flat spin.

A misfortune occurred in the combat: a midair collision between Capt. Eugene Barnum of the 61st Squadron, and Lt. Wyman A. Baker of the 63rd Squadron, who was on his first mission. Neither of

Lt. Russell Kyler's aircraft from the 61st Fighter Squadron. The nose of the aircraft was enhanced by a portrait of Lorene. USAAF

the pilots survived the incident. Lt. Donald Al-layaud of the 62nd Squadron was also killed on the mission.

December 4 marked a successful strafing mission but one that resulted in another near disaster for the group. The Wolfpack set out to provide withdrawal support for the bombers but was vectored to unidentified aircraft, which turned out to be friendly B-17s. Meanwhile Maj. Gordon Baker sighted an enemy aircraft but lost it in the clouds.

By now the group was down to low altitude. As it flew over Neuburg, Germany, airdrome some 35 miles from Munich, it sighted a promising target. Of the fifty to seventy aircraft that were present at least thirty were Me 262s. The balance were primarily twin- and four-engined aircraft. The best feature of the airfield was that it was only lightly defended by flak. The Thunderbolts roared down to the attack and destroyed eleven enemy aircraft, four of them Me 262s.

Then came misfortune: the group encountered very bad weather on its return home. Winds aloft reached up to 150mph and a 10/10 undercast spread all over the western areas of the Continent. When the

P-47s came home to roost, twenty-one were missing. When all was finalized, it was discovered that twelve of them had landed successfully on the Continent but nine of them had to bail out or crash-land. All pilots finally returned to base except for Maj. Robert W. Hall, who was injured in his bailout.

The next few missions were uneventful except for some further difficulty with the weather. The group went on a free-lance mission ahead of the bombers on December 18. Lt. Wilburn A. Haggard didn't return. He was later reported a prisoner of war.

December 23 found American troops fighting for their lives in what would become known as the Battle of the Bulge. Inclement weather had made Allied air operations almost impossible, and German armored columns pressed westward. St. Vith, Belgium, had fallen, and American troops were surrounded at Bastogne, Belgium. On this day, however, the skies began to clear, almost overnight, and air activity increased dramatically.

The 8th Air Force dispatched its bombers against communications in the area of Trier-Ehrang, Junkerath-Dahlem, and Ahrweiler, all in Germany.

Lt. Charles McBath taxis out in Dottie Dee II. *USAAF*

By midmorning a huge formation of Luftwaffe fighters had arisen to oppose these strikes. About ninety FW 190s and Me 109s from JGs 4, 11, 27, and 54 were airborne. As they flew over the Bruhl-Bonn-Euskirchen triangle in Germany, JG 4 proceeded on south unmolested. At this moment the balance of the formation was engaged by the 56th Fighter Group in one of its largest and most successful air battles of the war.

Lt. Col. Dave Schilling was leading the Wolfpack. He reported:

As the group reached a location approximately 30 miles west of Bonn at an altitude of 27,000 feet, MEW Control changed our previous vector of 103 degrees to 90 degrees magnetic, telling us that a large number of enemy aircraft was ahead to the east. In about 2 minutes a gaggle was sighted about 10 miles to the north flying west. We turned to a vector of 330 degrees in an effort to cut them off, but they managed to get away in [a] large patch of cirrus clouds. We then returned to the vector of 90 degrees and in 1 or 2 minutes sighted another large gaggle about 10 miles to the south with a heading of west. We turned south but lost them the same as the first.

I then called MEW and asked them why they had not picked the enemy aircraft up and to give us some help. Their reply was: "Don't worry. There is plenty straight east at 22[,000] to 23,000 feet." About 2 or 3 minutes later the 63rd Squadron leader [Maj. Harold Comstock] called and said a large formation of FW 190s was directly below me. At the same time I sighted a large number of enemy aircraft, approximately forty, flying south in a wide turn to the left about 1,500 feet below me and several miles ahead. I told the 63rd to attack and the 61st to aid, as I was going to hit the enemy aircraft ahead, since we had altitude and speed on both formations.

I flew straight ahead, pulled up, applied full power, and made a slow diving turn to the left to position my flight on the outside and allow the other three to cross over inside so that we might bring as many planes into position to fire as possible. In so doing I managed to hit the rear right Me 109 with about a 20-degree deflection shot at a range of about 700 yards. There was a large concentration of strikes all over the left side of the fuselage, and he fell off to the left. I then picked out another more or less ahead of the first and fired from about the same range as the first, causing him to smoke and catch on fire immediately. By this time the first

Lt. Col. Dave Schilling taxiing out for takeoff. The Hairless Joe character on the nose is from the Al Capp comic strip L'il Abner. USAAF

Me 109 was slightly ahead, below, and to the left, at which point he started to smoke and caught on fire. I then picked another and fired at about 1,000 yards and missed as he broke right and started to dive for the deck. At about 17,000 feet I had closed to about 500 yards and fired, resulting in a heavy concentration of strikes, and the pilot bailed out.

At this point I had become separated from the other three flights and had only my own with me. I heard Major Comstock of the 63rd Squadron in a hell of a fight and called to get his position. As I was attempting to locate him, I sighted another gaggle of thirty-five to forty FW 190s 1,000 feet below circling to the left. I repeated the same tactics as before and attacked one from 500 yards' range and slightly above and to the left. This plane immediately began to smoke and burn, spinning off to the left. I then fired at a second and only got two or three strikes. He immediately took violent evasive action, and it took me several minutes of maneuvering until I managed to get in a position to fire. I fired from about 300 yards from above and to the left, forcing me to pull through him and fire as he went out of sight over the cowling. I gave about a 5-second burst and began getting strikes all over him. The pilot immediately bailed out, and the ship spun down to the left, smoking and burning, until it blew up at about 15,000 feet.

By this time I was alone and saw a lone 63rd plane. I called, and he joined up just as a thirty-five—to forty-plane formation of FW 190s flew by heading west about 1,000 feet above. I had hoped to sneak by and turn upon their tails, but they saw me just as I started my climbing turn. I knew I would have to hit the deck sooner or later but thought I could get their tail-end man before I had to. My wingman lagged back, and just as I was getting set, he called and said two were on his tail. I thought I saw him get hit and told him to do vertical aileron rolls and hit the deck. At that time two got behind me and were getting set, so I did several rolls as I started down, hit the switch, and outran them by a mile as I got to the deck. I lost them and zoomed back up to 8,000 feet.

While Schilling was downing five of the enemy, the 62nd Squadron, which he was leading, and the 61st Squadron, which he led into battle, were meeting with great success against the enemy. Capt. Felix Williamson overshot the first gaggle but managed to down an Me 109 that emerged from the gaggle as a single. Williamson and his wingman then found another gaggle and shot the tail-end Charlie off the formation.

Lt. Robert E. Winters of the 62nd Squadron got into a gaggle and set one Me 109 on fire. As Winters closed on a second, the Luftwaffe pilot chopped throttle. Winters' closure was such that he hit the left wing of the enemy craft with his right wing. As Winters recovered, he saw his first target going down in flames, but he could not spot the plane that he struck, owing to the number of enemy aircraft in the vicinity.

Capt. Joseph H. Perry was leading the 61st Squadron, which stayed aloft for a time after Schilling took the 62nd Squadron down to do combat. As the gaggle was broken up, Perry began to spiral down on the enemy. He sighted a Thunderbolt with two FW 190s on its tail and attacked them. He drove them off the P-47, but they refused further combat. He and his wingman then appeared to be the only P-47s in a whole beehive of enemy aircraft. Perry fired in short bursts as enemy aircraft crossed his nose, and managed to get a lucky hit on one FW 190. This aircraft went into a sharp left-hand turn and pulled up, and the pilot bailed out.

Perry and his wingman decided that if they were to survive, they had to get out of the area, so they shoved full throttle and climbed up into the sun. Another straggling Thunderbolt joined them, and as they cruised around, Perry sighted an FW 190 going down. He immediately dived after the 190 and chased it down over a village at 500 feet where light flak opened up. Perry continued to chase the 190 on the deck until it crashed and blew up.

One pilot that didn't get back home that day was Lt. Lewis R. Brown. He attacked some FW 190s in a Lufbery and scored hits on two of them. When he left the Lufbery, he went after another 190, at which he expended the balance of his ammunition. At this moment his cockpit lit up like a torch and he saw the nose of an FW 190 right on his tail. Brown bailed out to become a prisoner of war.

The 63rd Squadron, led by Maj. Harold Comstock, had a great day. When Lieutenant Colonel Schilling told it to attack the gaggle of FW 190s, it did so with vigor. Comstock made his first pass through the middle of the formation and damaged one enemy aircraft in the wing. He then pulled up and turned head-on into another 190. They both began firing at about 1,000 yards. The 190's shots went below Comstock, but the fire from the Thunderbolt caught the 190 flush in the engine. The 190 pilot jettisoned his canopy and bailed out.

Comstock pulled up and tucked under another FW 190, whose pilot could not see him. He stayed with that 190 until he rolled out of his turn and then closed in directly astern. A burst from pointblank range was all that it took to send pieces flying off, and the 190 went down.

Lt. Randel L. Murphy, Jr., chased a long-nosed 190 but couldn't catch it. As he climbed back up, he sighted a 61st Squadron Thunderbolt with a 190 chasing it. Murphy turned and dived down to drive the 190 off. The 61st pilot turned the 190 back to Murphy in a head-on pass, on which Murphy was able to get strikes from stem to stern. The 190 went straight into the ground.

Lt. Walter Frederick of the 63rd Fighter Squadron on the
nose of his Quaker Sad Sack. USAAF

The Brat P-47 flown by Lt. Randel Murphy, Jr., of the 63rd
Fighter Squadron. Murphy destroyed two enemy aircraft
in the air and 11 on the ground. R. Murphy

As Murphy climbed back up, he had another
190 make a pass at him. Murphy dived for the deck
with the 190 after him. About 500 feet off the deck
Murphy made a tight diving bank to the right. As the
FW 190 tried to follow through, it stalled and
snapped into the ground.

Capt. Cameron Hart got caught up in some hot
action that he was lucky to get out of. He had
downed an FW 190 out of the initial gaggle, and he
related what happened next:

> I climbed back up and engaged . . . four more
> head-on. Slightly above them were seven more
> coming in on my tail as I started to fire. This
> encounter is sort of hazy in my mind, but I do
> remember seeing hits on one and possibly two
> enemy aircraft before I had to barrel-roll down to
> shake my "friends" in the rear. I came back up trying
> to find someone to join, but they were all in a big
> Lufbery at about 18,000 feet. I found several more
> targets, but each time I was about to fire, several
> 190s would come in from the rear and force me to go
> down again. This happened four or five times.
> These Jerries were really aggressive and good, hot
> pilots. I got too close to a formation of fifty-plus 190s
> coming in from the southeast, and four of them
> came after me, chasing me over past Aachen, where I
> shook them in the clouds.

The 63rd Squadron lost one pilot in the fight:
Lt. John E. Lewis, who when bounced by an FW 190
went into a cloud bank and was not seen again. The
62nd Squadron lost Lt. Charles E. Carlson, who was
last seen in the vicinity of Euskirchen airdrome.
Both of these pilots were later reported to have been
killed in action.

The good news was that the 56th Fighter Group
had scored a resounding victory. Thirty-four enemy

Capt. Cameron Hart scored one of his victories in this
aircraft on Christmas Day 1944. USAAF

aircraft had been downed, with seventeen being
credited to the 62nd Squadron and an even dozen to
the 63rd.

Christmas Day saw the Wolfpack flying a fighter
sweep in the Bonn-Coblenz area. MEW vectored the
Thunderbolts several times before they finally
found a target. Capt. Mike Jackson was leading the
62nd Squadron when they sighted a gaggle of
approximately thirty Me 109s. These were attacked
from above, with Jackson blowing one of the enemy
craft up at pointblank range.

Capt. Cameron Hart was leading the 63rd
Squadron when he heard that the 62nd was in
action. On arrival the 62nd found that the gaggle had

been pretty well broken up but Hart managed to catch an Me 109 by using water injection. Hart opened fire on the craft from 600 yards and closed rapidly, still using water. The 109 disintegrated in midair, with Hart having to barrel-roll to miss the debris.

The 56th was credited with eight enemy aircraft destroyed in the air for no losses.

Lt. Col. Dave Schilling receives the Distinguished Service Cross from Gen. Jesse Auton for his five-in-a-day victories on December 23, 1944. USAAF

A snow-covered aircraft of the 61st Fighter Squadron in early 1945. USAAF

The group returned to the Bonn-Cologne area the following day. Although a number of enemy aircraft were sighted, only a few were encountered, and these by the 62nd Fighter Squadron. In a brief, but sharp, action three FW 190s were downed—two by Lt. Alfred O. Perry and one by the squadron leader, Maj. Leslie Smith.

The group closed out 1944 with a penetration and withdrawal support mission. Maj. James Carter led the Thunderbolts, which made rendezvous with the bombers in the vicinity of Hanover. On the way out Nuthouse vectored the P-47s to the Quackenbruck area, where two Me 109s were seen at low altitude. The 62nd Squadron engaged and was in turn bounced by seven FW 190s that were flying high cover for the Me 109s.

In the ensuing engagement three FW 190s were shot down, with Capt. Francis A. Nolan getting two of them. On the other side of the coin the squadron suffered two losses: Lt. Andrew Chasko was shot down to become a prisoner, and Lt. William H. Stovall, Jr., was killed in action.

Chapter 11

Final Acts

The early part of the New Year for 1945 was marked with several uneventful escort and free-lance missions. One significant event took place in this period, however. The first P-47M arrived. The turbo-supercharged engine, the R-2800-57, vastly improved performance at high altitude. The aircraft was flown at speeds in excess of 450mph above 30,000 feet. Initially, the pilots were exuberant with the aircraft, but then engine troubles developed that really handicapped the new aircraft in combat. Ignition lead and turbo-performance correlation were the primary difficulties. It would be April of 1945 before the P-47M was ready for combat in quantity.

On January 14 Maj. Paul Conger led A Group and Maj. Mike Jackson led B Group on fighter

Two Thunderbolts get airborne from Boxted. Each is carrying a 150-gallon flat drop tank under each wing.
P. Conger

Maj. Paul Conger's P-47M Bernyce gets fitted with drop tanks in preparation for a mission. P. Conger

Lt. Felix Williamson of the 62nd Fighter Squadron got five enemy aircraft in one day on January 14, 1945. S. Sox

sweeps ahead of the bombers that were attacking Magdeburg, Germany. On the way in three gaggles of Me 109s were sighted forming up over Steinhuder Lake. The first of the enemy were encountered by the 63rd Squadron of B Group, which destroyed four Me 109s.

Major Jackson got a call when the 63rd Squadron became engaged, and he at once led his Thunderbolts to the scene. He and his element leader got into the middle of the fight and chased the enemy aircraft to the deck. Jackson caught an Me 109 with its wheels down that was trying to get into its airfield to land. A well-placed short burst caused it to roll over and crash on the field.

Jackson then swung left and sighted an FW 190 turning at the edge of the airfield. A short burst from Jackson's .50 calibers hit the enemy aircraft, and the 190 split-essed and went into the ground.

At this time Jackson found that he had an FW 190 on his tail. The two began to orbit with one and then the other, getting in a few hits. Finally Jackson ran out of ammunition. Just in the nick of time his element leader, Lt. William C. Daley, arrived on the scene and downed the enemy aircraft.

Altogether B Group destroyed ten enemy fighters and suffered no losses.

Maj. Paul Conger, leading A Group, made his rendezvous with the bombers. Capt. Felix Williamson of A Group had the 62nd Squadron wide to the left of Conger, and A Group was the first to sight the enemy. Williamson had his Thunderbolts at 28,000 feet sweeping to the right of the bomber stream. Many contrails were observed in front of the bombers at about two o'clock. The P-47s began to climb, and as the P-47s neared the contrails, most of the other aircraft were identified as Me 109s.

Williamson stated:

A couple of these 109s came down in front of the squadron, so I picked one and gave chase. This aircraft pulled up into the sun. I could not see him, so I flew straight into the sun until I saw the 109 come out of the left side. I fired a short burst at about 800 yards, and the 109 started a turn to the left. I turned with him and closed to about 600 yards, then fired again. This time I observed hits on the left wing and left side of the fuselage. The aircraft began to smoke, and the pilot bailed out.

As I pulled up, I observed [an] FW 190 going down in a shallow dive. I gave chase, and he saw me at the same time. The enemy aircraft began some of the most violent evasive action I have ever seen. This consisted of very fast rolls and vertical reverses. Every time I got in a position where I thought I could shoot, I was unable to find my sight. Finally we were both going straight down and the 190 was doing snap rolls. About this time I hit compressibility and could not control my aircraft. I then concentrated on pulling out. As I began to do

so, I passed the enemy aircraft about 50 feet out to my right, and the 190 was still dropping. After I pulled out, I observed a fire on the ground, and Lt. [Donald] Henley[, Jr.,] later informed me that the enemy aircraft continued to snap into the ground.

I pulled up and gave chase to another 109, but Lieutenant Henley was nearer, so he got between me and this 109. About this time I observed two 109s coming in on [Henley's] tail, so I broke into them and decided to take a head-on shot at one of them. I opened fire at about 800 yards, and by the time we were 600 yards apart, I observed many strikes on the nose and wings. The 109 slipped off into a falling turn to his right and then started tumbling into the ground.

As I turned 180 degrees, another 109 came head-on at me, so I fired again and got a few hits on the nose and wings. As the enemy aircraft went by me, I turned to follow and see if he needed another burst, but as I turned, the canopy of the 109 came off and the pilot bailed out. I called my wingman, who was still with me, and said we had better start trying to get out of there.

At this time two more 109s came in after us. I called for my wingman to break and reefed my aircraft hard to the left to try and get a shot. One aircraft broke off and took a deflection shot at my wingman [Lt. James Wither]. I did not see any strikes, but I observed my wingman going straight down smoking. I did a wingover and took a 45-degree deflection shot at this 109 and registered many hits on him. The enemy aircraft began to smoke badly and finally caught on fire, and the pilot bailed out.

Captain Williamson had destroyed four Me 109s and an FW 190, but his wingman, Lieutenant

A formation shot of Capt. Paul Conger taken at 30,000 feet by Capt. Mike Jackson. The pilots liked to play wing tip and often came home with bent tips. P. Conger

Wither, did not pull out of his smoking Thunderbolt. These Luftwaffe pilots from JG 26 also downed Lt. Jack D. Hedke in the combat. He, too, was killed in the conflict.

Major Conger arrived with the rest of the force, but by this time the gaggle had been dispersed and only singles were left. Conger chased one Me 109 up and down, and although Conger was getting super performance from the new P-47M, the 109 kept

Lt. Col. Dave Schilling's aircraft in early 1945. USAAF

overrunning him. Finally the enemy aircraft split-essed and escaped on the deck.

Conger then climbed back up to 18,000 feet, where he was attacked by three Me 109s. He spiraled up to 27,000 feet, easily pulling away from the enemy. Conger then peeled back down and got on the tail of the last 109 at 15,000 feet. The enemy aircraft were concentrating their attack on two Mustangs. Conger continued to close on the last enemy aircraft and opened fire on it at 400 yards. A concentration of strikes was observed on the fuselage and wing roots, and glycol began to pour out. The canopy then flew off, and the 109 went into a spiral. The pilot never bailed out.

B Group destroyed nine of the enemy for the loss of two of its own. The total of nineteen enemy fighters destroyed in the two air battles would mark the last big aerial victory for the group during the war.

The balance of the month of January saw little of consequence as far as action went for the group. Following an escort mission to Heilbronn, Germany, on the twenty-first, the 62nd Squadron went down to strafe an airfield and destroyed two aircraft on the ground. Another strafing attack on the twenty-ninth

Lt. Col. Lucien ("Pete") Dade's aircraft. Dade took over command of the 56th Group in January 1945. USAAF

destroyed some flak positions and caught some German buses loaded with troops. A number of the enemy soldiers were caught in the fire as they fled for the woods.

Several administrative changes took place during the month. Maj. Paul Conger took over command of the 63rd Fighter Squadron when Maj. Harold Comstock returned to the United States. Capt. Felix Williamson took over the 62nd Squadron on January 26 when Maj. Leslie Smith was moved up to deputy group commander. The following day Lt. Col. Lucien Dade took over the reins as group commander when Lt. Col. Dave Schilling moved up to 65th Wing Headquarters.

February 3 was a historic date for the Wolfpack, for it marked the first time that P-47s had been scheduled to Berlin. The targets were the Berlin Tempelhof marshaling yard and the Magdeburg synthetic oil plant. The 56th swept ahead of the bombers to Berlin, and Maj. Paul Conger, leading the group, sighted enemy aircraft flying at treetop level over a wooded area southeast of the city. Conger left one squadron up as top cover and went down to investigate.

The aircraft were identified as fifteen or more FW 190s and were climbing, flying in line-abreast flight of four or five at 3,000 feet. Once they sighted the Thunderbolts, the 190s broke to the left. The enemy aircraft went into a large Lufbery, and Conger went into a turn after one that was chasing a P-47. Conger's first burst missed. A few seconds later the 190 opened fire on Lt. David M. Magel, whose aircraft burst into flames. Lieutenant Magel was seen to bail out, but apparently he did not survive.

Conger went after the 190 again, this time moving in to close range, and hit it with a solid burst. The 190 broke to the right and went into a half roll with Conger still hot on its tail. As the 190 sliced the half roll into a steep diving turn, its right wing tore off and it went down to hit the ground and explode.

Later Conger chased an Me 109 across the suburbs of Berlin. In spite of light flak the Thunderbolt pilot continued his pursuit until he was able to close to 500 yards behind the enemy aircraft. At this time Conger opened fire. When the 109 was hit, a small explosion took place, white smoke came forth, and the aircraft hit some trees and crashed into the ground.

A colorful aircraft flown by F/Lt. Withold Lanowski, a Polish ace who flew with the 61st Fighter Squadron. USAAF

P-47Ms in all their two-tone splendor taxi out past the
rows of drop tanks on their way to a mission. P. Conger

Lt. Arthur Bux and his P-47M in the nearly black color
scheme of the 61st Fighter Squadron. P. Conger

Lt. Edgar Huff in Ole Miss Lib and Lt. Phil Kuhn in Fireball, two P-47Ms of the 63rd Fighter Squadron. USAAF

A P-47M of the 63rd Fighter Squadron gets airborne. The performance of this aircraft made it one of the fastest in the sky. Yes, it could outrun the P-51 Mustang. P. Conger

Capt. Cameron Hart also destroyed two enemy aircraft in the fight, and other pilots of the 63rd Squadron added three more victories.

Capt. Felix Williamson took the 62nd Squadron down to seek out the enemy and found himself over an airfield where some FW 190s were trying to land. He came in astern of one FW 190 and hit it with a heavy concentration of .50-caliber firepower. The 190 went into some trees and exploded. Williamson swiftly attached himself to another 190 with its wheels down. He got a burst into it, but this time the pilot managed to get his aircraft down in one piece.

Williamson then picked up an Me 109 that had just become airborne. Williamson opened fire, and the enemy pilot turned into him head-on. Hits were observed on the 109, and as Williamson pulled up, he saw the enemy aircraft on its back and thought perhaps he had done it in. The 109 managed to right itself, however, and Williamson went back after it. The enemy craft snapped once, leveled out, and then snapped again. One wing hit the ground, and the aircraft exploded.

For the most part the balance of the month of February was uneventful. Several escort missions were flown, but no enemy aircraft were encountered. Some strafing was done, and a large convoy of trucks was shot up on February 25 in the Giessen area.

Lt. Col. Leslie Smith led the group on a fighter sweep in the Halle area of Germany on February 27. The Thunderbolts carried 100-pound spike bombs, which were used against a bridge that was destroyed, and one railway cut was made. The group went in and strafed the Weimar-Norha Airdrome, which the 4th Fighter Group had just shot up, and destroyed four enemy aircraft on the west side of the field that the 4th had not touched.

On March 7 the U.S. 1st Army had captured the vital Remagen Bridge across the Rhine River. As American troops poured across the span, the Luftwaffe did its utmost to bomb the bridge and put it out of commission. Every type of bomber that the Luftwaffe possessed was put into the fray, and the 8th Air Force was asked to set up fighter patrols over the bridge to defend it from these attacks.

Two squadrons of Thunderbolts from the 56th Group were dispatched to patrol the bridge on the afternoon of March 10. The P-47s arrived with one squadron at 10,000 feet as top cover and the 62nd Squadron at 3,000 feet. Shortly after its arrival the 62nd Squadron encountered six Me 109s carrying bombs. The Thunderbolts swiftly attacked the 109s and caused them to drop their bombs in open country. Once the enemy aircraft got rid of their bombs, they split and tried to flee, but two of them were downed by the Thunderbolts. Lt. Norman D. Gould got one of them, but he was in turn bounced by an FW 190. This aircraft was immediately set upon by Lts. Dennis A. Carroll and Donald Henley, Jr., who dispatched it without delay. The German pilot bailed out.

Both A and B Groups escorted the bombers to Holzwickede, Germany, on March 14. The Thunderbolts had completed their escort mission and the 62nd Squadron was flying north in the Coblenz area when three aircraft were sighted flying north. As the P-47s approached, it became obvious that the bogeys were Ar 234 twin-engined jet bombers. They

Lt. Phil Kuhn and his colorful Fireball. *Kuhn destroyed four enemy aircraft on the ground and shot one down in the air.* USAAF

were attacked immediately. Lt. Norman Gould downed one of them, and Lts. Sanborn Hall and Warren S. Lear shared another. The Thunderbolts had no difficulty overtaking these aircraft, and the 234s proved to be no problem at all in the encounter.

On the way home Lt. Sherman Pruitt downed an Me 109 in the vicinity of Frankfurt. One pilot was lost on the mission: Lt. Earl Townsend suffered engine failure 10 miles west of Knocke, Germany. He bailed out, but his parachute was not seen to open.

On March 19 Capt. George Bostwick took command of the 63rd Fighter Squadron when Maj. Paul Conger departed for the United States. Three days later Lt. Col. Donald D. Renwick became deputy

group commander when Maj. Leslie Smith was moved up to 65th Wing Headquarters.

Maj. Felix Williamson led the group on an escort mission to Hitzacher, Germany, on March 25. As the Wolfpack took station on the sides of the bomber stream, six or seven Me 262 jets, flying line abreast, came from north of the Luneburg area of Germany. The 262s opened fire from about 200 yards on the rear box of B-24s and downed two of them.

Capt. George Bostwick was leading the 63rd Squadron, which set out after the Me 262s after they had made their attack on the bombers. Bostwick reported:

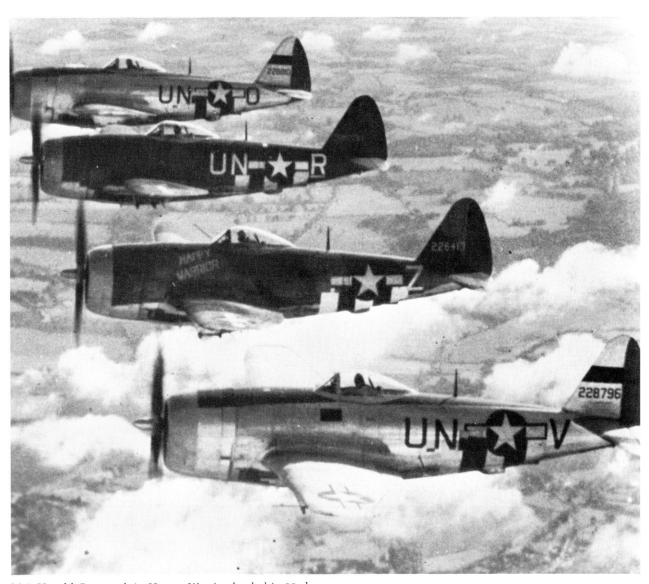

Maj. Harold Comstock in Happy Warrior *leads his 63rd Fighter Squadron in close formation late in 1944. via Sam Sox*

165

The Me 262s split up after their attack, most of them heading roughly east. I followed them until I lost sight of them and then proceeded to look over all the airfields in the area. I finally found the airdrome at Parchim, Germany, and orbited it at about 12,000 feet for some 20 minutes. There were between twenty and thirty aircraft visible on the field. After many wide orbits my number 4 man called in a bogey and I directed him to lead off.

This enemy aircraft was also [an] Me 262, and [it] led us back to the airdrome. Upon reaching the airdrome I spotted four more Me 262s milling around it, almost on the deck. I picked out one 262 who was flying parallel to the landing strip as if he was going to peel off to land. He did not, however, but flew straight down the runway.

As he reached the end of the runway, he passed over a second enemy aircraft which was taking off and which was just breaking ground. I pulled my nose through to get a shot at this enemy aircraft, but before I could, he apparently saw me and made a tight turn to the left. His left wing dug into the

ground and the plane cartwheeled, breaking into many pieces and strewing wreckage for some distance.

Lt. Edwin M. Crosthwait, Jr., also caught an Me 262 over the field and shot it down.

The group had two more engagements with the German jets—one on March 31 and another on April 2, on which damage claims were made—but not until April 5 was another confirmed victory scored over an Me 262.

On April 5 the Wolfpack was escorting the bombers to Plauen, Germany, when an Me 262 was sighted making an attack on the bombers. Capt. John C. Fahringer picked it up just as it hit the bombers from three o'clock, going through to nine o'clock, and dropping down to 14,000 feet. When the jet was clear of the bombers, it started a turn to the right about 3,000 feet below Fahringer's flight. The P-47s dropped their tanks and went into a diving turn to

A 61st Fighter Squadron formation in late Summer 1944. Note the varied paint schemes of the aircraft and the fact that there is still one razorback in the formation. USAAF

cut it off. Fahringer's element lead was on the inside, so he got the first shot at the target, but he overshot. Fahringer positioned himself on the tail of the jet when it rolled out. Initially, it was out of range, but as it went into a very shallow dive, the Thunderbolt pilot was able to close. Fahringer's first bursts got no results, but when the 262 went into a shallow turn, Fahringer hit it. The jet then rolled out and headed for a cloud.

When the jet came out of the cloud, Fahringer was right on its tail—dead astern at 500 yards. Another burst from the .50 calibers hit the 262 in the left wing and fuselage. The enemy craft then broke to the right, but Fahringer hung on and continued to pepper away. Finally debris began to come off the right jet engine. At about the same time something, thought to be the pilot, came out to the right. The aircraft continued to trail black smoke and fall off to the right. Lt. Philip G. Kuhn, Fahringer's wingman, saw the pilot bail out and the 262 crash into a river.

An escort mission to Duneburg and Krummel, Germany, on April 7 brought the Luftwaffe up in great numbers. It was not the fortune of the 56th to get into any of the gaggles that rose that day, however. Capt. George Bostwick was leading B Group in the Hamburg area when he sighted an Me 262 making a run at the bombers. Bostwick turned toward the 262 and got in a short burst that scored a few hits before the jet broke off and headed away from the Big Friends.

A few minutes later Nuthouse called in enemy aircraft above the bomber formation. Bostwick climbed to 30,000 feet to intercept. He initially closed in on an Me 109 and scored heavily with a short burst from 300 yards. Glycol was streaming back as Bostwick passed underneath the 109. He looked back and saw the pilot bail out.

Bostwick then picked out another contrail, but this one turned out to be from a P-51 Mustang. The Mustang, however, led him to a flight of six Me 109s. As Bostwick closed on one of the enemy aircraft, its pilot apparently sighted him and went into a steep dive. Both planes hurtled down at terrific speed. Suddenly, Bostwick saw a black object pass him, which may have been the pilot, but he could not be sure. The 109 stayed in its dive and crashed into a

The 62nd Fighter Squadron with two LM-Xs taxiing simultaneously. via H. Copic

Maj. George Bostwick of the 63rd Fighter Squadron.
G. Bostwick

Maj. George Bostwick's aircraft Ugly Duckling. G. Bost-wick

pond or reservoir. The Thunderbolt pilot pulled out and initially blacked out for a moment. When vision recovered, he was at 12,000 feet.

Three other 109s fell victim to the guns of the 63rd Squadron before the mission was over.

The Wolfpack went on a sweep ahead of the bombers en route to Berlin on April 10. The Thunderbolts broke into squadrons and strafed behind the bombers at Reichlin Airdrome and Neuruppen Airdrome and also shot up flying boats on Muritz Lake.

The 62nd Squadron was vectored to the vicinity of Oranienburg where four Me 262s were attacking B-17s. Two of the 262s were attacked, and one of them was destroyed. Lt. Walter J. Sharbo was credited with the jet, as he scored the telling strikes that resulted in the pilot bailing out.

The big story for the day was the amount of damage that the group did on the ground. The airfields looked like funeral pyres when the Americans departed. When the final assessment had been made, forty-seven enemy aircraft were credited as having been destroyed in the attacks. Leading the field as strafers for the day were Capts. George Bostwick and Walter Flagg, with four apiece.

Three Thunderbolts were lost on the mission. Two of the pilots hit by flak managed to land in Allied territory. Lt. Paul Stitt was not so lucky; he crashed in Belgium and died in a hospital there the following day.

April 13 would go down in the annals of the 56th Fighter Group as its most successful strafing mission and its last real numerical triumph over the Luftwaffe. This mission also marked the second anniversary of the initial combat mission of the group. The bombers were routed against targets in northern Germany, and the Wolfpack was ordered to give free-lance support in the target area, which included the German-Danish peninsula, Hamburg, Berlin, and northwest to the Baltic Sea.

The group made landfall north of Hamburg and swept north to Eggebeck Airdrome at 1510 hours. The squadrons then took their positions, with the 62nd flying top cover at 15,000 feet, the 61st at 10,000 feet, and Blue Section of the 63rd Squadron with eight P-47s orbiting the field at 5,000 feet. The last force was to strafe any gun positions that opened fire on the White and Red Flights of the 63rd, which were to initiate the strafing attacks.

The first pass caught some fire before the flak installations were silenced and cost the only casualty of the day. Lt. William R. Hoffman's Thunderbolt was hit, and although he pulled up to bail out, his altitude was not sufficient for his parachute to open. This pass was made with aircraft in line

abreast indicating between 400mph and 450mph. Three flak positions were silenced, and both flights recovered about 2 miles north of the airdrome. An estimated 150 to 200 aircraft of all descriptions were on the field.

White and Red Flights then made another pass over the field from the south. After this pass no serious flak was encountered and both Blue and Yellow Flights were called down to strafe. Five passes were made by the 63rd Squadron, with at least forty enemy aircraft being destroyed. By this time the area was covered with smoke rising from the burning aircraft.

The 61st Squadron then went down to strafe, making ninety-four individual passes. It claimed more than twenty enemy aircraft destroyed.

The 62nd Squadron finished things up as it struck at what areas it could find that were not completely up in flames. In the course of 105 individual passes it claimed more than twenty enemy aircraft destroyed.

The total of the group, as reported by Lt. Col. Lucien Dade, who led the mission, was 339 individ-

Lt. Darrell McMahan of the 62nd Fighter Squadron scored 1.5 aerial victories and got an additional four enemy aircraft on the ground. USAAF

*Eggebeck airdrome ablaze following the strafing attack on
April 13, 1945. USAAF*

*Lt. Randel Murphy, Jr., who set the 8th Air Force scoring
record with 10 enemy aircraft destroyed on one mission.
R. Murphy*

ual strafing runs while expending 78,073 rounds of ammunition. The final 8th Air Force assessment of damage was ninety-one enemy aircraft destroyed on the ground. Leading the pack individually with the unbelievable total of ten aircraft destroyed was Lt. Randel J. Murphy. Other high scorers were Lt. Russell S. Kyler with five and the following pilots with four each: Lt. Burton O. Blodgett, Capt. Philip Fleming, Lt. Lloyd F. Geren, Lt. Philip G. Kuhn, and Lt. Vernon A. Smith.

The group ended its brilliant scoring record on April 16 when it escorted the bombers to Rosenheim, Germany. When the uneventful escort was broken off, the Thunderbolts made strafing passes on Muldorf Airdrome, where two enemy aircraft were destroyed on the ground. Capt. Edward H. Appel was shot down but managed to belly in and evade capture.

Missions continued through April 21, but all were uneventful. The 56th Fighter Group saw the war in Europe come to a successful conclusion on May 8, 1945. In just over two years it had advanced from the doubtful Thunderbolt unit to the triumphant top aerial scoring group in the 8th Air Force. It had taken the fight to the cream of the Luftwaffe and defeated the German air force in its own skies. Through superlative leadership, the tenacity of its pilots, the dedication of its ground echelon, and the ruggedness of its beloved Thunderbolt the 56th had accomplished what had been considered an impossibility. Its combat record ranks at the pinnacle of the achievements of the U.S. Army Air Forces in World War II.

This Thunderbolt was painted up at the end of the war for display purposes. USAAF

King of the Strafers

Lt. Randel L. Murphy, Jr., became the top scoring one-mission strafer in the 8th Air Force when he destroyed ten enemy aircraft on the ground during the strafe fest at Eggebeck Airdrome on April 13, 1945. Murphy credited a great deal of his success that day to the ammunition that was used. The official designation of this ammunition was T-48, and it was a highly incendiary type of round that had been designed to ignite the low-grade fuel that was used in the German jets.

Earlier several pilots from the 56th Fighter Group had been detached to work with RAF pilots flying the new Gloster Meteor jets in an attempt to combat primarily the German Me 262 fighter. The 56th was flying the Republic P-47M, which, with its new engine, could hit 465mph at altitude. The only other Allied fighters that could compete with it in the speed category were the new Meteor and the Hawker Tempest. A few missions were flown with the Meteors without result.

The group, squadron, and element leaders in the 56th Group were issued the new "jet" ammunition in April of 1945. In the course of some strafing they discovered that the ammunition was so incendiary that it would set the grass on fire in strafing attacks. When the airdrome at Eggebeck was attacked, the aircraft of the leaders were loaded with the new ammunition. Murphy was a crack shot. In his passes at the enemy aircraft he was able to hit and whatever he hit immediately went up in flames.

Following his outstanding success, Murphy was sent back to the United States to brief new pilots on combat and strafing techniques. At that time it was thought that an invasion of Japan would be necessary. Had it been, the "jet" ammunition would have been a boon for the strafers.

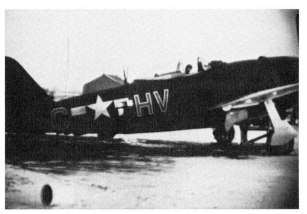

Lt. Fred Barrett's aircraft of the 61st Fighter Squadron with 1945 markings. USAAF

Appendix

Combat Commanders

Group Commanders
Col. Hubert Zemke	9-16-42 to 10-30-43
Col. Robert H. Landry	10-30-43 to 1-19-44
Col. Hubert Zemke	1-19-44 to 8-12-44
Lt. Col. David Schilling	8-12-44 to 1-27-45
Lt. Col. Lucien Dade	1-27-45 to 5-8-45

Deputy Group Commanders
Maj. Loren G. McCollom	6-9-43 to 8-21-43
Maj. David Schilling	8-21-43 to 8-12-44
Maj. Lucien Dade	8-12-44 to 3-22-45
Maj. Donald Renwick	3-22-45 to 5-8-45

61st Fighter Squadron Commanders
Maj. Loren G. McCollom	-42 to 6-9-43
Maj. Francis S. Gabreski	6-9-43 to 1-13-44
Maj. James Stewart	1-13-44 to 4-13-44
Maj. Francis S. Gabreski	4-13-44 to 7-20-44
Maj. Gordon Baker	7-20-44 to 9-26-44
Maj. Donovan Smith	9-26-44 to 1-10-45
Maj. James Carter	1-10-45 to 5-8-45

62nd Fighter Squadron Commanders
Maj. David Schilling	-42 to 8-21-43
Maj. Horace C. Craig	8-21-43 to 2-9-44
Maj. Leroy Schreiber	2-9-44 to 4-15-44
Maj. Lucien Dade	4-15-44 to 8-13-44
Maj. Michael Quirk	8-13-44 to 9-10-44
Maj. Leslie C. Smith	9-10-44 to 1-26-45
Maj. Felix Williamson	1-26-45 to 5-8-45

63rd Fighter Squadron Commanders
Maj. Philip E. Tukey, Jr.	-42 to 9-30-43
Maj. Sylvester V. Burke, Jr.	9-30-43 to 2-19-44
Maj. Gerald W. Johnson	2-19-44 to 3-27-44
Maj. Robert Lamb	3-27-44 to 5-25-44
Maj. Don Goodfleisch	5-25-44 to 7-17-44
Maj. Joseph L. Egan	7-17-44 to 7-19-44
Maj. Harold E. Comstock	7-19-44 to 1-20-45
Maj. Paul Conger	1-20-45 to 3-19-45
Maj. George Bostwick	3-19-45 to 5-8-45

Group Markings

Initially the group aircraft were marked in the white identity stripes that were used by all American fighters at the time. These consisted of a 24-inch white cowling lip measured from the front lip, a 12-inch white band 26 inches from the tip of the fin that was painted on the vertical tail, and an 18-inch-wide white band that was painted around the horizontal stabilizer, centered 33 inches from the outer edge.

The 56th Group was the first to request individual group markings. Permission was granted in February 1944. The 61st Fighter Squadron painted its cowlings red, the 62nd Fighter Squadron yellow, and the 63rd Fighter Squadron a pale blue.

Squadron codes from the beginning were 61st Fighter Squadron, HV; 62nd Fighter Squadron, LM; and 63rd Fighter Squadron, UN.

In March 1944 all fighter groups were given distinctive group markings, with the 56th taking the red cowling. At this time colors were designated for squadron rudders. The 61st had red rudders, and the 62nd had yellow rudders. The 63rd did not paint its rudders until September 1944, when it adopted blue rudders.

In the spring of 1944 a number of the Thunderbolts were painted in dark green and light gray camouflage paints, which were much the same as those used by the RAF.

When the P-47Ms arrived in 1945, the squadrons went wild on paint colors. The 61st painted many of its aircraft an all-matte black, the 62nd used dark green and light gray, and the 63rd used two shades of blue.

Distinguished Service Cross Recipients

Maj. Paul Conger
Maj. Francis S. Gabreski
Capt. Gerald W. Johnson
Capt. Robert S. Johnson
Lt. Robert J. Keen
Lt. Vance P. Ludwig
Capt. Walker Mahurin
Lt. Darrell E. McMahan
Lt. Robert J. Rankin
Lt. Col. David C. Schilling (2)
Lt. Glenn D. Schlitz, Jr.
Capt. Leroy A. Schreiber
Lt. Donovan F. Smith
Maj. James C. Stewart
Lt. John H. Truluck, Jr.
Capt. John W. Vogt, Jr.
Capt. Felix D. Williamson
Col. Hubert Zemke

56th Fighter Group Aces

Rank	Name	Air Victories	Ground Victories	Total Number	Remarks
Col.	David C. Schilling	22.5	11.5	35.5	
Lt. Col.	Francis S. Gabreski	28	2.5	30.5	POW 7-20-44
Maj.	Robert S. Johnson	27	0	27	
Col.	Hubert Zemke	17.75*	8.5	26.25	POW 10-30-44, 479th FG
Capt.	Fred J. Christensen, Jr.	21.5	0	21.5	
Maj.	Walker M. Mahurin	20.75†	0.25	21	MIA 3-27-44, Evadee
Maj.	Gerald W. Johnson	16.5‡	0	16.5	POW 3-27-44
Capt.	Michael J. Quirk	11	5	16	POW 9-11-44
Maj.	George E. Bostwick	8	7	15	
Capt.	Joseph H. Powers	14.5	0	14.5	
Maj.	Leroy A. Schreiber	12	2	14	KIA 4-15-44
Maj.	Michael J. Jackson	8	5.5	13.5	
Capt.	Robert J. Keen	6	7	13	
Lt.	Randel L. Murphy	2	11	13	
Capt.	Felix D. Williamson	13	0	13	
Lt. Col.	James C. Stewart	11.5	1	12.5	
Maj.	Paul A. Conger	11.5	0	11.5	
Lt. Col.	Leslie C. Smith	7	4.5	11.5	
Maj.	B. Michael Gladych	10	1	11	Polish Air Force
Lt.	Billy G. Edens	7	3	10	POW 9-10-44
Lt.	Russell S. Kyler	3	7	10	
Capt.	Robert J. Rankin	10	0	10	
Lt. Col.	Lucien A. Dade, Jr.	3	6	9	
Capt.	Stanley B. Morrill	9	0	9	
Capt.	Joseph H. Bennett	8.5§	0	8.5	POW 5-25-44, 4th FG
Capt.	Walter L. Flagg	2	6	8	
Capt.	Glen D. Schlitz, Jr.	8	0	8	
Capt.	John H. Truluck, Jr.	7	1	8	
Maj.	John W. Vogt, Jr.	8‖	0	8	
Lt.	Donald Henley, Jr.	3	4.5	7.5	
Maj.	Donovan F. Smith	5.5	2	7.5	
Maj.	Harold E. Comstock	5	2	7	
Capt.	Steven N. Gerick	5	2	7	
Lt.	Frank W. Klibbe	7	0	7	
Maj.	Robert A. Lamb	7	0	7	
F/O	Evan D. McMinn	5	2	7	
Lt.	Charles M. Rotzler	1	6	7	
Capt.	Mark L. Moseley	6.5	0	6.5	
Lt.	Eugene M. Beason	1	5	6	

Rank	Name	Air Victories	Ground Victories	Total Number	Remarks
Lt.	Claude A. Chinn	0	6	6	
Maj.	James R. Carter	6	0	6	
Capt.	Walter V. Cook	6	0	6	
Capt.	George F. Hall	6	0	6	
Capt.	Cameron M. Hart	6	0	6	
Capt.	Witold A. Lanowski	6	0	6	Polish Air Force
Lt.	Roy L. Patterson	1	5	6	
Capt.	John B. Eaves	3.5	2	5.5	
Capt.	Frank E. McCauley	5.5	0	5.5	
Lt.	Darrell E. McMahan	1.5	4	5.5	
Lt.	Sanborn N. Ball, Jr.	1.5	3.5	5	
Lt.	George H. Butler	3	2	5	
Lt.	Burton O. Blodgett	0	5	5	
Capt.	Joseph L. Egan, Jr.	5	0	5	
Capt.	John C. Fahringer	4	1	5	
Lt.	Joseph W. Icard	5	0	5	
Lt.	James M. Jure	3.5	1.5	5	
Lt.	Herman E. King	1	4	5	
Lt.	Philip G. Kuhn	1	4	5	
Lt.	Thomas W. Queen, Jr.	0	5	5	
Lt.	Walter J. Sharbo	3	2	5	
Lt.	Vernon A. Smith	0	5	5	
Lt.	Eugene A. Timony	1	4	5	

Note: POW stands for prisoner of war; FG stands for fighter group; MIA stands for missing in action; KIA stands for killed in action.
*Includes 2 victories with the 479th Fighter Group.
†Includes 1 victory with the 5th Air Force.
‡Includes 1 victory with the 356th Fighter Group.
§Includes 3 victories with the 4th Fighter Group.
‖Includes 3 victories with the 356th Fighter Group.

Since this work is a World War II–vintage narrative history, I have chosen to include ground victories in the chart of aces. The air-to-air victories were taken from Dr. Frank Olynyk's *USAAF Credits (European Theater) for the Destruction of Enemy Aircraft in Air-to-Air Combat World War II*, which is by far the most comprehensive and accurate study ever done. I have gone through the 8th Air Force Final Victories Credits thoroughly to form the ground credits. If anyone has information that might change any of the figures in this chart, please contact me at the publisher's address.

56th Fighter Group Confirmed Victories

Date	Name	Squadron	Type	Location
6-12-43	Capt. Walter V. Cook	62	FW 190	V. Ypres
6-13-43	Lt. Robert S. Johnson	61	FW 190	SE Bergues
	Col. Hubert Zemke	HQ	2 FW 190	V. Kassel
6-26-43	Lt. Gerald W. Johnson	61	FW 190	N. Dieppe
	Lt. Charles R. Harrison	62	FW 190	NE Rouen
7-30-43	Lt. Joe H. Powers	61	Me 109	Arnhem
	Capt. Leroy A. Schreiber	61	2 Me 109	Arnhem
8-17-43	Capt. Gerald W. Johnson	61	Me 109	Nr. Hasselt
	Capt. Gerald W. Johnson	61	Me 109	Nr. Diest
	Capt. Gerald W. Johnson	61	0.5 Me 109	N. Liege
	Lt. Frank E. McCauley	61	0.5 Me 109	N. Liege
	Capt. Walker M. Mahurin	63	2 FW 190	Eupen
	Lt. Harold E. Comstock	63	Me 109	Nr. Ans

Date	Name	Squadron	Type	Location
	Lt. Glen D. Schlitz, Jr.	63	3 FW 190	Ans–St. Nicholas
	Lt. John H. Truluck	63	FW 190	Ans–St. Nicholas
	Lt. Edgar D. Whitley	63	Me 110	Ans
	Lt. Frank E. McCauley	61	FW 190	Nr. Hasselt
	Col. Hubert Zemke	HQ	Me 110	V. St. Trond
	Capt. Donald D. Renwick	61	Me 109	Liege
	Lt. Charles R. Harrison	62	Me 110	V. Ans
	Lt. Caleb L. Reeder	62	Me 110	V. Ans
8-19-43	Lt. Joseph L. Egan, Jr.	63	FW 190	Tholen Is.
	Lt. John W. Vogt, Jr.	63	Me 109	Nr. Walcheren Is.
	Capt. Robert A. Lamb	61	FW 190	Breda
	Capt. Gerald W. Johnson	61	Me 109	Nr. Gilze-Rijen
	Lt. Robert S. Johnson	61	Me 109	NE Woendrecht
	Lt. Frank E. McCauley	61	Me 109	Oosterhout
	Lt. Frank E. McCauley	61	Me 109	Schoonhaven
	Lt. Michael J. Quirk	62	FW 190	V. Gilze-Rijen
	Lt. Edgar D. Whitley	63	Me 109	Walcheran Is.
8-24-43	Capt. Francis S. Gabreski	61	FW 190	Dreux, Fr.
	Lt. James M. Jones, Jr.	62	FW 190	S. Paris
	Capt. Leroy A. Schreiber	62	FW 190	S. Paris
9-3-43	Col. Hubert Zemke	HQ	FW 190	NW Romilly
	Capt. Lyle A. Adrianse	63	FW 190	Nr. Romilly
	Capt. Don M. Goodfleisch	63	FW 190	SE Paris
	Maj. Francis S. Gabreski	61	FW 190	St. Germain
9-7-43	Lt. Anthony R. Carcione	62	Me 109	Tessel Is.
	Lt. Ralph A. Johnson	62	Me 109	Tessel Is.
9-9-43	Capt. Walker M. Mahurin	63	FW 190	S. Beauvais
9-16-43	Lt. George G. Goldstein	62	Me 109	V. Vitre
	Lt. Robert B. Taylor	62	FW 190	V. Fougeres
9-27-43	Lt. John H. Truluck	63	FW 190	Nr. Borkum Is.
	Lt. John H. Truluck	63	Me 109	Nr. Borkum Is.
	Lt. Wayne J. O'Connor	63	Me 109	Nr. Borkum Is.
	Lt. John E. Coenen	63	2 FW 190	S. Juist Is.
10-2-43	Maj. David C. Schilling	HQ	Me 109	SE Groningen
	Maj. David C. Schilling	HQ	FW 190	NE Emden
	Col. Hubert Zemke	HQ	FW 190	V. Groningen
10-4-43	Lt. Frank E. McCauley	61	Me 110	E. Aachen
	Lt. John W. Vogt, Jr.	63	Me 110	E. Duren
	Lt. John D. Wilson	63	Me 110	E. Duren
	Maj. David C. Schilling	HQ	Me 110	E. Duren
	Capt. Don M. Goodfleisch	63	Me 110	E. Duren
	Lt. Vance P. Ludwig	63	3 Me 110	E. Duren
	Capt. Walker M. Mahurin	63	3 Me 110	E. Duren
	Lt. Jack D. Brown	63	Me 110	E. Duren
	Lt. Harold E. Comstock	63	Me 110	Bruhl
	Lt. Bernard R. Smith	63	Me 110	Bruhl
	Lt. Glen D. Schlitz, Jr.	63	Me 110	E. Duren
	Lt. William A. Marangello	61	Me 110	W. Aachen
10-8-43	Maj. David C. Schilling	HQ	FW 190	V. Quackenbruck
	Lt. Robert S. Johnson	61	FW 190	Nr. Lingen
	Lt. Harry Coronios	62	FW 190	V. Quackenbruck
	Lt. Michael J. Quirk	62	FW 190	V. Quackenbruck
	Capt. Leroy A. Schreiber	62	FW 190	V. Quackenbruck
10-10-43	Maj. David C. Schilling	HQ	FW 190	V. Altenberge

Date	Name	Squadron	Type	Location
	Capt. Walter V. Cook	62	Me 210	V. Altenberge
	Lt. John B. Eaves	62	Me 109	V. Altenberge
	Lt. James M. Jones, Jr.	62	FW 190	V. Altenberge
	Lt. Robert B. Taylor	62	FW 190	V. Altenberge
	Lt. Anthony R. Carcione	62	Me 109	V. Nienburg
	Lt. Robert S. Johnson	61	Me 110	N. Munster
	Lt. Robert S. Johnson	61	FW 190	N. Munster
	Capt. Gerald W. Johnson	61	Me 110	N. Munster
	Capt. Gerald W. Johnson	61	Me 210	N. Munster
10-14-43	Capt. Gerald W. Johnson	61	FW 190	V. Eupen
	Lt. Norman E. Brooks	61	Me 110	W. Aachen
	Lt. Frank E. McCauley	61	Me 110	W. Aachen
10-18-43	Maj. James C. Stewart	61	0.5 Me 210	NE Maastricht
	Lt. Melvin C. Wood	61	0.5 Me 210	NE Maastricht
10-20-43	Lt. John W. Vogt, Jr.	63	FW 190	N. Ans
	Col. Hubert Zemke	HQ	FW 190	Eindhoven
11-3-43	Capt. Walker M. Mahurin	63	0.5 Me 109	N. Essens
	Lt. Wayne J. O'Connor	63	0.5 Me 109	N. Essens
	Lt. Robert S. Johnson	61	Me 109	N. Ameland Is.
	Capt. Walker M. Mahurin	63	Me 110	N. Juist
11-5-43	Lt. Eugene E. Barnum	61	FW 190	S. Rheine
	Maj. Francis S. Gabreski	61	FW 190	S. Rheine
	Lt. John D. Wilson	63	FW 190	Rheine-Munster
	Lt. Charles W. Reed	63	FW 190	Rheine-Munster
	Col. Hubert Zemke	HQ	FW 190	Enscheda-Rheine
	Lt. George F. Hall	63	Me 210	Nr. Enscheda
11-11-43	Capt. Sylvester V. Burke	63	Me 109	NW Munster
	Lt. George G. Goldstein	62	FW 190	V. Munster
	F/O Joe W. Icard	62	FW 190	V. Munster
	Capt. Eugene W. O'Neill, Jr.	62	FW 190	V. Munster
	Capt. Walter V. Cook	62	2 FW 190	V. Bocholt
11-26-43	Lt. Col. David C. Schilling	HQ	2 FW 190	SE Oldenburg
	Capt. Walker M. Mahurin	63	2 Me 110	S. Oldenburg
	Lt. Harold E. Comstock	63	Me 110	Friesoythe
	Maj. James C. Stewart	61	Do 217	SE Oldenburg
	Maj. Francis S. Gabreski	61	2 Me 110	SE Oldenburg
	Lt. John P. Bryant	62	Me 110	V. Papenburg
	Lt. Anthony R. Carcione	62	Me 210	V. Papenburg
	Lt. Fred J. Christensen	62	Me 110	V. Papenburg
	Capt. Walter V. Cook	62	2 Me 110	V. Papenburg
	Capt. Ralph A. Johnson	62	2 Me 110	V. Papenburg
	Lt. Stanley B. Morrill	62	Me 109	V. Papenburg
	F/O Irvin E. Valenta	62	2 Me 110	V. Papenburg
	Capt. Eugene W. O'Neill, Jr.	62	0.5 Me 110	V. Papenburg
	Lt. Mark K. Boyle	62	0.5 Me 110	V. Papenburg
	Capt. Eugene W. O'Neill, Jr.	62	FW 190	V. Papenburg
	Lt. John H. Truluck	63	FW 190	Friesoythe
	F/O Frank W. Klibbe	61	Me 109	SE Oldenburg
	Capt. Walker M. Mahurin	63	Me 110	Zuider Zee
11-29-43	Capt. Walker M. Mahurin	63	Me 109	Leer-Papenburg
	Maj. Francis S. Gabreski	61	2 Me 109	NE Bremen
	Lt. Joe H. Powers	61	Me 109	NE Bremen
	Lt. Harry M. Pruden	62	0.5 Me 210	S. Oldenburg

Date	Name	Squadron	Type	Location
	Capt. Leroy A. Schreiber	62	0.5 Me 210	S. Oldenburg
	Lt. Col. David C. Schilling	HQ	0.5 FW 190	S. Oldenburg
	Lt. Felix D. Williamson	62	0.5 FW 190	S. Oldenburg
12-1-43	Lt. Dick H. Mudge	61	Me 109	Ruhr Valley
	Lt. Fred J. Christensen	62	Me 109	SE Roermond
	Lt. Justus D. Foster	61	FW 190	Beverloo
12-11-43	Lt. Paul A. Conger	61	2 Me 109	Langeoog Is.
	Lt. Paul A. Conger	61	Ju 88	Langeoog Is.
	Maj. Francis S. Gabreski	61	Me 110	Essens
	Capt. Robert A. Lamb	61	3 Me 110	N. Langeoog Is.
	Lt. Robill W. Roberts	61	Me 110	Langeoog Is.
	Lt. Robill W. Roberts	61	Ju 88	Langeoog Is.
	Lt. Donovan F. Smith	61	2 Me 110	Emden
	Lt. Donovan F. Smith	61	0.5 FW 190	Emden
	F/O William R. Aggers	61	0.5 FW 190	Emden
	Col. Robert H. Landry	HQ	Me 109	NE Emden
	Lt. Joe H. Powers	61	Me 110	N. Norderney Is.
	Lt. Joe H. Powers	61	Me 109	N. Aurich
	Lt. Stanley B. Morrill	62	Me 109	V. Eelde
	Lt. Glen D. Schlitz, Jr.	63	Me 210	V. Emden
12-20-43	Lt. Michael J. Quirk	62	Me 109	S. Bremen
	Capt. Joseph H. Bennett	61	Me 110	Falkenberg
	Lt. Joe H. Powers	61	Me 109	NE Bremen
	Maj. Horace C. Craig	62	Do 217	SE Bremen
	Capt. Eugene W. O'Neill, Jr.	62	Me 109	V. Vegesack
12-22-43	Lt. Robert S. Johnson	61	Me 109	N. Almelo
	Capt. Walker M. Mahurin	63	2 Me 109	V. Hespe
	Lt. Felix D. Williamson	62	Me 109	W. Rheims
12-30-43	Lt. Robert S. Johnson	61	FW 190	Soissons
12-31-43	Lt. Robert S. Johnson	61	2 FW 190	N. St. Gilles
1-4-44	Lt. Michael J. Quirk	62	FW 190	V. Stadtlohn
1-5-44	Lt. Stanley B. Morrill	62	Me 109	V. Duren
	Lt. Robert S. Johnson	61	FW 190	N. Liege
	Lt. Fred J. Christensen	62	FW 190	V. Ans
	Maj. James C. Stewart	61	FW 190	SW Bonn
1-11-44	Capt. James R. Carter	61	Me 109	N. Osnabruck
	Lt. Stanley B. Morrill	62	Me 109	V. Bramsche
	Lt. Col. David C. Schilling	HQ	FW 190	Nr. Osnabruck
	Lt. Justus D. Foster	61	Me 109	NE Osnabruck
	Maj. Sylvester V. Burke	63	Me 109	N. Osnabruck
	Lt. Archie R. Robey	63	Me 109	N. Osnabruck
	Lt. Glen D. Schlitz, Jr.	63	3 Me 109	N. Osnabruck
	Lt. Bernard R. Smith	63	FW 190	N. Osnabruck
1-21-44	Lt. Robert S. Johnson	61	FW 190	N. Rouen
1-29-44	Lt. Anthony S. Cavallo	63	Me 210	SW Coblenz
	Lt. Col. Francis S. Gabreski	61	Me 210	S. Coblenz
	Capt. Joseph H. Bennett	61	Me 110	Simmern
	Lt. Praeger Neyland	61	0.5 Me 110	Simmern
	Capt. Joseph H. Bennett	61	0.5 Me 110	Simmern
	Lt. Melvin C. Wood	61	Me 210	Simmern
1-30-44	Lt. Joseph L. Egan, Jr.	63	Me 210	S. Quackenbruck
	Lt. George F. Hall	63	2 Me 109	S. Quackenbruck
	Lt. Lloyd M. Langdon	63	2 Me 109	S. Quackenbruck

Date	Name	Squadron	Type	Location
	Capt. Walker M. Mahurin	63	Ju 88	S. Quackenbruck
	Lt. Eugene E. Barnum	61	Me 210	V. Lingen
	Lt. Robert S. Johnson	61	Me 210	E. Lingen
	Lt. Robert S. Johnson	61	Me 109	E. Lingen
	Lt. Anthony R. Carcione	62	0.5 Ju 88	V. Twente
	Lt. Stanley B. Morrill	62	0.5 Ju 88	V. Twente
	Lt. Michael J. Quirk	62	Me 109	V. Almelo
	Lt. Col. Francis S. Gabreski	61	Me 210	Lingen
	Lt. Col. Francis S. Gabreski	61	Me 109	Lingen
	Lt. Frank W. Klibbe	61	Me 109	Lingen
	Capt. James R. Carter	61	FW 190	Leeuwen
	Lt. Joe H. Powers	61	FW 190	V. Meppen
2-3-44	Capt. Walker M. Mahurin	63	Me 109	SE Ruhlertwist
	Lt. Charles W. Reed	63	Me 109	SE Ruhlertwist
2-4-44	Lt. Fred J. Christensen	62	FW 190	V. Charleroi
	Lt. James E. Fields	62	FW 190	V. Charleroi
	Capt. Michael J. Quirk	62	FW 190	V. Charleroi
	Capt. Michael J. Quirk	62	TE A/C	E. St. Omer
2-6-44	Capt. Robert A. Lamb	61	Me 109	Beauvais
	Lt. Joe H. Powers	61	Me 109	V. Beauvais
	Lt. Samuel D. Hamilton, Jr.	61	Me 109	Nr. Paris
	Lt. Robert J. Rankin	61	Me 109	Paris
	Capt. Eugene W. O'Neill, Jr.	62	FW 190	Paris
2-8-44	Lt. Joe W. Icard	62	Me 109	V. Cambrai
2-11-44	Lt. Stanley B. Morrill	62	Me 109	V. Dison
	Lt. Joe W. Icard	62	Me 109	V. Bierset
	Maj. Sylvester V. Burke	63	Me 109	Hody-Spa
	Maj. James C. Stewart	61	FW 190	S. Duren
	Lt. Fred J. Christensen	62	Me 109	V. Bierset
	Col. Hubert Zemke	HQ	Me 109 Grd	Juvincourt A/D
2-20-44	Capt. James R. Carter	61	Me 110	SW Steinhuder Lk.
	Lt. Col. Francis S. Gabreski	61	2 Me 110	W. Hanover
	Lt. Robert S. Johnson	61	2 Me 110	W. Hanover
	Lt. Donovan F. Smith	61	2 Me 110	Steinhuder Lk.
	Capt. Robert A. Lamb	61	Ju 88	E. Minden
	Lt. Stanley B. Morrill	62	Me 110	Steinhuder Lk.
	Lt. Stanley B. Morrill	62	0.5 Do 217	E. Steinhuder Lk.
	Lt. Fred J. Christensen	62	0.5 Do 217	E. Steinhuder Lk.
	Capt. Leroy A. Schreiber	62	3 Me 109	Steinhuder Lk.
	Lt. Fred J. Christensen	62	Ju 88	Steinhuder Lk.
2-21-44	Capt. John W. Vogt, Jr.	63	Me 110	N. Munster
	F/O Evan D. McMinn	61	Me 109	Zuider Zee
	Lt. Charles R. Harrison	62	Me 109	V. Soesterberg
	Maj. Gerald W. Johnson	HQ	FW 190	NW Zwolle
	Lt. Frank W. Klibbe	61	Me 109	Zuider Zee
	Lt. Donald M. Funcheon	61	Me 109	Zuider Zee
	Lt. Claude E. Mussey	61	Me 109	Zuider Zee
	Lt. Roy B. Bluhm, Jr.	62	Me 109	V. Zwolle
	Lt. Joe W. Icard	62	FW 190	V. Soesterberg
	Lt. Joseph L. Egan, Jr.	63	Me 109	E. Zuider Zee
	Capt. B. Michael Gladych	61	2 Me 109	Zuider Zee
2-22-44	Lt. James E. Fields	62	0.5 FW 190	V. Breda
	Capt. Michael J. Quirk	62	0.5 FW 190	V. Breda

Date	Name	Squadron	Type	Location
	Lt. James E. Fields	62	0.5 Me 109	V. Breda
	Capt. Leroy A. Schreiber	62	0.5 Me 109	V. Breda
	Capt. Michael J. Quirk	62	FW 190	V. Breda
	Lt. Frederick L. Roy	62	FW 190	Breda
	Capt. Leslie C. Smith	61	2 FW 190	Lippstadt
	Lt. Joseph L. Egan, Jr.	63	Me 109	Munster
	Lt. George F. Hall	63	2 Me 110	V. Raderborn
	Capt. John W. Vogt, Jr.	63	Me 110	V. Raderborn
	Lt. Col. Francis S. Gabreski	61	FW 190	N. Lippstadt
	F/O Evan D. McMinn	61	FW 190	Lippstadt
	Maj. James C. Stewart	61	Me 109	SW Munster
	Capt. Lyle A. Adrianse	63	Me 110	Raderborn
	Lt. Donovan F. Smith	61	FW 190	Lippstadt
	Lt. Anthony R. Carcione	62	Me 109 Grd	Soesterberg A/D
2-24-44	Lt. Gordon J. Blake	61	FW 190	N. Minden
	Maj. Gerald W. Johnson	63	FW 190	N. Minden
	Lt. John H. Truluck, Jr.	63	FW 190	Herford
	Lt. Donald M. Funcheon	61	FW 190	Holzminden
	Maj. James C. Stewart	61	FW 190	Kassel
	Lt. William P. Gordon, Jr.	62	FW 190	SW Hanover
	Lt. Stanley B. Morrill	62	Me 109	E. Asnabruck
	Lt. Joe H. Powers	61	FW 190	Minden
2-25-44	Capt. Robert A. Lamb	61	Me 109	Landau
	Capt. Michael J. Quirk	62	FW 190	Homburg
	Lt. Donald M. Funcheon	61	Me 109	V. Landau
2-29-44	Maj. Gerald W. Johnson	63	Ju 52	Horderwijk
3-2-44	Maj. Gerald W. Johnson	63	Me 109	SE Aachen
3-6-44	Lt. Robert S. Johnson	61	FW 190	N. Dummer Lk.
	Maj. James C. Stewart	61	2 FW 190	N. Dummer Lk.
	Col. Hubert Zemke	HQ	FW 190	Minden–Dummer Lk.
	Col. Hubert Zemke	HQ	Me 109	Minden–Dummer Lk.
	Col. Hubert Zemke	HQ	0.25 Me 109	Minden–Dummer Lk.
	Lt. Marvin H. Becker	63	0.25 Me 109	Minden–Dummer Lk.
	Lt. Donald V. Peters	63	0.25 Me 109	Minden–Dummer Lk.
	Lt. Charles W. Reed	63	0.25 Me 109	Minden–Dummer Lk.
	Lt. Joe W. Icard	62	FW 190	Dummer Lk.
	Lt. George F. Hall	63	FW 190	V. Ulzen
	Capt. Walker M. Mahurin	63	FW 190	Wenzendorf A/D
	Lt. Fred J. Christensen	62	FW 190	N. Dummer Lk.
	Capt. B. Michael Gladych	61	FW 190 Grd	Yechta A/D
3-8-44	Lt. Felix D. Williamson	62	FW 190	Minden
	Capt. Joseph H. Bennett	61	FW 190	Munstorf A/F
	Capt. Joseph H. Bennett	61	2 Me 109	E. Steinhuder Lk.
	Lt. Marvin H. Becker	63	Me 109	E. Dummer Lk.
	Maj. Gerald W. Johnson	63	2 Me 109	Dummer Lk.
	Lt. Archie R. Robey	63	Me 109	V. Dummer Lk.
	Maj. James C. Stewart	61	FW 190	S. Steinhuder Lk.
	Lt. Mark L. Moseley	62	FW 190	Dummer Lk.
	Capt. Leroy A. Schreiber	62	FW 190	Steinhuder Lk.
	Capt. Leroy A. Schreiber	62	Me 109	Steinhuder Lk.
	Lt. Gordon J. Blake	61	FW 190	NE Steinhuder Lk.
	Maj. James C. Stewart	61	Me 110	S. Steinhuder Lk.
	Lt. Robert S. Johnson	61	2 Me 109	NE Steinhuder Lk.

Date	Name	Squadron	Type	Location
	Lt. John B. Eaves	62	0.5 FW 190	V. Celle
	Capt. Michael J. Quirk	62	0.5 FW 190	V. Celle
	Lt. John H. Truluck	63	Me 109	V. Dummer Lk.
	Lt. Frank W. Klibbe	61	FW 190	Steinhuder Lk.
	Capt. Walker M. Mahurin	63	2 FW 190	Wesendorf A/D
	Capt. Walker M. Mahurin	63	Ju 88	Wesendorf A/D
	Lt. Bernard R. Smith	63	Me 110	NW Steinhuder Lk.
	Lt. Claude E. Mussey	61	Me 109	E. Steinhuder Lk.
	Lt. Robert C. Cherry	62	FW 190	Steinhuder Lk.
	Lt. James E. Fields	62	FW 190	Steinhuder Lk.
	Capt. B. Michael Gladych	61	FW 190	Dummer Lk.
	Lt. Col. Francis S. Gabreski	61	FW 190 Grd	Wunstdorf A/D
	Lt. Col. David C. Schilling	HQ	Me 210 Grd	Wunstdorf A/D
3-15-44	Capt. Michael J. Quirk	62	FW 190	Dummer Lk.
	Lt. James E. Fields	62	FW 190	V. Dummer Lk.
	Lt. John P. Bryant	62	FW 190	V. Dummer Lk.
	Lt. Fred J. Christensen	62	2 FW 190	V. Dummer Lk.
	Lt. James M. Jones, Jr.	62	FW 190	V. Dummer Lk.
	Lt. Mark L. Moseley	62	FW 190	V. Dummer Lk.
	Lt. Robert S. Johnson	61	2 FW 190	NE Dummer Lk.
	Lt. Robert S. Johnson	61	Me 109	NE Dummer Lk.
	Lt. Frank W. Klibbe	61	FW 190	S. Barenburg
	Maj. Gerald W. Johnson	63	2 Me 109	Nr. Nienburg
	Capt. Leslie C. Smith	61	Me 109	Dummer Lk.
	F/O Steven Gerick	61	Me 109	Dummer Lk.
	Lt. Robert J. Rankin	61	2 Me 109	NE Dummer Lk.
	Lt. Donald V. Peters	63	Me 109	V. Hanover
	Lt. Archie R. Robey	63	2 FW 190	Vechta
	Lt. John H. Truluck	63	FW 190	V. Hanover
	Lt. Joe H. Powers	61	FW 190	NE Dummer Lk.
	Lt. Joe H. Powers	61	Me 109	NE Dummer Lk.
	Lt. Joseph L. Egan, Jr.	63	FW 190	Nienburg
3-16-44	F/O Evan D. McMinn	61	FW 190	N. St. Dizier
	Lt. Thaddeus S. Buszko	62	FW 190	V. St. Dizier
	Lt. Stanley B. Morrill	62	FW 190	V. St. Dizier
	Lt. Col. Francis S. Gabreski	61	2 FW 190	Nancy
	Lt. Joe H. Powers	61	Me 109	V. St. Dizier
	Capt. Leroy A. Schreiber	62	Me 109	V. St. Dizier
	Capt. Leroy A. Schreiber	62	0.5 FW 190	V. St. Dizier
	Lt. Arlington W. Canizares	62	0.5 FW 190	V. St. Dizier
	Lt. Fred J. Christensen	62	2 FW 190	V. St. Dizier
	Lt. Felix D. Williamson	62	FW 190	V. St. Dizier
3-18-44	Lt. Joe H. Powers	61	FW 190	Cambrai
	Lt. Dale E. Stream	61	FW 190	Cambrai
3-20-44	Maj. James C. Stewart	61	2 Me 109	S. Charleville
	Lt. Dale E. Stream	61	U/I T/E Grd	Charleville
3-27-44	Lt. Willard D. Johnson	63	0.25 Do 217	S. Chartres
	F/O Samuel J. Lowman	63	0.25 Do 217	S. Chartres
	Maj. Walker M. Mahurin	63	0.25 Do 217	S. Chartres
	Lt. Isadore T. Porowski	63	0.25 Do 217	S. Chartres
	Lt. Col. Francis S. Gabreski	61	2 Me 109	NE Nantes
	Capt. B. Michael Gladych	61	Me 109	S. Angers
	Lt. Col. David C. Schilling	HQ	Ju 52 Grd	Chartres

Date	Name	Squadron	Type	Location
3-29-44	Lt. Col. David C. Schilling	HQ	Me 109	NE Dummer Lk.
	Lt. Robert J. Rankin	61	Me 109	NE Nienburg
4-8-44	Capt. James M. Jones, Jr.	62	Ju 88 Grd	Hespe
	Lt. Arlington W. Canizares	62	0.5 Ju 88 Grd	Hespe
	Maj. Leroy A. Schreiber	62	0.5 Ju 88 Grd	Hespe
	Lt. Arlington W. Canizares	62	0.5 Me 109 Grd	Hespe
	Maj. Leroy A. Schreiber	62	0.5 Me 109 Grd	Hespe
4-9-44	Capt. Tadeusz Andersz	61	Me 109	SE Kiel
	Lt. Samuel D. Hamilton, Jr.	61	FW 190	NW Kiel
	Capt. Robert S. Johnson	61	FW 190	NW Kiel
	Capt. Leslie C. Smith	61	Me 109	E. Neumunster
	Capt. Joe H. Powers	62	Me 109	S. Kiel
	Lt. Arlington W. Canizares	62	0.5 Me 109	A/D V. Lubeck
	Maj. Leroy A. Schreiber	62	0.5 Me 109	A/D V. Lubeck
	Lt. Harold L. Matthews	63	0.5 U/I 4E FlyBt Grd	Schleswig
	Lt. Col. Francis S. Gabreski	61	0.5 U/I 4E FlyBt Grd	Schleswig
	F/O Walter E. Frederick	61	He 115 Grd	V. Schleswig
	Lt. Col. David C. Schilling	HQ	Ar 196 Grd	NE Schleswig
	Lt. Vernon E. Kerr, Jr.	63	Ar 196 Grd	NE Schleswig
4-11-44	Lt. Mark K. Boyle	62	He 115 Grd	Courcelles
4-13-44	Lt. Col. David C. Schilling	HQ	Me 109	V. Ludwigshafen
	Lt. Mark K. Boyle	62	Me 109	V. Ludwigshafen
	Capt. Robert S. Johnson	61	2 FW 190	Kaiserslautern
4-15-44	Lt. Willard D. Johnson	63	0.5 FW 190	Flensburg
	Lt. Samuel O. Stamps	63	0.5 FW 190	Flensburg
	Capt. Paul A. Conger	61	FW 190	Elmshorn area
	Lt. William P. Chattaway	62	FW 190	V. Altona
	Capt. Fred J. Christensen	62	Me 109	V. Altona
	Capt. Fred J. Christensen	62	FW 190	V. Altona
	Lt. Marvin H. Becker	63	He 111 Grd	Flensburg A/D
	F/O Evan D. McMinn	61	He 111 Grd	Flensburg A/D
	F/O Evan D. McMinn	61	Me 210 Grd	Flensburg A/D
	Col. Hubert Zemke	HQ	4 He 111 Grd	Flensburg A/D
	Maj. Leroy A. Schreiber	62	He 111 Grd	Flensburg A/D
	F/O Samuel J. Lowman	63	He 111 Grd	Flensburg A/D
	Capt. Leslie C. Smith	61	He 111 Grd	Flensburg A/D
	Lt. Charles W. Reed	63	He 111 Grd	Flensburg A/D
	Lt. Edward A. Sison	61	He 111 Grd	Flensburg A/D
4-20-44	Lt. Wendel A. McClure	62	0.5 Ju 88	NE Paris
	Capt. Felix D. Williamson	62	0.5 Ju 88	NE Paris
4-24-44	Maj. James C. Stewart	62	Ju 87 Grd	Thronville A/D
	Lt. Adam J. Wisniewski	63	0.5 Me 210 Grd	Thalhein A/D
	Lt. Donald W. Marshall	63	0.5 Me 210 Grd	Thalhein A/D
	Lt. Donald W. Marshall	63	Ju 52 Grd	Thalhein A/D
	Lt. Harry F. Warner	63	Ju 87 Grd	Thalhein A/D
	Lt. Sam B. Dale, Jr.	63	Me 109 Grd	Thalhein A/D
	Lt. Sam B. Dale, Jr.	63	FW 190 Grd	Thalhein A/D
	Capt. John H. Truluck	63	Do 217 Grd	Thalhein A/D
	Lt. John A. Aranyos	63	Do 217 Grd	Thalhein A/D
	Lt. Donald V. Peters	63	Me 210 Grd	Thalhein A/D
	Lt. Donald V. Peters	63	Me 109 Grd	Thalhein A/D
	Lt. Warren E. Kerr, Jr.	63	2 Me 109 Grd	Thalhein A/D
	Lt. Warren E. Kerr, Jr.	63	Me 110 Grd	Thalhein A/D

Date	Name	Squadron	Type	Location
4-25-44	Col. Hubert Zemke	HQ	2 Ju 88 Grd	Metz A/D
	F/O Steven Gerick	61	Me 109 Grd	Metz A/D
5-4-44	Capt. Joe H. Powers	62	Me 109	V. Quackenbruck
	Lt. Eugene E. Bennett	62	0.5 FW 190	V. Nordhausen
	Lt. Robert C. Cherry	62	0.5 FW 190	V. Nordhausen
	Lt. Robert C. Cherry	62	Me 410	V. Nordhausen
5-8-44	Lt. Frank W. Klibbe	61	Me 109	W. Celle
	Lt. Frank W. Klibbe	61	FW 190	W. Celle
	Capt. Robert S. Johnson	62	Me 109	Brunswick area
	Capt. Robert S. Johnson	62	FW 190	Brunswick area
	Lt. Gordon H. Lewis	62	FW 190	V. Oschersleben
	Lt. Col. Francis S. Gabreski	61	Me 109	Celle
5-12-44	Capt. Paul A. Conger	61	2 FW 190	N. Marburg
	Lt. Arthur C. Maul	61	Me 109	N. Marburg
	Lt. Anthony S. Cavallo	63	2 FW 190	Coblenz
	Col. Hubert Zemke	HQ	Me 109	S. Coblenz
	F/O Steven Gerick	61	FW 190	NW Marburg
	Lt. Robert J. Rankin	61	2 Me 109	NW Marburg
	Lt. Robert J. Rankin	61	3 FW 190	S. Coblenz
	Lt. J. Carroll Wakefield	63	3 Me 109	NW Frankfurt
	Lt. Cleon C. Thornton	61	Me 109	Marburg
	Lt. Jack E. Green	62	Me 109	Frankfurt
	Lt. Herman E. King	62	Me 109	V. Frankfurt
	Capt. Joe H. Powers	62	0.5 Me 109	V. Frankfurt
	F/O Joseph Vitale	62	0.5 Me 109	V. Frankfurt
5-13-44	Lt. James M. Jure	61	FW 190	NE Hamburg
	Lt. Robert J. Keen	61	3 FW 190	W. Hagenow
	Maj. Lucien A. Dade, Jr.	62	FW 190	V. Lubeck
5-19-44	Capt. John B. Eaves	62	2 FW 190	N. Hanover
	Lt. Richard M. Heineman	61	FW 190	V. Halberstadt
	Maj. Leslie C. Smith	61	2 FW 190	N. Wernigerode
5-22-44	F/O Evan D. McMinn	61	2 FW 190	Rotenberg
	Capt. James R. Carter	61	FW 190	V. Hoperhofen
	F/O Witold A. Lanowski	61 (PAF)	FW 190	Hoperhofen A/D
	Lt. Richard M. Heineman	61	2 FW 190	Hoperhofen A/D
	Lt. Reginald A. Herin	61	FW 190	Hoperhofen A/D
	Lt. Praeger Neyland	61	FW 190	Hoperhofen A/D
	Lt. Col. Francis S. Gabreski	61	3 FW 190	Hoperhofen A/D
	Lt. James C. Clark	61	FW 190	Hoperhofen A/D
5-31-44	Col. Hubert Zemke	HQ	2 FW 190	Gutersloh area
	Lt. Wendel A. McClure	62	FW 190	Meldorf area
	Capt. Charles E. Tucker	62	FW 190	Meldorf area
	Lt. Donald V. Peters	63	FW 190	NW Kessel
6-6-44	Lt. William W. McElhare	62	FW 190	V. Rambouillet
	Col. Hubert Zemke	HQ	FW 190	NE Bernay
	Capt. B. Michael Gladych	61 (PAF)	Me 109	Croisy
6-7-44	Lt. Joseph R. Curtis	63	FW 190	Forrest Lyones
	Lt. Col. Francis S. Gabreski	61	Me 109	E. Dreux
	Lt. Col. Francis S. Gabreski	61	FW 190	E. Dreux
	F/O Steven Gerick	61	Me 109	SE Houdan
	Capt. B. Michael Gladych	61 (PAF)	Me 109	SE Houdan
	Lt. Joel I. Popplewell	61	Me 109	SE Houdan
	Lt. George E. Bostwick	62	Me 109	Grandvilliers A/D

Date	Name	Squadron	Type	Location
	Lt. Mark L. Moseley	62	0.5 Ju 88	St. Andre de L'Eure
	Lt. Jack W. Pierce	62	0.5 Ju 88	St. Andre de L'Eure
	Lt. Robert J. Rankin	61	Me 109	SE Senlis
	Col. Hubert Zemke	HQ	2 FW 190	Chartres
	Lt. Marvin H. Becker	63	0.5 FW 190	Les Andleys
	Lt. Sam B. Dale	63	0.5 FW 190	Les Andleys
6-8-44	Lt. Billy G. Edens	62	2 Me 109	St. Andre de L'Eure
	Lt. Billy G. Edens	62	FW 190	St. Andre de L'Eure
	Lt. Mark L. Moseley	62	2 FW 190	St. Andre de L'Eure
	Lt. George H. Butler	62	Me 109	St. Andre de L'Eure
	Lt. George H. Van Noy, Jr.	62	Me 109	St. Andre de L'Eure
6-12-44	Lt. Oscar W. Belk	61	Me 109	Quittebeuf
	Lt. Col. Francis S. Gabreski	61	2 Me 109	V. Evreux
	F/O Steven Gerick	61	2 Me 109	V. Evreux
6-16-44	Lt. Edward A. Sison, Jr.	61	Me 109	V. Rouen
6-24-44	Col. Hubert Zemke	HQ	Ju 88 Grd	Sally-Laurette
6-27-44	Lt. Warren S. Patterson, Jr.	61	Me 109	Connantre
	Lt. James M. Jure	61	Me 109	Nr. Esternay
	Lt. Robert C. Cherry	62	Me 109	V. La Perth
	Capt. Fred J. Christensen	62	Me 109	Cambrai
	Lt. Col. Francis S. Gabreski	61	Me 109	La Perth A/F
	F/Lt. Witold A. Lanowski	61 (PAF)	Me 109	La Perth A/F
6-30-44	Lt. Marvin H. Becker	63	Ju 88	S. Novon
7-4-44	F/O Robert W. Magel	63	Me 109	SW Evreux
	Lt. Joseph R. Curtis	63	Me 109	Bernay-Evreux
	Capt. James R. Carter	61	Me 109	W. Louviers
	Maj. Gordon E. Baker	62	Me 109	Conches area
	Lt. George E. Bostwick	62	3 Me 109	Conches area
	Maj. Lucien A. Dade, Jr.	62	2 Me 109	Conches area
	Capt. Michael J. Jackson	62	Me 109	Conches area
	Lt. Albert P. Knafelz	62	Me 109	Conches area
	Lt. Baird M. Knox	62	Me 109	Conches area
	Lt. William W. McElhare	62	Me 109	Conches area
	Lt. Darrell E. McMahan	62	0.5 Me 109	Conches area
	Lt. Frank C. Newell	62	0.5 Me 109	Conches area
	Lt. Wiley H. Merrill	62	2 Me 109	Conches area
	Capt. Mark L. Moseley	62	Me 109	Conches area
	Lt. Dayton C. Sheridan	62	Me 109	Conches area
	Lt. Joseph R. Curtis	63	0.5 Me 109	Bernay-Evreux
	Lt. Walter E. Frederick	63	0.5 Me 109	Bernay-Evreux
7-5-44	Lt. Billy G. Edens	62	FW 190	N. Evreux
	Lt. George H. Butler	62	FW 190	N. Evreux
	Capt. Fred J. Christensen	62	FW 190	N. Evreux
	Lt. Jack W. Pierce	62	FW 190	Evreux area
	F/Lt. Witold A. Lanowski	61 (PAF)	Me 109	Conches A/D
	Maj. B. Michael Gladych	61 (PAF)	Me 109	Evreux
	Lt. Robert J. Keen	61	3 Me 109	Evreux
	Lt. Col. Francis S. Gabreski	61	Me 109	Evreux area
	Lt. Robert C. Cherry	62	FW 190	W. Paris
	Lt. Walter L. Flagg	63	Me 109	Evreux
7-6-44	Lt. George E. Bostwick	62	Me 109	V. Beaumont
	Capt. Mark L. Moseley	62	Me 109	V. Beaumont
	Lt. Joseph R. Curtis	63	Me 109	N. Evreux
	Lt. Barney P. Casteel	63	FW 190	E. Chartres

Date	Name	Squadron	Type	Location
	Lt. Thomas Guerrero	63	FW 190	E. Chartres
7-7-44	Capt. Fred J. Christensen	62	6 Ju 52	Gardelegen A/D
	Lt. Billy G. Edens	62	3 Ju 52	Gardelegen A/D
	Capt. Michael J. Jackson	62	Ju 52	Gardelegen A/D
	Lt. Steven Gerick	61	U/I T/E Grd	Peine A/D
7-20-44	Lt. Col. Francis S. Gabreski	61	He 111 Grd	Bassenheim A/D
	Capt. Donovan F. Smith	61	He 111 Grd	Bassenheim A/D
	Lt. Stuart H. Getz	61	2 He 111 Grd	Bassenheim A/D
	Lt. William H. Barnes	61	3 He 111 Grd	Bassenheim A/D
	Lt. Warren S. Patterson	61	He 111 Grd	Bassenheim A/D
7-24-44	Lt. Col. David C. Schilling	61	0.5 Me 410 Grd	Villaroche A/D
	Lt. Arthur J. Bux	61	0.5 Me 410 Grd	Villaroche A/D
8-3-44	Lt. Richard B. Anderson	63	FW 190	SW Sarrebourg
8-4-44	Lt. Arthur C. Maul	61	Me 109	S. Hamburg
	Maj. Gordon E. Baker	61	0.5 4/E F/B Grd	Selenter Lk.
	Lt. Carl E. Westman	61	0.5 4/E F/B Grd	Selenter Lk.
	Lt. James M. Jure	61	0.5 4/E F/B Grd	Selenter Lk.
	Lt. Stuart H. Getz	61	0.5 4/E F/B Grd	Selenter Lk.
	Col. Hubert Zemke	HQ	0.5 U/I T/E Grd	Plantlunne A/D
	Lt. John W. Ferguson	62	0.5 U/I T/E Grd	Plantlunne A/D
	Lt. Billy G. Edens	62	2 He 111 Grd	Plantlunne A/D
8-9-44	Lt. Lewis R. Brown	62	U/I T/E Grd	V. Coblenz
	Maj. Gordon E. Baker	61	U/I T/E Grd	Euskirchen A/D
8-12-44	Maj. B. Michael Gladych	61	Ju 88	V. Cambrai
	Capt. Roy T. Fling	63	Me 109	Mauberge
8-15-44	Capt. Russell W. Campbell	63	Me 109 Grd	St. Trond A/D
8-28-44	Capt. Paul A. Conger	63	0.5 He 111	S. Saarbrucken
	Lt. James M. Jure	63	0.5 He 111	S. Saarbrucken
	Capt. Michael J. Jackson	62	Ju 88	V. Irsch
	Lt. Walter R. Groce	63	He 111	N. Kaiserslautern
	Lt. Edward M. Albright	63	He 111	N. Saarbrucken
	Lt. Col. David C. Schilling	HQ	He 111	S. Trier
	Maj. Gordon E. Baker	61	U/I T/E Grd	V. Koch
	Lt. Walter L. Flagg	63	Me 109	Charleroi
9-5-44	Lt. Richard B. Anderson	63	2 Me 109	NE Coblenz
	Lt. Robert J. Daniel	63	Me 109	NE Coblenz
	Lt. Cameron M. Hart	63	Me 109	NE Coblenz
	Lt. James A. Kyle	63	Me 109	NE Coblenz
	Lt. Richard T. Warboys	63	Me 109	NE Coblenz
	Lt. George H. Butler	62	FW 44	NE Gelnhausen A/D
	Lt. Eugene A. Timony	63	FW 190	S. Coblenz
	Lt. Cleon C. Thomton	61	0.5 Me 110 Grd	Merzhausen A/D
	Lt. William D. Clark, Jr.	61	0.5 Me 110 Grd	Merzhausen A/D
	Maj. Lucien A. Dade, Jr.	61	He 111 Grd	Merzhausen A/D
	Maj. Lucien A. Dade, Jr.	61	2 Me 110 Grd	Merzhausen A/D
	Lt. James M. Jure	61	He 111 Grd	Merzhausen A/D
	Lt. William D. Clark, Jr.	61	Me 110 Grd	Merzhausen A/D
	Lt. William D. Clark, Jr.	61	Me 410 Grd	Merzhausen A/D
	Capt. Benjamin E. Cathers	61	Ju 88 Grd	Merzhausen A/D
	Lt. Richard T. Warboys	63	Me 109 Grd	Gelnhausen A/D
	Lt. Thomas W. Queen	63	2 FW 190 Grd	Gelnhausen A/D
	Lt. Everett A. Henderson	63	FW 190 Grd	Gelnhausen A/D
	Lt. Eugene A. Timony	63	2 Bucher 131 Grd	Gelnhausen A/D

Date	Name	Squadron	Type	Location
	Lt. Eugene A. Timony	63	Me 109 Grd	Gelnhausen A/D
	Lt. Claude A. Chinn	63	U/I TR Grd	Gelnhausen A/D
	Col. David C. Schilling	63	3 FW 190 Grd	Gelnhausen A/D
	Lt. Charles M. Rotzler	63	2 FW 190 Grd	Gelnhausen A/D
	Lt. Charles M. Rotzler	63	Me 109 Grd	Gelnhausen A/D
	Lt. Charles M. Rotzler	63	2 FW 190 Grd	Gelnhausen A/D
	Lt. Edward M. Albright, Jr.	63	Ju 52 Grd	Gelnhausen A/D
	Lt. Edward M. Albright, Jr.	63	U/I S/E Grd	Gelnhausen A/D
	Lt. Robert J. Daniel	63	FW 190 Grd	Gelnhausen A/D
	Col. David C. Schilling	63	2 U/I S/E Grd	Gelnhausen A/D
	Capt. Michael J. Quirk	62	4 FW 190 Grd	Gelnhausen A/D
	Lt. Trevor A. Edwards	62	2 FW 190 Grd	Gelnhausen A/D
	Lt. Darrell E. McMahan	62	4 FW 190 Grd	Gelnhausen A/D
	Lt. Eugene M. Beason	62	FW 190 Grd	Gelnhausen A/D
	Lt. Eugene M. Beason	62	U/I LAI Grd	Gelnhausen A/D
	Lt. Jack W. Pierce	62	2 FW 190 Grd	Gelnhausen A/D
	Lt. Frederick B. McIntosh	62	2 FW 190 Grd	Gelnhausen A/D
	Lt. Robert E. Winters	62	FW 190 Grd	Gelnhausen A/D
	Capt. Robert J. Keen	62	6 FW 190 Grd	Gelnhausen A/D
	Lt. George H. Butler	62	2 Me 109 Grd	Gelnhausen A/D
	Lt. George H. Butler	62	FW 190 Grd	Gelnhausen A/D
	Lt. Roy L. Patterson	62	2 FW 190 Grd	Gelnhausen A/D
	Lt. Roy L. Patterson	62	U/I BI Grd	Gelnhausen A/D
	Lt. James C. Clark	61	FW 190 Grd	Gelnhausen A/D
	Lt. William M. Hartshorn	61	FW 190 Grd	Gelnhausen A/D
	Lt. Herschel C. Womack	62	Me 110 Grd	Merzhausen A/D
	Capt. Herman E. King	62	Me 110 Grd	Merzhausen A/D
	Capt. William F. Wilkerson	62	He 111 Grd	Merzhausen A/D
	Lt. Steven T. Murray	62	2 Ju 88 Grd	Merzhausen A/D
	Lt. Frederick B. McIntosh	62	Me 110 Grd	Merzhausen A/D
	Lt. Frederick B. McIntosh	62	U/I T/E Grd	Merzhausen A/D
	Capt. Michael J. Jackson	62	2 Ju 88 Grd	Limburg A/D
	Capt. Michael J. Jackson	62	Me 109 Grd	Limburg A/D
	Capt. Michael J. Jackson	62	Me 210 Grd	Limburg A/D
	Lt. Steven T. Murray	62	0.5 Me 110 Grd	Limburg A/D
	Capt. Michael J. Jackson	62	0.5 Me 110 Grd	Limburg A/D
	Lt. Steven T. Murray	62	2 Fi. Storch Grd	Limburg A/D
9-8-44	Lt. Eugene A. Timony	63	Ju 88 Grd	Euskirchen A/D
	Lt. George E. Bostwick	62	3 FW 190 Grd	Euskirchen A/D
	Lt. Jackie L. Carwell	62	Me 109 Grd	Euskirchen A/D
	Lt. Billy G. Edens	62	U/I T/E Grd	Euskirchen A/D
9-10-44	Lt. Jack W. Pierce	62	He 111 Grd	Selingenstadt
	Capt. Michael J. Quirk	62	He 111 Grd	Selingenstadt
9-12-44	Lt. Darrell E. McMahan	62	Me 109	V. Sachau A/D
	Lt. James C. Clark	61	Me 109	N. Brandenburg
	Lt. James M. Jure	61	Me 109	N. Brandenburg
9-16-44	Capt. Donovan F. Smith	61	He 177 Grd	Ahlhorn A/D
	Capt. Robert J. Keen	62	Ju 88 Grd	V. Dummer Lk.
	Capt. Harold E. Comstock	63	He 177 Grd	Ahlhorn A/D
9-21-44	Capt. Michael J. Jackson	62	FW 190	NE Arnhem
	Lt. Robert E. Winters	62	FW 190	NE Arnhem
	Lt. Walter R. Groce	63	FW 190	Lochem
	Lt. Walter H. Pitts	63	2 FW 190	Lochem

Date	Name	Squadron	Type	Location
	Lt. Stuart H. Getz	61	0.5 FW 190	E. Deventer
	Lt. William J. Osborne	61	0.5 FW 190	E. Deventer
	Maj. B. Michael Gladych	61	2 FW 190	E. Arnhem
	Lt. Russell S. Kyler	61	FW 190	Deventer area
	Lt. Lewis R. Brown	62	FW 190	Arnhem area
	Lt. Col. David C. Schilling	HQ	3 FW 190	Lochem
	Lt. Donald Henley, Jr.	62	FW 190	SE Arnhem
	Lt. Roy L. Patterson	62	FW 190	V. Arnhem
10-5-44	Lt. James A. Kyle	63	Me 109 Grd	V. Geseke
	Lt. Robert E. Winters	62	Me 109 Grd	V. Geseke
	Lt. Col. David C. Schilling	HQ	3 Me 210 Grd	V. Geseke
	Lt. Francis A. Nolan	62	Ju 88 Grd	V. Geseke
	Lt. Charles M. Rotzler	63	Me 109 Grd	V. Geseke
	Lt. Roy L. Patterson	62	Ju 88 Grd	V. Geseke
	Lt. Roy L. Patterson	62	Me 109 Grd	V. Geseke
	Capt. John B. Eaves	62	FW 190 Grd	V. Geseke
	Lt. Eugene M. Beason	62	Me 110 Grd	V. Geseke
	Lt. Reigel W. Davis	62	Me 109 Grd	V. Geseke
	Lt. Reigel W. Davis	62	Ju 88 Grd	V. Geseke
	Lt. George R. Choate	62	Me 110 Grd	V. Geseke
10-12-44	Lt. James E. Lister	63	FW 190	Dummer Lk.
10-15-44	Lt. James A. Kyle	63	0.5 Me 109 Grd	Rheine A/D
	Lt. Thomas W. Seling III	63	0.5 Me 109 Grd	Rheine A/D
11-1-44	Lt. Walter R. Groce	63	0.5 Me 262	E. Arnhem
11-18-44	Capt. James R. Carter	61	Me 109	E. Hanau
	Lt. Robert A. Baughman	61	FW 190	E. Hanau
	Lt. Arthur H. Gerow	61	FW 190	E. Hanau
	Lt. Russell S. Kyler	61	FW 190	E. Hanau
	Capt. Withold A. Lanowski	61 (PAF)	FW 190	E. Hanau
	Lt. Charles R. Raymond	61	FW 190	E. Hanau
	Capt. Michael J. Jackson	62	FW 190	V. Hanau
	Capt. William F. Wilkerson	62	FW 190	V. Hanau
	Lt. John W. Ferguson	62	FW 190	V. Hanau
	Lt. Norman D. Gould	62	Me 109	V. Hanau
	Lt. Ramon R. Davis	63	FW 190	E. Hanau
	Maj. Harold E. Comstock	63	He 111 Grd	Gross Ostheim A/D
	Lt. Randel L. Murphy, Jr.	63	FW 190 Grd	Gross Ostheim A/D
	Lt. Claude A. Chinn	63	3 Me 109 Grd	Gross Ostheim A/D
11-27-44	Lt. Russell Frederickson	63	2 Me 109	SE Dummer Lk.
	Lt. James E. Lister	63	Me 109	SE Dummer Lk.
12-2-44	Lt. Samuel K. Batson	63	Me 109	S. Marburg
	Maj. Paul A. Conger	63	2 Me 109	S. Marburg
	Capt. John C. Fahringer	63	2 Me 109	S. Marburg
	Lt. Russell Frederickson	63	Me 109	S. Marburg
	Lt. Walter R. Groce	63	Me 109	S. Marburg
	Lt. Pershing B. Trumble	63	Me 109	S. Marburg
	Lt. Richard B. Anderson	63	Me 109	S. Marburg
	Capt. Reigel W. Davis	62	2 Me 109	E. Coblenz
12-4-44	Capt. Francis A. Nolan	62	FW 200 Grd	Neuburg A/D
	Lt. Andrew Chasko	62	0.5 He 177 Grd	Neuburg A/D
	Lt. William C. Daley	62	0.5 He 177 Grd	Neuburg A/D
	Lt. Eugene M. Beason	62	He 177 Grd	Neuburg A/D
	Lt. Eugene M. Beason	62	FW 190 Grd	Neuburg A/D
	Lt. Donald Henley, Jr.	62	0.5 U/I S/E Grd	Neuburg A/D

Date	Name	Squadron	Type	Location
	Lt. Sanborn Ball	62	0.5 U/I S/E Grd	Neuburg A/D
	Lt. Charles A. Wook	62	U/I S/E Grd	Neuburg A/D
	Capt. Michael J. Jackson	62	Me 262 Grd	Neuburg A/D
	Lt. Norman D. Gould	62	Me 262 Grd	Neuburg A/D
	Capt. William F. Wilkerson	62	He 111 Grd	Neuburg A/D
	Lt. Claude A. Chinn	62	2 Me 262 Grd	Neuburg A/D
12-23-44	Col. David C. Schilling	HQ	3 Me 109	Euskirchen A/D
	Col. David C. Schilling	HQ	2 FW 190	Euskirchen A/D
	Capt. Joseph H. Perry	61	2 FW 190	Coblenz area
	Lt. Lloyd F. Geren	62	0.5 FW 190	Euskirchen A/D
	Lt. Don A. Westover, Jr.	62	0.5 FW 190	Euskirchen A/D
	Lt. Samuel K. Batson	63	FW 190	NW-Coblenz
	Lt. Charles R. Clark	63	FW 190	NW Coblenz
	Maj. Harold E. Comstock	63	2 FW 190	SW Bonn
	Lt. Robert J. Daniel	63	FW 190	NW Coblenz
	Capt. Cameron M. Hart	63	2 FW 190	NW Coblenz
	Lt. William R. Hoffman	63	FW 190	NW Coblenz
	Lt. Randel L. Murphy	63	2 FW 190	NW Coblenz
	Lt. Willard C. Scherz	63	FW 190	NW Coblenz
	F/O Melvin J. Hughes	63	FW 190	NW Coblenz
	Lt. Alfred O. Perry	62	FW 190	Bonn-Coblenz
	Lt. William C. Daley	62	Me 109	Euskirchen A/D
	Lt. Victor E. Bast	61	FW 190	Coblenz area
	Lt. John F. Frazier	61	2 FW 190	Coblenz area
	Lt. Eugene M. Beason	62	Me 109	Bonn-Coblenz
	Lt. Andrew Chasko	62	Me 109	Euskirchen A/D
	Lt. Norman D. Gould	62	FW 190	V. Euskirchen A/D
	Lt. Warren S. Lear	62	FW 190	Euskirchen A/D
	Capt. Felix D. Williamson	62	Me 109	Euskirchen A/D
	Capt. Felix D. Williamson	62	FW 190	Euskirchen A/D
	Lt. Charles E. Carlson	62	FW 190	Euskirchen A/D
	Lt. Sanborn N. Ball, Jr.	62	FW 190	Euskirchen A/D
	Lt. Alfred O. Perry	62	FW 190	Bonn-Coblenz
12-25-44	Lt. William D. Clark, Jr.	61	FW 190	Cologne
	Lt. William C. Daley	62	2 Me 109	Bonn-Coblenz
	Capt. Michael J. Jackson	62	Me 109	Bonn-Coblenz
	F/O Walter J. Sharbo	62	2 Me 109	Bonn-Coblenz
	Capt. Cameron M. Hart	63	Me 109	SE Cologne
12-26-44	Lt. Alfred O. Perry	62	2 FW 190	V. Cologne
	Maj. Leslie C. Smith	62	FW 190	V. Coblenz
12-31-44	F/O Leo F. Butiste	62	FW 190	V. Quackenbruck
	Capt. Francis A. Nolan	62	2 FW 190	V. Quackenbruck
	Lt. William H. Stovall, Jr.	62	2 FW 190	V. Burgsteinfort
1-14-45	Lt. Russell S. Kyler	61	Me 109	E. Rheine
	Lt. Robert E. Walker	61	Me 109	Rheine area
	Lt. William C. Daley	62	Me 109	Rheine area
	Maj. Michael J. Jackson	62	Me 109	Rheine area
	Maj. Michael J. Jackson	62	FW 190D	Rheine area
	Lt. Kenneth L. Smith	62	Me 109	Rheine area
	Lt. Ramon R. Davis	63	Me 109	V. Munster
	Lt. Charles T. McBath	63	2 Me 109	V. Munster
	Lt. Charles M. Rotzler	63	Me 109	V. Munster
	Capt. Felix D. Williamson	62	4 Me 109	N. Burg
	Capt. Felix D. Williamson	62	FW 190D	N. Burg

Date	Name	Squadron	Type	Location
	Lt. Donald Henley, Jr.	62	Me 109	Magdeburg area
	Lt. Donald Henley, Jr.	62	0.5 Me 109	Magdeburg area
	Lt. Herschel C. Womack	62	0.5 Me 109	Magdeburg area
	Maj. Paul A. Conger	63	Me 109	Stendal
	Lt. Pershing B. Trumble	63	Me 109	Stendal
1-21-45	Maj. Leslie C. Smith	62	Ju 88 Grd	Mutzingen A/D
	Maj. Leslie C. Smith	62	0.5 Ju 52 Grd	Oberthalheim A/D
	Lt. Norman D. Gould	62	0.5 Ju 52 Grd	Oberthalheim A/D
2-3-45	Maj. Paul A. Conger	63	FW 190	SE Berlin
	Maj. Paul A. Conger	63	Me 109	SE Berlin
	Capt. John C. Fahringer	63	Me 109	SE Berlin
	Capt. Cameron M. Hart	63	2 FW 190	SE Berlin
	Lt. Philip G. Kuhn	63	FW 190	SE Berlin
	Lt. Frank M. Ogden III	63	FW 190	SE Berlin
	Capt. Felix D. Williamson	62	FW 190	Berlin area
	Capt. Felix D. Williamson	62	Me 109	Berlin area
	Capt. John C. Fahringer	63	Me 109 Grd	Friedersdorf A/D
2-27-45	Lt. Robert A. Baughman	61	2 U/I T/E Grd	Weimannorha A/D
	Lt. Col. Leslie C. Smith	61	2 U/I T/E Grd	Weimannorha A/D
3-10-45	Lt. Norman D. Gould	62	Me 109	Remagen area
	Lt. Dennis A. Carroll	62	0.5 FW 190	Remagen area
	Lt. Donald Henley, Jr.	62	0.5 FW 190	Remagen area
3-14-45	Lt. Sanborn N. Ball, Jr.	62	0.5 Ar 234	V. Coblenz
	Lt. Warren S. Lear	62	0.5 Ar 234	V. Coblenz
	Lt. Norman D. Gould	62	Ar 234	V. Coblenz
	Lt. Sherman Pruitt, Jr.	62	Me 109	V. Frankfurt
3-25-45	Maj. George E. Bostwick	63	Me 262	Parchim A/D
	Lt. Edwin M. Crosthwait, Jr.	63	Me 262	Parchim A/D
4-5-45	Capt. John C. Fahringer	63	Me 262	N. Regensburg
4-7-45	Lt. Charles T. McBath	63	Me 109	N. Celle
	Maj. George E. Bostwick	63	2 Me 109	S. Bremen
	Capt. Robert E. Winters	62	Me 109	S. Hamburg
4-10-45	Lt. Walter J. Sharbo	62	Me 262	SW Muritz Lk.
	Lt. Clarence A. Tingen	62	Ju 88 Grd	Rechlin A/D
	Lt. Leo F. Butiste	62	U/I S/E Grd	Rechlin A/D
	Lt. Leo F. Butiste	62	He 111 Grd	Rechlin A/D
	Lt. Frank G. Koch	62	2 U/I T/E Grd	Rechlin A/D
	Lt. Robert B. Jones, Jr.	62	He 111 Grd	Rechlin A/D
	Lt. Donald Henley, Jr.	62	Ju 88 Grd	Rechlin A/D
	Lt. William J. Stevenson	62	Ju 88 Grd	Rechlin A/D
	Lt. Walter J. Sharbo	62	2 He 111 Grd	Rechlin A/D
	Lt. Herschel C. Womack	62	He 111 Grd	Rechlin A/D
	Lt. Dennis A. Carroll	62	Ju 88 & Me 109 Pikabak Grd	Rechlin A/D
	Capt. William F. Wilkerson	62	He 111 Grd	Rechlin A/D
	F/O Clinton R. Albright	62	U/I T/E Grd	Rechlin A/D
	Lt. Boss E. Vest	63	Ju 88 Grd	Rechlin A/D
	Lt. John A. Arnold	63	FW 190 Grd	Rechlin A/D
	Lt. Arthur T. Shupe	63	FW 190 Grd	Rechlin A/D
	Capt. George E. Bostwick	63	2 Ju 88 Grd	Rechlin A/D
	Capt. George E. Bostwick	63	2 U/I T/E Grd	Rechlin A/D
	Lt. James C. Naylor	63	FW 190 Grd	Rechlin A/D
	Lt. James C. Naylor	63	Me 109 Grd	Rechlin A/D
	Lt. Thomas W. Smith, Jr.	63	Ju 88 Grd	Rechlin A/D

Date	Name	Squadron	Type	Location
	Capt. Walter L. Flagg	63	2 Do 217 Grd	Rechlin A/D
	Capt. Walter L. Flagg	63	Me 109 Grd	Rechlin A/D
	Capt. Walter L. Flagg	63	U/I T/E Grd	Rechlin A/D
	Lt. William R. Hoffman	63	2 U/I T/E Grd	Rechlin A/D
	Lt. Vernon A. Smith	63	Ju 88 Grd	Rechlin A/D
	Lt. Emmett S. Barrentine	63	2 Ju 88 Grd	Rechlin A/D
	Capt. Charles E. Bond	61	Ju 88 Grd	Rechlin A/D
	Capt. Charles E. Bond	61	Do 24 Grd	Rechlin A/D
	Lt. Russell S. Kyler	61	Me 109 Grd	Rechlin A/D
	Lt. Russell S. Kyler	61	U/I T/E Grd	Rechlin A/D
	Lt. Longfin M. Winski	61	He 115 Grd	Rechlin A/D
	Lt. Richard W. Higgins	61	U/I S/E Grd	Rechlin A/D
	Lt. Philip J. Clinton, Jr.	61	Do 24 Grd	Rechlin A/D
	Lt. Burton O. Blodgett	61	Do 24 Grd	Rechlin A/D
	Lt. Fred H. Barrett	61	2 Ju 88 Grd	Rechlin A/D
	Lt. Charles R. Raymond	61	U/I T/E Grd	Rechlin A/D
	Lt. Edmund T. Ellis	61	Do 217 Grd	Rechlin A/D
	Lt. Edmund T. Ellis	61	He 111 Grd	Rechlin A/D
	Lt. Edmund T. Ellis	61	U/I T/E Grd	Rechlin A/D
4-13-45	Lt. Russell S. Kyler	61	4 Ju 88 Grd	Eggebeck A/D
	Lt. Russell S. Kyler	61	Me 410 Grd	Eggebeck A/D
	Capt. Victor E. East	61	3 Ju 88 Grd	Eggebeck A/D
	Lt. Ernest E. Traff	61	3 Ju 88 Grd	Eggebeck A/D
	Lt. Burton O. Blodgett	61	3 Ju 88 Grd	Eggebeck A/D
	Lt. Burton O. Blodgett	61	U/I T/E Grd	Eggebeck A/D
	Lt. Franklin E. Ruder	61	He 111 Grd	Eggebeck A/D
	Lt. William G. Bartle	61	2 Ju 88 Grd	Eggebeck A/D
	F/Lt. Longfin W. Winski	61	Ju 88 Grd	Eggebeck A/D
	Lt. William F. Smith	61	Me 110 Grd	Eggebeck A/D
	Lt. Charles R. Raymond	61	U/I T/E Grd	Eggebeck A/D
	Capt. Charles B. Cole	61	Ju 88 Grd	Eggebeck A/D
	Lt. Robert W. Heoflein	61	Me 109 Grd	Eggebeck A/D
	Lt. Donald Henley, Jr.	62	U/I T/E Grd	Eggebeck A/D
	Lt. Donald Henley, Jr.	62	2 Ju 88 Grd	Eggebeck A/D
	Lt. William M. Carrington	62	Ju 87 Grd	Eggebeck A/D
	Lt. Irving Rich	62	Me 109 Grd	Eggebeck A/D
	Lt. Ben A. Westover, Jr.	62	FW 190 Grd	Eggebeck A/D
	Lt. Ben. A Westover, Jr.	62	2 Do 217 Grd	Eggebeck A/D
	Lt. Robert E. Jones	62	FW 190 Grd	Eggebeck A/D
	Lt. Robert E. Jones	62	He 111 Grd	Eggebeck A/D
	Capt. Philip F. Fleming	62	He 111 Grd	Eggebeck A/D
	Capt. Philip F. Fleming	62	3 Do 217 Grd	Eggebeck A/D
	Lt. Lloyd F. Geren	62	4 He 111 Grd	Eggebeck A/D
	Lt. Virgil L. Elliot	62	2 Do 217 Grd	Eggebeck A/D
	Lt. Sanborn Ball	62	2 Do 217 Grd	Eggebeck A/D
	Lt. Sanborn Ball	62	He 111 Grd	Eggebeck A/D
	Lt. Donald M. Gramer	62	He 111 Grd	Eggebeck A/D
	Lt. Col. Donald D. Renwick	HQ	He 111 Grd	Eggebeck A/D
	Lt. Dennis A. Carroll	62	He 111 Grd	Eggebeck A/D
	Lt. Hugh F. Besler	62	FW 190 Grd	Eggebeck A/D
	Lt. William J. Stevenson	62	Ju 88 Grd	Eggebeck A/D
	Lt. Thomas W. Queen	63	U/I T/E Grd	Eggebeck A/D
	Lt. Thomas W. Queen	63	Me 410 Grd	Eggebeck A/D

Date	Name	Squadron	Type	Location
	Lt. Thomas W. Queen	63	U/I S/E Grd	Eggebeck A/D
	Lt. Randel L. Murphy, Jr.	63	3 He 111 Grd	Eggebeck A/D
	Lt. Randel L. Murphy, Jr.	63	Me 210 Grd	Eggebeck A/D
	Lt. Randel L. Murphy, Jr.	63	5 U/I T/E Grd	Eggebeck A/D
	Lt. Randel L. Murphy, Jr.	63	FW 200 Grd	Eggebeck A/D
	Lt. Philip G. Kuhn	63	FW 190 Grd	Eggebeck A/D
	Lt. Philip G. Kuhn	63	2 Me 410 Grd	Eggebeck A/D
	Lt. Philip G. Kuhn	63	U/I T/E Grd	Eggebeck A/D
	Lt. John A. Arnold	63	U/I T/E Grd	Eggebeck A/D
	Lt. Col. Lucien Dade	HQ	2 Me 110 Grd	Eggebeck A/D
	Lt. Col. Lucien Dade	HQ	U/I T/E Grd	Eggebeck A/D
	Lt. Thomas B. Hennessey	63	2 Me 110 Grd	Eggebeck A/D
	Lt. Charles R. Clark	63	Me 110 Grd	Eggebeck A/D
	Lt. Charles R. Clark	63	Ju 88 Grd	Eggebeck A/D
	Lt. Robert E. Bailey	63	2 Me 110 Grd	Eggebeck A/D
	Lt. Vernon A. Smith	63	2 Ju 88 Grd	Eggebeck A/D
	Lt. Charles T. McBath	63	Me 109 Grd	Eggebeck A/D
	Lt. Edgar H. Huff	63	U/I S/E Grd	Eggebeck A/D
	Capt. Walter L. Flagg	63	Ju 88 Grd	Eggebeck A/D
	Capt. Walter L. Flagg	63	FW 190 Grd	Eggebeck A/D
	Lt. John W. Keeler	63	U/I T/E Grd	Eggebeck A/D
	Lt. John W. Keeler	63	Me 110 Grd	Eggebeck A/D
	Lt. Emmett S. Barrentine	63	Me 110 Grd	Eggebeck A/D
	Lt. Carter Taylor	63	Me 110 Grd	Eggebeck A/D
	Capt. Samuel F. Stebelton	63	U/I T/E Grd	Eggebeck A/D
4-16-45	Lt. Boss E. Vest	63	Ju 88 Grd	Muldorf A/D
	Lt. Clarence A. Tingen	62	He 177 Grd	Muldorf A/D

Index

Adrianse, Capt. Lyle A., 22, 175, 179
Aggers, F/O William R., 177
Aggers, Lt. Sam, 131, 137
Albright, F/O Clinton R., 188
Albright, Lt. Edward M., 140, 184-185
Allayaud, Lt. Donald, 150
Anderson, Lt. Milton, 13
Anderson, Lt. Richard B., 132, 149, 184, 186
Andersz, Capt. Tadeusz, 66, 181
Appel, Capt. Edward H., 171
Aranyos, Lt. John A., 100-101, 181
Arnold, Lt. John A., 188, 190
Auton, Brig. Gen. Jesse, 85, 155

Bailes, Lt. Albert, 13
Bailey, Lt. Robert E., 190
Baker, Maj. Gordon, 132, 137, 142, 150, 172, 183-184
Baker, Lt. Wyman A., 149
Ball, Lt. Sanborn N., Jr., 174, 187, 188, 189
Barnes, Lt. William H., 134, 184
Barnum, Capt. Eugene E., 46, 89, 149, 178
Barrentine, Lt. Emmett S., 189-190
Bartle, Lt. William G., 141, 189
Batson, Lt. Samuel K., 186, 187
Beason, Lt. Eugene M., 173, 185-187
Becker, Lt. Marvin H., 116, 121, 179, 183
Bennett, Capt. Joseph H., 60, 81, 173, 177, 179
Bennett, Lt. Eugene E., 114, 182
Bevens, Lt. Hiram O., 26, 27
Blake, Lt. Gordon J., 89, 147, 179
Blodgett, Lt. Burton O., 171, 174, 189
Bluhm, Lt. Roy B., Jr., 178
Bostwick, Maj. George E., 115, 123, 165, 168, 169, 172, 182-183, 185, 188
Boyle, Lt. Mark K., 181
Brainard, Lt. Wayne A., 41
Brooks, Lt. Norman E., 49, 176
Brown, Lt. Cleve M., 50
Brown, Lt. Jack D., 46, 175
Brown, Lt. Lewis R., 184, 186
Bryant, Lt. John P., 46, 176, 180
Burke, Maj. Sylvester V., Jr., 29, 172, 176-178
Buszko, Lt. Thaddeus S., 56, 180
Butiste, F/O Leo F., 187-188
Butler, Lt. George H., 117, 174, 183-185
Bux, Lt. Arthur J., 162, 184

Cagle, Lt. Oscar, 142
Calmes, Lt. Alben G., 148
Campbell, Capt. Russell W., 184
Campbell, Lt. Robert B., Jr., 62
Canizares, Lt. Arlington W., 97, 99, 180-181
Carclone, Lt. Anthony, 24-25, 27, 46, 68, 84, 139, 175-176, 178-179

Carlson, Lt. Charles E., 154, 187
Carter, Maj. James R., 56-57, 108, 116, 172, 174, 178, 182-183, 186
Casteel, Lt. Barney P., 183
Cathers, Capt. Benjamin E., 184
Cavallo, Lt. Anthony S., 107, 139, 177, 182
Chasko, Lt. Andrew, 156, 186-187
Chattaway, Lt. William P., 181
Cherry, Lt. Robert C., 123, 180, 182-183
Chinn, Lt. Claude A., 174, 185-187
Choate, Lt. George R., 144, 186
Christensen, Capt. Fred, 33, 62, 70, 86, 88, 100, 114, 119, 120-121, 123-126, 173, 176-181, 183-184
Clamp, Lt. Charles, 52, 74, 137
Clark, Lt. Charles R., 187, 190
Clark, Lt. James C., 108, 182, 185
Coenen, Lt. John E., 175
Comstock, Col. Harold E., 8, 21, 23, 32, 46, 48, 52, 60, 139-140, 152, 161, 172, 174-176, 185-187
Conger, Maj. Paul A., 8, 50, 79, 83, 89, 105, 157-159, 161, 164-165, 172, 177, 181-182, 184, 186, 188
Cook, Capt. Walter V., 14, 42, 44, 46, 174, 176
Coronlos, Lt. Harry, 33, 175
Craig, Maj. Horace C., 24, 66, 172, 177
Crosswaithe, Col. John C., 7
Curtis, Lt. Joseph R., 92, 115, 126, 182-183
Czarnota, Lt. Leo J., 148

Dade, Lt. Col. Lucien, 100, 134-135, 160-161, 172, 182-184, 190
Dale, Lt. Sam B., Jr., 116, 181, 183
Daley, Lt. William C., 158, 186-187
Daniel, Lt. Robert J., 136, 184-185, 187
Dauphin, Capt. Ray, 33
Davis, Lt. Ramon R., 147, 186-187
De Mayo, Lt. Julius, 144
Dieppe, 17
Dimmick, Lt. Allen, 60
Doublebolt, The, 138
Duncan, Col. Glenn C., 111
Dyar, Capt. Roger, 11-12, 18, 21

Eaves, Capt. John B., 84, 174, 176, 179, 182, 186
Eby, Capt. Merle, 13, 18
Edens, Lt. Billy G., 117, 128, 139, 173, 183-185
Edwards, Lt. Trevor A., 185
Egan, Maj. Joseph L., Jr., 53, 61, 63, 72, 172, 174-175, 177-180
Elliot, Lt. Virgil L., 189
Evans, Lt. Alfred, Jr., 114
Everett, Lt. Evert, 91-92

Fahringer, Capt. John C., 166, 174, 186, 188
Fields, Lt. James E., 63, 93, 178-180
Flagg, Capt. Walter L., 134, 173, 183-184, 189-190
Fleming, Capt. Philip F., 171, 189
Fling, Capt. Roy T., 184
Foster, Lt. Justus D., 69, 103, 177
Frederick, Lt. Walter E., 52, 153, 181, 183
Frederickson, Lt. Russell, 186
Frederickson, Lt. Walter, 123
Frye, Lt. Chester, 136
Funcheon, Lt. Donald M., 91, 178, 179
Furlong, Lt. Donald, 114

Gabreski, Col. Francis S., 8, 27, 40-41, 44-46, 48-51, 59-60, 65-66, 69, 72, 82, 84, 87-88, 91, 97, 100, 102-103, 105-109, 111, 115, 117-120, 124-125, 128-129, 175, 177-180, 182-184
Garth, Lt. Winston, 12
Gerbe, Lt. William, 145
Geren, Lt. Lloyd F., 171, 187, 189
Gerick, Capt. Steven N., 89, 105, 115, 117-118, 173, 180, 182-184
Gerow, Lt. Arthur H., 186
Getz, Lt. Stuart H., 184, 186
Gladych, Capt. Michael B., 66, 70, 73, 80, 84, 91, 114-115, 127, 173, 178-180, 182-184, 186
Godfrey, Lt. Hillyar S., 57, 137
Goldstein, Lt. George C., 27, 42, 51, 175-176
Goodfleisch, Maj. Don M., 25, 31-32, 109, 128, 172, 175
Gordon, Lt. William P., Jr., 77, 179
Gould, Lt. Norman D., 165, 186-188
Graves, Maj. David D., 7
Green, Lt. Jack E., 106, 182
Groce, Lt. Walter R., 184-186

Haggard, Lt. Wilburn A., 150
Hall, Capt. George F., 41, 60-61, 92, 174, 176-177, 179
Hamilton, Lt. Samuel D., Jr., 88, 97, 178, 181
Hannigan, Lt. Walter T., 25
Harrison, Capt. Charles R., 100, 174-175, 178
Hart, Capt. Cameron, 135-136, 154, 163, 174, 184, 187-188
Hartshorn, Lt. William M., 141, 185
Healy, Lt. Robert E., 145
Hedke, Lt. Jack D., 160
Heineman, Lt. Richard M., 109, 182
Henderson, Lt. Everett A., 137, 184
Henley, Lt. Donald, Jr., 159, 164, 173, 186, 188-189
Henry, Aalbert L., 145
Hertel, Lt. Earl, 136
Hodges, Lt. Glen, 23

Hoffman, Lt. William R., 169, 187, 189
Horton, Lt. Jack, 20
Huff, Lt. Edgar H., 163, 190
Hunter, Brig. Gen. Frank O'D., 66

Icard, Lt. Joe W., 42, 65, 82, 176, 178-179

Jackson, Maj. Michael J., 146, 173, 183-187
Janicki, F/O Z., 118
Johnson, Maj. Gerald W., 8, 15, 17, 21, 23, 27, 30, 33-34, 36, 69-70, 72-75, 78, 80, 86, 89-91, 93, 108-109, 112, 172, 174-176, 178-180
Johnson, Capt. Ralph A., 16-17, 25, 27, 46, 175-176
Johnson, Lt. Col. Robert S., 5, 15-17, 34, 52, 60-61, 78, 82, 84-85, 90, 97, 99, 102-103, 173-182
Johnson, Lt. Willard D., 104, 180, 181
Jones, Lt. James M., Jr., 34-36, 175-176, 180-181
Jure, Lt. James M., 136, 174, 182-185

Keeler, Lt. John W., 190
Keen, Capt. Robert J., 89, 106, 125, 136, 173, 182-183, 185
Kepner, Maj. Gen. William E., 66, 85
Kerr, Lt. Vernon E., Jr., 100-101, 181
Kerr, Lt. Warren E., Jr., 181
King, Capt. Herman E., 135, 185, 174, 182
Klibbe, Lt. Frank W., 46, 59-60, 67, 72, 102-103, 140, 173, 176, 178, 180, 182
Kling, Lt. David, 141
Knafelz, Lt. Albert P., 96, 183
Knox, Lt. Baird M., 183
Kozey, Lt. John, 86
Kruer, Lt. Edward J., 50
Kuhn, Lt. Philip G., 163, 167, 171, 174, 188, 190
Kyle, Lt. James A., 184, 186
Kyler, Lt. Russell S., 149, 171, 173, 185-187, 189

Lamb, Maj. Robert A., 50-51, 58, 63, 74, 172, 175, 177-179
Landry, Col. Robert H., 38, 43, 59, 172, 177
Langdon, Lt. Lloyd M., 60-61, 177
Lanowski, Capt. Withold A., 66, 120, 125, 127, 174, 182-183, 186
Lewis, Lt. Gordon H., 104, 182
Lewis, Lt. John E., 154
Lewis, Lt. Kenneth, 60
Lister, Lt. James E., 186
Lowman, F/O Samuel J., 180, 181
Ludwig, Lt. Vance P., 30, 173, 175

Magel, Lt. Robert W., 123, 133, 161, 183
Mahurin, Col. Walker M., 5, 12, 27, 30-32, 39-40, 46-48, 52, 61, 78, 84-85, 91-93, 112, 174-180
Marangello, Lt. William A., 175
Marcotte, Lt. John C., 82
Matthews, Lt. Harold L., 120, 181
Maul, Lt. Arthur C., 134, 182, 184
McBath, Lt. Charles T., 150, 190
McCauley, Capt. Frank E., 20, 22-23, 38, 174-176
McClure, Capt. John E., 11-12, 96-97, 99, 115, 181-182
McCollom, Maj. Loren G., 9, 14, 16, 24, 172
McElhare, Lt. William W., 182-183
McMahan, Lt. Darrell E., 169, 173, 183, 185
McMinn, F/O Evan D., 71, 87, 107-108, 114, 173, 178-182
Merrill, Lt. Wiley H., Jr., 122-123, 183
Mitchel Field, 7

Morrill, Lt. Byron L., 43, 46-47, 70, 85, 176-180
Morrill, Capt. Stanley B., 173
Moseley, Capt. Mark L., 100, 115, 117, 121, 126, 173, 179-180, 183
Mudge, Capt. Dick H., 100, 177
Murphy, Lt. Randel L., Jr., 152, 154, 170-171, 186-187, 190
Murray, Lt. Steven T., 185
Mussey, Lt. Claude E., 69, 91, 178, 180

Neale, Lt. Cletus B., 109
Neyland, Lt. Praeger, 60, 110, 182
Nolan, Capt. Francis A., 156, 186-187

O'Connor, Lt. Wayne J., 29, 43, 53, 175
O'Neill, Capt. Eugene W., 11, 42, 46, 64-65, 133, 176-178
Olynyk, Dr. Frank, 174
Operation Pointblank, 69
Osborne, Lt. William J., 144, 186

Palmer, Lt. James, 128
Parson, Lt. Townsend, 148
Patterson, Lt. Roy L., 174, 185-186
Patterson, Lt. Warren S., Jr., 183, 184
Perry, Lt. Alfred O., 156, 187
Perry, Capt. Joseph H., 152, 187
Peters, Lt. Donald V., 100-101, 179-182
Pierce, Lt. Jack W., 115, 183, 185
Piper, Lt. Col. Preston, 104
Pitts, Lt. Walter H., 142, 185
Polish No. 315th Fighter Squadron, 65
Popplewell, Lt. Joel I., 115, 182
Porowski, Lt. Isadore T., 180
Powers, Capt. Joseph H., 18, 23, 41, 52, 86-87, 173-174, 176-182
Price, Lt. Jack, 134
Pruden, Lt. Harry M., 176
Pruitt, Lt. Sherman, Jr., 165, 167, 188

Queen, Lt. Thomas W., Jr., 174, 184, 189-190
Quirk, Maj. Michael B., 54, 60, 62-63, 83-84, 95, 134, 172, 175, 177-180, 185

Rankin, Lt. Robert J., 29, 64, 86, 93, 104-105, 173, 178, 180-183
Raymond, Lt. Charles R., 186, 189
Raymond, Lt. Elwood R., 141
Reed, Lt. Charles W., 47, 52, 61, 137, 178-179, 181
Reeder, Lt. Caleb L., 84, 175
Renwick, Maj. Donald D., 165, 172, 175, 189
Roberts, Lt. Robill W., 177
Robey, Lt. Archie R., 91-93, 177, 179-180
Rotzler, Lt. Charles M., 141, 173, 185-187
Rougeau, Lt. Edward N., 76
Roy, Lt. Frederick L., 82, 179
Ruder, Lt. Franklin E., 189

Sawicz, F/Lt., 66
Scherz, Lt. Willard C., 187
Schilling, Col. David C., 8-9, 11-12, 14, 24, 29-30, 32-33, 43-44, 46-47, 50, 54-56, 60, 69, 80-81, 88, 91-93, 97, 129, 144, 151, 155, 160, 172, 175-177, 180-181, 184
Schlitz, Capt. Glen D., Jr., 20, 21, 29, 57, 173, 175
Schreiber, Maj. Leroy A., 18, 31, 33, 66, 69-70, 82, 87, 97, 99, 172, 174, 177-181
Schweinfurt, Germany, 20, 36, 144
Sharbo, Lt. Walter J., 174, 187-188

Sheridan, Lt. Daylon C., 122, 183
Shupe, Lt. Arthur T., 188
Sison, Lt. Edward A., 181, 183
Smith, Lt. Bernard R., 84, 175, 177, 180
Smith, Maj. Donovan F., 39, 49, 68-69, 72, 94, 131, 141-142, 172, 177-179, 184-185
Smith, Lt. Kenneth L., 187
Smith, Lt. Col. Leslie C., 71-72, 87, 107, 161, 164, 172, 179-182, 187-188
Smith, Lt. Thomas W., Jr., 188
Smith, Lt. Vernon A., 171, 174, 189-190
Smith, Lt. William F., 189
Spicer, Lt. Harold, 142
Stamps, Lt. Samuel O., 111, 181
Stevens, Capt. Gordon S., 141
Stevenson, Lt. William J., 188-189
Stewart, Lt. Col. James C., 36, 46, 59, 72, 76, 82, 100, 172, 178, 179-181
Stewart, Lt. Roach, 130, 132
Stitt, Lt. Paul, 169
Stovall, Lt. William H., 156, 187
Stover, Robert, 20
Strand, Lt. Lawrence R., 50
Stream, Lt. Dale E., 89, 91, 180
Sullivan, Lt. Timothy, 118, 125

Taylor, Lt. Robert B., 29, 54, 175-176
Thomton, Lt. Cleon C., 182, 184
Timony, Lt. Eugene A., 116, 136, 174, 184-185
Tingen, Lt. Clarence A., 188, 190
Truluck, Capt. John H., 21, 23, 28, 45, 82, 173, 175-176, 179-181
Trumble, Lt. Pershing B., 186, 188
Tucker, Capt. Charles E., 120, 182
Tukey, Maj. Philip E., Jr., 9, 29, 172

Valenta, F/O Irvin E., 44, 46, 176
Van Abel, Lt. Wilfred A., 18, 25
Van Meter, Lt. Malcolm, 43
Van Noy, Lt. George H., Jr., 117, 183
Vest, Lt. Boss E., 188, 190
Vitale, F/O Joseph, 117, 182
Vogt, Capt. John W., Jr., 25-26, 31, 38, 72, 175-176, 178-179

Wakefield, Lt. J. Carroll, 105, 182
Walker, Lt. Joseph P., 40, 58
Warboys, Lt. Richard T., 184
Warner, Lt. Harry F., 114, 184
Westfall, Capt. Russel B., 61, 114
Westman, Lt. Carl E., 184
Wetherbee, Robert, 18
Whitley, Lt. Edgar D., 175
Wilkerson, Capt. William F., 185-188
Williamson, Maj. Felix D., 47, 100, 158-159, 161, 163, 165, 172-173, 177, 179-181, 187-188
Wilson, Lt. John D., 41, 48-49, 175
Windmayer, Lt. Frederick, 49
Winski, Lt. Longfin M., 189
Winters, Capt. Robert E., 185-186, 188
Wisniewski, Lt. Adam J., 31, 181
Wither, Lt. James, 159
Womack, Lt. Herschel C., 141, 185, 188
Wood, Lt. Melvin C., 42-43, 78, 91, 176-177
Wook, Lt. Charles A., 187

Zemke, Col. Hubert, 5, 8, 10-11, 13, 15, 17, 20-21, 24, 30, 37-38, 40, 54, 58-59, 65, 69-70, 72, 76, 78, 93, 96, 99, 101, 104-107, 109, 112-116, 125-126, 174-176, 178-179, 181-184